791.4309415

KT-488-819

GAELIC
GAMES
ON FILM

GAELIC
GAMES
ON FILM

From silent films to Hollywood hurling, horror
and the emergence of Irish cinema

Seán Crosson

CORK UNIVERSITY PRESS

First published in 2019 by
Cork University Press
Youngline Industrial Estate
Pouladuff Road, Togher
Cork T12 HT6V, Ireland

© Seán Crosson

All rights reserved. No part of this book may be reprinted
or reproduced or utilised in any electronic, mechanical or other
means, now known or hereafter invented, including photocopying
and recording or otherwise, without either the prior written
permission of the publisher or a licence permitting restricted
copying in Ireland issued by the Irish Copyright Licensing Agency
Ltd, 25 Denzille Lane, Dublin 2.

The right of the author to be identified as originator of this work
has been asserted by him in accordance with Copyright and
Related Rights Acts 2000 to 2007.

British Library Cataloguing in Publication Data

A CIP catalogue record for this book is available from
the British Library.

ISBN-978-1-78205-247-0

Typeset by Studio 10 Design
Printed by Hussar Books in Poland

This publication was grant-aided by the Publications Fund of National
University of Ireland Galway/Rinneadh maoiniú ar an bhfoilseachán seo
trí Chiste Foilseachán Ollscoil na hÉireann, Gaillimh.

This publication was grant-aided by the National University of Ireland's
Publications Scheme.

CONTENTS

ACKNOWLEDGEMENTS

The research and writing of this book would not have been possible without the support of friends and colleagues in the National University of Ireland Galway and further afield. Since joining the staff of NUI Galway, I have been the fortunate beneficiary of a positive research-support culture, including the university's Millennium Minor Project fund which facilitated my initial research on this topic. This research really began when David Doyle, then a PhD student in the Centre for Irish Studies at NUI Galway, invited me in late 2006 to present at the Third Annual Conference of Sports History Ireland (hosted at NUI Galway) on the topic of Gaelic games in film. At that time, I had limited knowledge of the subject, and few expectations of there being many relevant films, but a journey began that twelve years later has resulted in this book. I am grateful to David for his initial invitation and to many others along the way who have facilitated and supported the research. In particular I should acknowledge the collaborative work undertaken with Dónal McAnallen on newsreels and Gaelic games, particularly Dónal's groundbreaking research on the GAA's history that provides important context for the analysis in Chapter Two. As with some of the material in that chapter, elements of this publication have appeared previously in other works associated with this topic, as has my engagement with the topic of sport cinema internationally in my monograph *Sport and Film* (Routledge, 2013) – I am grateful to all those who have supported my research and publication in this area as it has developed. NUI Galway also generously contributed to the publication of this book through the Grant-in-aid of Publication Fund, while I also received important support from the National University of Ireland through its Publication Scheme. I would also like to acknowledge the support of colleagues within the School of Humanities and across the College of Arts, Social Sciences and Celtic Studies in NUI Galway, in particular Philip Dine for his invaluable advice and collaboration on previous sport-related symposia and publications. Within the Huston School of Film & Digital Media, where this research was primarily undertaken, I am grateful to my colleagues Tony Tracy, Conn Holohan and Dee Quinn – and former director Rod Stoneman – for their support in the development of my research. Others who assisted in the completion of this book and to whom I am also grateful include Charles Barr, Marcus Free, Alan Bairner, Mike Cronin, Bill Morrison, Cormac Hargaden, Eamonn Sweeney, Ruth Barton, Paul Balbirnie (for kindly providing me with a copy of the fascinating publicity sheet for the

MGM short *Hurling* (1936)), Paul Rouse, Lance Pettitt, Aonghus Meaney (for the great care and attention he brought to the copy-editing process), William Murphy, Máire Harris (from Gael Linn for her advice regarding the material in Chapter Five, and Gael Linn for permission to reproduce the images included there), Tyrone Productions Ltd (and in particular Dara Parkes-Kenna and Patricia Carroll for providing me with the stills from *Laochra* in Chapter Nine and allowing me to reproduce them), Sheila Jepson and Portland Public Schools, Portland, Maine (for permission to reproduce a photograph of the school's 1913 state-champions football team, which included director John Ford), Richard Holt, Edward Fletcher (at Thunderbird Releasing, and Eeva Lennon for permission to reproduce images from *Rocky Road to Dublin* (1968)), Joseph McBride, Louis Marcus, Phelim O'Neill, Hedwig Schwall, Irene Gilsenan Nordin, Martin McLoone, Jimmy Brohan, Pat Comer, Fergus Tighe, Conor McMahon, and Mike Collins and Maria O'Donovan at Cork University Press for all their advice and hard work along the way in bringing this work to publication. I am also grateful to the Laboratoire sur les Vulnérabilités et l'Innovation dans le Sport at Université Claude-Bernard Lyon 1, and in particular to Professor Philippe Liotard, for their support, via a Visiting Research Fellowship, that provided me with invaluable time and space to develop this book. Several individuals who supported the research in this work have sadly passed on, including former Meath footballer Mattie Gilsenan; former Cavan footballer Mick Higgins; former National Film Institute cameraman and pioneering researcher of Irish cinema Robert Monks; the late journalist and director Peter Lennon; and former professor of English and American language and literature at the University of Vienna, Werner Huber – *ar dheis Dé go raibh a n-anamacha uasal*. I also want to acknowledge the generous support of the staff of the Irish Film Archive in the Irish Film Institute, including Kasandra O'Connell, Sunniva O'Flynn and Rebecca Grant, during the many hours I spent in the archive undertaking my research – the institute also kindly allowed me to reproduce the images from the National Film Institute Gaelic games films included in Chapter Five. Finally, I would like to thank my parents for their support down through the years and my partner Anne Karhio for her patience and encouragement during the research and completion of this book.

FIGURES AND TABLES

Figures

Tables

INTRODUCTION

On 24 April 2016, to commemorate the 1916 Easter Rising, the organisation responsible for administering Gaelic games, the Gaelic Athletic Association (GAA), hosted a major pageant in the GAA's main stadium Croke Park precisely one hundred years to the day since the first shots were fired in the key nationalist revolutionary event of the twentieth century. Entitled *Laochra*, which can be translated as 'Warriors' or 'Heroes', the pageant followed the playing of the GAA's Allianz Football League Division 1 and 2 finals and consisted of a specially commissioned half-hour stadium production featuring a cast of more than 3,500 performers.

While *Laochra* was broadcast to one of the largest audiences to date to watch a programme on the Irish-language broadcaster TG4,[1] delivery of this pageant involved significant cinematic elements for those present in Croke Park for the performance. The cinematic aspects were evident in the combination of different forms of live performance (including re-enactments from episodes in Irish mythology featuring hurling, Irish dancing and live reading/singing performance), rendered for television broadcast through pitch-side camera, dynamic Steadicam sequences, and pre-recorded archive footage screened on three of the largest high-definition outdoor screens in Europe. Though not screened within a cinema space, this in-stadium experience was nonetheless the culmination of over one hundred years of cinematic depictions of Gaelic games. Indeed, it marked the movement and integration of cinematic elements from the cinema space into the stadium experience of followers of Gaelic games today in Ireland; major matches in Croke Park are always accompanied by the relaying of the on-pitch action onto the stadium's two permanent big screens. Furthermore, *Loachra* revealed the continuing relevance of a range of themes in association with Gaelic games explored in this book: the employment of Gaelic games as a key marker of Irish identity; the engagement of features associated with a 'tourist gaze' on Ireland; and the association of hurling with violence. This book will chart the progression of cinematic depictions of Gaelic games, exploring some of the key features evident and the fascinating (and sometimes problematic) perspectives that surviving film footage of Gaelic games provides.

SPORT AND CINEMA

The depiction of Gaelic games in the cinema dates from the beginning of the twentieth century and from the start reflected an international fascination with capturing sporting activity on film. From the earliest days of moving-image technology, sport has been a frequent subject of representation, with initial experiments often engaged with sporting topics. In 1870s France, the pioneering gymnast Georges Demenÿ assisted French scientist Étienne-Jules Marey in his early experiments at capturing movement photographically, including serving as the subject for Marey's work.[2] In the same period in the United States, attempts to capture motion in photography, in the work of English photographer Eadweard Muybridge, were also focused on sport, including images featuring members of the Olympic Athletic Club based in San Francisco engaged in various athletic activities from boxing to jumping.[3] Even before the first public projections of this new art form to audiences, the early experiments to capture movement on film in Thomas Edison's laboratories in West Orange, New Jersey, featured athletes and sporting contests. Primarily due to the efforts of William K.L. Dickson, who directed most of the early Edison Company films, a rudimentary motor-powered camera called the kinetograph was invented in late 1890, and the first experimental films were shot the following year. Among these early films was a short entitled *Men Boxing*, directed by Dickson and William Heise, and boxing would continue to be a popular subject of representation in subsequent years.[4]

This new moving-image technology may have initially attracted audiences due to its novelty, but it was sport, and particularly boxing in the United States, which contributed considerably to its continued popularity for much of the first decade of film production. Film historian Luke McKernan identifies in the early boxing films 'the very birth of American cinema realism and drama, newsfilm and fakery, commercialism, populism, professionalism, two protagonists battling within the perfect staging, the ring'.[5] Indeed, the first feature-length films, the first use of actors and the first commercial cinema exhibitions in the United States were all concerned with the subject of boxing.[6]

While the sports film may have been largely defined in Hollywood in the early twentieth century, national cinemas across the world have also made important contributions. From Asia to Australia and Africa, Europe to South America, sport has featured prominently throughout world cinema. The Internet Movie Database (IMDb) lists seventy-one countries other than the United States that have produced sports films, with over 200 United Kingdom productions alone to date. The sports film also has a long history internationally; one of the most commercially successful Chinese silent films of the 1930s was *Ti yu huang hou* (*Queen of Sports*) (1934), which foregrounded a strong female lead protagonist as an athlete at a time when women rarely featured in such roles in the West. Sport also featured prominently in the formative years of sub-Saharan African film production; *Lamb* (1963), a film released three years after Senegalese independence by a pioneer of film production in West Africa, Paulin Soumanou Vieyra, concerned traditional wrestling in Senegal and was part of a general pattern in newly emerging independent African states to 'reassert the value of the cultural heritage from the perspective of a search for identity'.[7] This relationship between sport and national culture and identity will be the subject of further examination in the following section.[8]

SPORT AND NATIONAL CULTURE

The question of national culture and identity has been a recurring concern of films featuring sport. The relationship between sport and identity is a complex yet crucial one in understanding the popularity and passions that sport evokes internationally. The relationship between sport and national identity is perhaps more complex still. The complexities here relate to the idea of the nation itself. Even today, nations are defined by often quite different criteria, many of which are neither straightforward nor uncontested. As Lincoln Allison notes:

We refer to nations defined by religion (Israel, Pakistan, Belgium), by language (Germany, Italy) and by ideology (the United States of America), though in all cases the common characteristic is attached to a defined territory. Perhaps the most coherent concept is that developed by such German writers as J.G. Fichte in arguing for German unification in the nineteenth century. According to this version, a nation possesses a common language and shares a common territory; it has a common 'spirit', the Volkgeist.[9]

However, particularly since the 1980s, in the work of Ernest Gellner (1983), Benedict Anderson (1983), Anthony D. Smith (1986), John Hutchinson (1987) and Eric J. Hobsbawm (1992), essentialist approaches to the nation have been increasingly questioned. Rather than nations being viewed as in the past as timeless phenomena, they are now more commonly seen to comprise, in Benedict Anderson's familiar formulation, 'imagined communities'[10] conceptualised as nations, post the Enlightenment. Nationalism is today regarded as a relatively recent development emerging in the late eighteenth century and associated with romanticism and the celebration of the virtues of distinctive cultures and a shared (often) heroic past as well as a utopian impulse to realise an 'ideal society the national movement wants to will into existence'.[11] Such 'nations' that have emerged have been largely constructed around invented histories and traditions, formulated by movements aimed at constructing them in their own interests.[12] In the words of Eugene Weber, states try to transform 'peasants into Frenchmen' by emphasising a common language, history and culture and by denying or suppressing those features that may contradict this, such as the Basque and Breton cultures in France.[13] In other words, national identity as we understand it today is a modern creation for which a pre-modern history has been largely rewritten.

A crucial determinant in the formation of nations is cultural activities. As Gellner notes, 'culture is now the necessary shared medium' for members of a nation-state.[14] Benedict Anderson has referred to the importance of the role of the printing press and the consolidation of capitalism in the process of nation building, noting that the 'development of print-as-commodity is the key to the generation of wholly new ideas of simultaneity' by allowing people to access the same information and ideas in different locations concurrently in a manner not possible previously.[15] For Anderson, this brought a sense of unity and collective identity to disparate groups bound together by ideas. As the nineteenth century developed, organised sport and, subsequently, film were both important in consolidating such collectivities as national identities became increasingly significant. Indeed, in emphasising nationalism's 'banality' as a natural and often unnoticed part of everyday life, Michael Billig has argued for the 'social and political significance' of modern sport in this context, 'extending through the media beyond the player and the spectator' by providing luminous moments of national engagement and national heroes whom citizens can emulate and adore.[16] As Billig's remarks suggest, the mass media (including the cinema) has played a crucial role in the popularisation of sport and in asserting its political significance.

SPORT, FILM AND NATIONAL CULTURE

Film's potential as a powerful vehicle for the articulation and affirmation of the nation has been long recognised in critical studies.[17] Susan Hayward in her examination of French cinema identified how film may function

> as a cultural articulation of a nation ... [it] textualises the nation and subsequently constructs a series of relations around the concepts, first, of state and citizen, then of state, citizen and other ... a 'national' cinema ... is ineluctably 'reduced' to a series of enunciations that reverberate around two fundamental concepts: identity and difference.[18]

Whether of American origin or not, a recurring theme across films featuring sport is its employment within narratives concerned with affirming, or less often contesting, established constructions of national identity. In the United States, this has most often been associated with the theme of the American dream of opportunity, upward social mobility and material success, as exemplified in the Oscar-winning production *Rocky* (1976).[19] Given the popularity of American cinema internationally, it is not surprising to find that the theme of the 'underdog' overcoming seemingly impossible odds also recurs in many other national cinemas, including in Ireland.

Sport's ability to mobilise and sustain a sense of national identity has, at various points, been exploited by film-makers in differing contexts. International sporting victories may contribute to a sense of national solidarity and pride in one's country, but filmic depictions of such victories can also add significantly to this process. The recuperation of German identity in the post-Second World War era was helped greatly by World Cup victories, particularly in 1954 and 1990. While the 1954 victory was concurrent with the beginning of Germany's economic recovery after the war, the 1990 victory coincided with German unification after the fall of the Berlin Wall. However, both moments have been evocatively rendered and affirmed in two of the most commercially successful German films in the post-war era, *Das Wunder von Bern* (*The Miracle of Bern*) (2003), concerning West Germany's unexpected victory in the 1954 World Cup, and *Good Bye Lenin!* (2003), which features a German nation enthralled by West Germany's path to World Cup victory in 1990. Other examples include the 2009 film *Invictus*, which explores Nelson Mandela's attempts to bring his divided nation together, after the abolition of apartheid, through South Africa hosting, and eventually winning, the 1995 Rugby Union World Cup. *Invictus* (a Warner Bros. Pictures production) also indicates how this pattern may be evident even where individual films – such as the Oscar-winning production *Chariots of Fire* (1981) – are primarily funded from outside the national context. *Chariots of Fire* – a fact-based narrative concerning the attempts of British athletes to achieve Olympic glory at the 1924 Paris Olympics – was one of the most acclaimed British films of the past fifty years, winning four Academy Awards (including for Best Picture) and taking almost $60 million at the US box office alone, a rare achievement for a British-themed production. The film was also viewed as the beginning of a revival (largely unrealised) of British cinema, with the screenwriter Colin Welland announcing 'the British are coming' at the Academy Awards ceremony after he received his Oscar for Best Original Screenplay.[20] Indeed, the film was celebrated as achieving success while maintaining one's own national distinctiveness, 'winning on your own terms', as the film's producer, David Puttnam, remarked at the time.[21] However, in reality *Chariots of Fire* was largely funded not by British backers – who were hesitant to get involved – but by a Hollywood studio, 20th Century Fox, who reaped most of the financial benefits of the film's success.[22] Nonetheless, as Alan Tomlinson has observed, the film reveals 'a set of social divisions and inner conflicts and then provid[es] a resolution in the form of nationalist integration'.[23]

However, film's articulation of the nation and national identity is often rife with tensions and sometimes contradictions, including those productions featuring sport. Following from Mette Hjort and Scott MacKenzie's formulation within their collection *Cinema & Nation*, national cinema is perhaps best comprehended 'in terms of notions of conflict'. As they continue, films

> do not simply represent or express the stable features of a national culture, but are themselves one of the loci of debates about a nation's governing principles, goals, heritage, and history. It follows that critics should be attuned not only to the expressive dimensions of a nation's films, but to what these films and their categorisation as elements of a national cinema may elide or strategically repress.[24]

Indeed, sport has on occasion provided a means for film-makers to contest hegemonic constructions of the nation and national identity, particularly in instances where such constructions obscured or elided identities – sporting, cultural, social, gendered or otherwise – that may not concur with established understandings of the nation itself. Relevant international examples include the British films *The Loneliness of the Long Distance Runner* (1962), *This Sporting Life* (1963) and the Iranian film *Offside* (2006), all works which challenge established constructions of national identity in their respective contexts.[25] A further example is the Australian biopic of Olympic swimming champion Dawn Fraser, *Dawn!* (1979). Fraser won gold medals at the Melbourne (1956), Rome (1960) and Tokyo (1964) Olympics in the 100-metres freestyle event. However, she was a controversial figure who was suspended for ten years by the Australian Swimming Union after being arrested for stealing an Olympic flag from a flagpole outside Emperor Hirohito's palace during the 1964 Olympics, an incident depicted in the film. *Dawn!* questions gender categories (Fraser is depicted in the film as being critical of conventional gender typing) and sexual conventions, particularly those associated with a central stereotype within Australian culture, the larrikin. In the film's portrayal of Fraser as an anti-authoritarian and working-class 'battler', who prefers drinking pints in the primarily male domain of the local pub to female company, *Dawn!* evokes characteristics associated with the larrikin figure. However, larrikinism, as John Rickard observes, is 'bound up with understandings of masculinity'.[26] While this does not exclude women, or female sexuality, Fraser's engagement in a lesbian relationship (also suggested within the film) challenges the stereotype. As noted by Phillips and Osmond, Fraser's bisexuality is 'inconsistent with dominant masculine interpretations of larrikinism, with normative sexuality, with sport and sexuality and ultimately with Fraser herself'.[27] The suggestion of such a relationship in the film, if more implied than depicted, was nonetheless a radical departure at a time when homosexuality was still a criminal offence in Australia. In common with *Dawn!*, this book will explore in Chapter Seven Fergus Tighe's *Clash of the Ash* (1987), which might similarly be considered to contest hegemonic constructions of Gaelic games and those who play them.

Film has also engaged with distinctive national and ethnic sporting cultures; one of France's most commercially successful and critically acclaimed animated films, *Les Triplettes de Belleville* (*Belleville Rendez-vous*) (2003), concerns the kidnap of a cyclist competing in the annual Tour de France, a race which Roland Barthes viewed as occupying a mythological place in French culture.[28] The most popular film ever at the Norwegian box office is the stop-motion animated feature film *Flåklypa Grand Prix* (*Pinchcliffe Grand Prix*) (1975) about a motor race and how local interests overcome an international elite. In its successful evocation of the Norwegian landscape and rendering of a range of idiosyncratic characters created by popular Norwegian cartoonist Kjell Aukrust, *Flåklypa Grand Prix* struck a chord with Norwegian people in particular, though it also attracted large audiences across Scandinavia. The fascinating documentary *Trobriand Cricket* (1975) reveals the manner through which Trobriand Islanders off the eastern coast of Papua New Guinea transformed the English sport of cricket – introduced in the early twentieth century by the British Methodist missionary Reverend Gilmour – into their own distinctive sport, which has become a conduit for tribal rivalry and simulated combat. The depiction of Gaelic games in film, therefore, can be placed within an international and historical context where distinctive indigenous sporting practices have provided revealing and popular material for film-makers' work.[29]

SPORT, POLITICS AND THE MEDIA IN IRELAND[30]

The depiction of sport in film internationally, discussed in the previous section, has been the subject of increasing academic research, some of which will be considered shortly. However, this relationship remains under-researched in the Irish context, though there is a growing body of relevant work focused on the representation of sport in the media more broadly in Ireland. This includes contributions by Raymond Boyle (1992), Luke Gibbons (1996), Mike Cronin (2007), Mark Duncan (2009), Paul Rouse (2009), John Connolly and Paddy Dolan (2012), and Marcus Free (2013), with each study emphasising the crucial relationship between sport and media, particularly in terms of the popularisation of sport in Irish life.

Most of these commentators were concerned with those most distinctive of Irish indigenous sports, Gaelic games, the principal focus of this book. In Ireland, the development and consolidation of Irish nationalism and the emergence of the independent Irish state were inextricably linked with sport, in particular the Gaelic Athletic Association, still the largest sporting organisation on the island today. The Gaelic games of hurling and Gaelic football would eventually become the principal sports promoted by the association; however, in its formative years, as its title suggests, the association was concerned with facilitating and encouraging Irish men in a broad range of athletic pursuits, including the hammer-throw (a sport also featured prominently in the first fiction film to depict Gaelic games, discussed in Chapter One). However, hurling in particular has been viewed as a key sport of the association, with a reputed ancient pedigree associated with the mythological figure of Cúchulainn, as evoked (discussed in Chapter Eight) in the contemporary horror film *Dead Meat* (2004). Interestingly, in terms of the representation of Gaelic games in film, particularly in international productions, depictions of hurling have also far exceeded those of Gaelic football, the more popular indigenous game in Ireland promoted by the GAA.[31]

Despite attempts by leaders of the association to avoid the GAA being politicised, the emergence of many of the most prominent figures, and still more of the active Volunteers, within republicanism in the years leading up to and including the Irish War of Independence from the ranks of the GAA affirmed that association's nationalist credentials. While leading republicans – including Michael Collins – were associated with the GAA, the British government imprisoned many GAA members after 1916, including the association's president, James Nowlan.[32] Furthermore, hurling sticks were used by republican Volunteers for both training and drilling sessions, in the absence of sufficient arms, throughout the 1910s, as depicted in several major films discussed later, including Neil Jordan's *Michael Collins* (1996) and Ken Loach's *The Wind that Shakes the Barley* (2006).[33]

Yet, while sport may feature prominently in Irish society, one cannot underestimate the role of the media (including cinema) in popularising and affirming this position. Indeed, the GAA was founded at a point when Gaelic games were in considerable decline, with the distinct possibility that they would not survive beyond the turn of the twentieth century. The initial ban on members or players of the association attending or participating in 'foreign' games was at least partly a response to the growing popularity of sports perceived as 'British', such as cricket, in Ireland during the nineteenth century. In his letter of acceptance in 1884 to Michael Cusack to become the first patron of the association, Archbishop Thomas Croke of Cashel highlighted precisely this development:

Ball-playing, hurling, football-kicking, according to Irish rules, 'casting', leaping in various ways, wrestling, handy-grips, top-pegging, leap-frog, rounders, tip-in-the-hat, and all such favourite exercises and amusements amongst men and boys, may now be said to be not only dead and buried, but in several localities to be entirely forgotten and unknown. And what have we got in their stead? We have got such foreign and fantastic field sports as lawn tennis, polo, croquet, cricket, and the like – very excellent, I believe, and health-giving exercises in their way, still not racy of the soil, but rather alien, on the contrary, to it, as are, indeed, for the most part the men and women who first imported and still continue to patronise them.[34]

A crucial ingredient in Gaelic games' development was the role of popular media, particularly newspapers and sporting publications of the 1880s and 1890s, and the fortune that the association had in attracting journalists of the highest calibre to write on its games. As Paul Rouse observes, at least three of the seven (though, as Rouse notes, there may have been up to fourteen) people, including its founder and first secretary Michael Cusack, at the celebrated founding meeting of the association in Hayes' Commercial Hotel in Thurles on Saturday 1 November 1884 were journalists. Their contributions, particularly those of Cusack, were crucial in spreading the word regarding, and thus popularising, Gaelic games in Irish life. Rouse also highlights the fascinating and tumultuous period in which the association was founded, and the many challenges it faced, including that of a media initially largely hostile towards the association and its aims.[35]

Sport already had a number of publications dedicated to it in Ireland prior to the foundation of the GAA in 1884, namely the sporting papers the *Irish Sportsman* and *Farmer and Sport*, though neither gave coverage to Gaelic games but focused rather on sports such as hunting and horse-related activities, rugby, tennis and cricket.[36] Within a few short years of the foundation of the association, there were two more, *Celtic Times*, initiated by the GAA's founder Michael Cusack, and *The Gael*, both, though short-lived, a testament to the growing popularity of Gaelic games in this period.[37]

The media would continue to be a crucial contributor to the growing popularity of Gaelic games in the early twentieth century. As Luke Gibbons has noted:

> … far from passively relaying the activities of a thriving sporting body to an already captive audience, both radio and the press contributed substantially to creating a *nationwide* audience for Gaelic games, thus establishing the Gaelic Athletic Association as a truly national organisation.[38]

Radio in particular affirmed the popular communal engagement with Gaelic games as they grew in popularity in Ireland, with the Kilkenny-versus-Galway All-Ireland senior hurling semi-final one of the first live broadcasts of a sporting event in Europe, when transmitted by 2RN (Ireland's first indigenous radio broadcaster) on 29 August 1926. In post-partition Southern Ireland, the state's control of the media played a significant part in affirming and promoting a particular, and quite insular, version of Irishness. In this context, Gaelic games played a pivotal role as a marker of Irish culture particularly as distinct from that of Britain, evident in the frequent broadcasting of Gaelic games via 2RN, and the exclusion of perceived non-Irish games such as soccer and rugby. As Raymond Boyle notes in his pioneering study of the relationship between Irish radio and Gaelic games post-partition:

> ... sports coverage played a key role in the formative years of Irish broadcasting. The selective treatment given by radio to specific sporting events not only helped to amplify their importance, but actually played a central role in creating national events and organisations.[39]

In the North of Ireland, the BBC began transmitting from 1924, though its efforts to advance distinctive local cultural practices, such as sport, were hampered by 'intense political and public hostility to anything suggestive of an "Irish" identity'.[40]

Radio in the south of Ireland was quick to exploit sport as a means of attracting audiences, though Irish newspapers were slower to realise its importance. However, with the launch of the *Irish Press* in 1931 and its growing popularity, significantly contributed to by its extensive coverage of sporting events, particularly Gaelic games, both the *Irish Independent* and *Irish Times* increased their coverage of sport in Ireland substantially.[41] The *Irish Press*, in particular, played an important role not just in affirming the antiquity and centrality of Gaelic games in Irish life, but also the position of sport in general in Ireland as an important marker of identity. Boyle has also observed the

> important interrelationship that exists between radio and newspapers in helping to construct national pastimes. They transform sport from a simple rule-governed game into a tangible activity which can generate a degree of collective sensibility that in turn helps to legitimise more abstract political structures such as 'state' and 'nation' ... The effects of radio and newspaper coverage of sport were twofold. They elevated awareness of sport while also contributing to the building of the country's national passion for sport.[42]

Thus, political and economic factors are crucial to understanding the development of the relationship between sport and the media in Ireland.

The prominent images of families gathered around a radio in the first indigenous cinematic coverage of an All-Ireland final by the National Film Institute of Ireland, in 1948 (discussed in Chapter Five), reflected an awareness of the importance of radio to people's engagement with sport and also the fact that many people in the audience would probably have listened to the match live on the radio in the first instance. The hiring of Micháel O'Hehir to provide the commentary for this footage, famous across Ireland for his sporting commentary on radio since 1938, further affirmed this connection. With the arrival of Ireland's first dedicated national television broadcaster, Telefís Éireann (now Raidió Teilifís Éireann (RTÉ)) on 31 December 1961, O'Hehir would continue to play a crucial role in the commentary on Gaelic games until his retirement due to illness in 1986. Despite the popularity of sport on television subsequently, radio coverage of sporting events has continued to have a huge following among Irish listeners. While Mícheál Ó Muircheartaigh earned a reputation until his retirement in 2010 as one of the finest commentators on live sport in any country for his Gaelic-games commentaries on RTÉ Radio 1, the centrality of Gaelic-games coverage on local radio, and particularly of soccer on national radio stations Today FM and Newstalk (both established in the early 2000s), all testify to the continuing importance of this medium in Ireland for sporting enthusiasts.[43]

THEORISING SPORT AND FILM

The critical engagement discussed above with the representation of sport in the Irish media is less evident with regard to film productions. Internationally, however, there has been increasing academic focus on sport cinema, though research of the experience outside of the American context remains underdeveloped.[44] The most comprehensive academic studies of sport cinema are to be found in the works of Babington (2014), Crosson (2013), Baker (2003) and Tudor (1997).[45] Of these studies, only Crosson and Babington consider films outside of the American experience, reflecting a more general bias in academic engagements. As is evident in studies to date of relevant European film cultures, most research has focused on individual case studies of exemplary films (e.g. *Olympia* (Germany, 1938),[46] *Chariots of Fire* (UK, 1981),[47] *Les Triplettes de Belleville* (France, 2003))[48] or the development of sport cinema within specific national contexts (e.g. Jones re the British sports film;[49] Romaguera re the Spanish sports film;[50] Cunningham on Hungarian football films;[51] McDougall on East German football films[52]).

Methodologically, cultural studies has been the predominant approach adopted to date to analyses of sport and cinema and it is the approach that informs this volume. A central concern within cultural studies is the meanings particular cultural products, such as film, produce and how they are circulated and received. Cultural studies shares with film studies a concern with the textual analysis of popular forms and the historical context of their creation, and indeed there has been considerable cross-over here in terms of the works theorists in both areas have drawn on for their analyses. However, whereas film studies has tended to focus on the aesthetic value of individual films, cultural studies has been more concerned with the examination of 'the popularity of popular cinema',[53] within which we might include representations of sport. While individual depictions of sport may be of limited or questionable aesthetic value (including some depictions of Gaelic games considered in this volume), their very popularity requires us to examine further their prominence in contemporary society and the reasons for it. The interdisciplinary nature of cultural studies also makes it particularly appropriate to a study encompassing two popular cultural forms such as film and sport, and this has been reflected in recent studies of sport in film.

The development of the representation of Gaelic games has encompassed print, radio, cinema, television and the virtual (via the Internet) world; while this book will touch upon most of these media occasionally, the primary focus is on theatrically exhibited productions, including early actualities, newsreels, documentaries and fiction films. An in-depth study of the depiction of Gaelic games on television in particular remains to be written (and is certainly a project worthy of consideration), though it is beyond the scope of this volume. A further aspect not considered here is that of amateur productions featuring Gaelic games; as the production of films became increasingly possible on cheaper formats, particularly from the 1940s onwards (including 8mm, 16mm, video and eventually digital), amateur enthusiasts turned their cameras to Gaelic games, with significant results. A relevant early example is the footage recorded by Vincent Daly of Coalisland in Tyrone of his local community in the 1940s, including the opening of the local GAA grounds, MacRory Park and Pomeroy Park. Daly also captured the only footage of the homecoming of the victorious 1947 Tyrone minor[54] team, the first team from across the border to win a national GAA title.[55] A further 16mm production of note from the 1940s is the only surviving footage of the 1946 All-Ireland football final, produced by the film production company Comhar Cíno, set up in that year by Colm Ó Laoghaire and Kevin O'Kelly. Both O'Kelly and Ó Laoghaire would go on to make important contributions to the development of Irish film in subsequent decades, with Ó Laoghaire centrally involved in the filming of many of the Gael Linn newsreels discussed in Chapter Six. Comhar Cíno's silent footage, though limited in quality with shaky camera shots positioned in close proximity to play (and therefore unable to capture clearly much of the unfolding action), does include a fascinating – and robust – encounter between protesting teachers and gardaí at half-time, one of the few instances where wider social issues were captured in depictions of Gaelic games in this period.

In the chapters to come this study will explore the evolution of Gaelic games in surviving footage, and the distinctive role this depiction has played, both in films made outside Ireland and within the country. Gaelic games have repeatedly provided film-makers and producers with a resonant motif through which they have represented perceived aspects of Irish identity, perceived as this representation has been neither straightforward nor unproblematic: in international productions in particular, Gaelic games have provided on occasion a shorthand for regressive stereotypes associated with Irish people, including their alleged propensity for violence. For indigenous producers, on the other hand, Gaelic games provided distinctive Irish cultural practices and as such were employed to promote and affirm the Irish nation, particularly as an indigenous film culture began to develop in the aftermath of the Second World War. As we entered the late twentieth century, a critical turn was evident within indigenous productions featuring Gaelic games, though the dominant stereotypes of the past continued to appear.

This book adopts a chronological structure to provide the most effective framework for understanding the continuities and shifts in the relationship between different periods and contexts. Chapter One traces the evolution of depictions of Gaelic games in early cinema. As in other national contexts, Gaelic games featured prominently in early cinematic productions, and were often popular fare with audiences of the period. The chapter will explore these evolving depictions and includes a case study of the first feature-length indigenous film to include hurling, *Knocknagow* (1918), a production which offers a fascinating insight into distinctive features of both hurling and the hammer-throw.

Chapter Two will examine the place and function of Gaelic games in newsreels in the interwar period. In Ireland, the relationship between sport and the media has been complicated by the fact that much of this media emerged, and continues to emanate, from non-indigenous sources, particularly British and American production companies. Indeed, in his 1884 letter of acceptance to Michael Cusack to become the first patron of the GAA, Archbishop Thomas Croke of Cashel indicated his awareness of the popularity of British media in Ireland when he remarked on what he called the 'vicious literature' which 'we are daily importing from England' and the need for 'our national journals ... to give suitable notices of those Irish sports and pastimes which your society means to patronise and promote'.[56] While an indigenous film culture was slow to develop, the representation of Gaelic games in film during the interwar years depended almost entirely on foreign newsreel companies. The surviving footage provides an important record of Gaelic games in these years, though their presentation sometimes reveals prejudiced perspectives and a limited understanding among producers of the games being filmed.

The interwar years also saw a range of Hollywood production companies take an interest in Gaelic games, the subject of Chapter Three. The presence of a large Irish-American audience and significant Irish-American figures within Hollywood contributed to the considerable interest in Irish subjects throughout the classical Hollywood period. These films often relied heavily on dominant stereotypes of the Irish, and were also informed by a 'tourist gaze' on Ireland, though American directors (particularly evident in the work of John Ford) also employed the comic potential of hurling to diffuse anxieties regarding the Irish, and to help integrate Irish-American culture into mainstream American life.

Gaelic games have featured in a considerable number of films across a wide range of genres, though few have foregrounded a hurling-playing lead protagonist. Chapter Four provides a case study of one apposite example, the Rank Organisation's 1958 production *Rooney*. Starring Liverpool-born John Gregson as a hurling-playing Dublin binman, and featuring scenes from the 1957 All-Ireland hurling final, *Rooney* is a fascinating exemplar of the tension that resides between national culture and international representation, with particular consequences for the depiction of indigenous sporting practices, such as hurling.

The first sustained period of indigenous filming of Gaelic games began in 1948, when the National Film Institute of Ireland (NFI) decided to film the All-Ireland hurling final. Chapter Five explores the productions that emerged subsequently and their role in affirming the Irish nation in the aftermath of the Second World War. Gael Linn also depicted Gaelic games during the 1950s and 1960s, and Chapter Six will examine the Irish-language organisation's hugely important contributions, including the *Amharc Éireann* newsreel series and coaching films *Peil* (1962) and *Christy Ring* (1964), during a transitional period for Irish society.

The arrival of indigenous television in 1961 with the launch of Teilifís Éireann would bring a fundamental change to the depiction of Gaelic games in Ireland. From the first live broadcast – which occurred on 5 August 1962 with the All-Ireland football semi-final between Dublin and Kerry – television would become the main medium through which moving images of Gaelic games would be captured and communicated. The discontinuation by the 1970s of the NFI films of Gaelic games and the *Amharc Éireann* series both reflected this development. Eventually, both drama and, particularly, documentary productions focused on Gaelic games would be produced primarily with a view to televisual broadcast rather than theatrical exhibition. As with other aspects of television, the coverage of Gaelic games was informed by previous cinematic depictions, and parallels are evident in the focus on the prematch ceremony and the crowd attending, as well as the positioning of the camera, even in today's televised matches. These parallels are partly accounted for by the movement of individuals into television production who were previously to the forefront of filmic depictions of Gaelic games, including the director of *Peil* and *Christy Ring*, Louis Marcus. Marcus would direct a range of RTÉ documentaries in the 1970s and 1980s, including the GAA centenary production *Sunday after Sunday* (1985). However, Gaelic games continued to feature in cinematic work – both fiction and documentary – though less so than in previous decades, and Chapters Seven and Eight will consider relevant cinematic depictions from the 1960s onwards.

The 1960s to the 1980s was a period of great change in Ireland, a time when a critical and revisionist turn in considerations of the nation and national identity were more evident in the public discourse. This would also be reflected in depictions of Gaelic games, and Chapter Seven will explore some of the relevant productions to emerge in this period, including *Rocky Road to Dublin* (1967) and *Clash of the Ash* (1987), works that might be considered postnationalist in their re-evaluation of Gaelic games in Irish society.

Gaelic games have continued to feature in contemporary depictions of Ireland in film; Chapter Eight will examine some relevant examples, as well as the increasing role of television in such depictions. These representations continue to feature the dominant paradigms of representing Ireland and Irishness, including the continuing popularity of established stereotypes; however, there is also evidence of the occasional employment of aspects of Gaelic games within a larger critique of these stereotypes themselves. While today television is undoubtedly the primary medium capturing and relaying moving images of Gaelic games, this book will conclude by reflecting on the manner in which these contemporary depictions (and the experience of Gaelic games for those attending matches in Croke Park) reveal the fascinating integration of the cinematic into Gaelic-games events themselves.

1

Gaelic Games
in Early Cinema

From the earliest days of the moving image, sport was one of the most popular subjects of representation, a crucial part of what Tom Gunning has referred to as the 'cinema of attractions'.[1] The preceding chapter has already referred to the early experiments to capture motion in photography, experiments often engaged with sporting subjects.[2] Boxing in particular was a frequent subject, with 'fight films' (as they were known at the time) popular with audiences during the first two decades of cinema. This coincided with a period when Irish and Irish-American boxers (and athletes more generally) enjoyed considerable success, and some of the most successful early films featured pugilists from an Irish background. The film that is regarded by some commentators as the first ever feature-length production and first box-office smash, *The Corbett–Fitzsimmons Fight* (1897), featured the reigning world champion, Irish-American 'Gentleman' Jim Corbett.[3] Furthermore, the fight itself was held on 17 March 1897, the date chosen not just reflecting the Irish ethnicity of the champion but also the popularity of boxing among the large urban Irish-American community.

The Corbett–Fitzsimmons Fight was also the first US feature-length film to be screened in Ireland, and this and subsequent fight films enjoyed considerable popularity with Irish audiences.[4] However, these screenings were not without controversy, and Kevin Rockett has noted that the first major contention regarding the cinema in Ireland concerned the screening of the 1910 world heavyweight bout between James J. Jeffries and the African-American boxer Jack Johnson, which prominent Irish political and religious figures tried to have banned lest its interracial subject cause offence to visitors from America, where the film had prompted protests from white Americans, leading to its banning in several cities.[5]

Unsurprisingly, Irish sport, including Gaelic games, featured prominently in early film and attracted considerable interest. The earliest record we have of the filming of a Gaelic game – a clip that does not survive, unfortunately – is a 1901 Cullen's Challenge Cup hurling game between 'Rovers' and 'Grocers' played at Jones' Road – now Croke Park – on 8 December 1901. The film was produced by the Irish Animated Photo Company (which was increasingly referred to in newspapers as the decade progressed as the Irish Animated Picture Company), an Irish actualities firm founded and directed by an early pioneer of film exhibition in Ireland, James T. Jameson. The film was shown as part of a 'Grand Gaelic Night' at the Rotunda on Wednesday 11 December.[6] Gaelic games, and other Irish sporting events, would continue to feature subsequently in both early actualities and newsreels throughout the silent period and enjoyed a significant following among Irish audiences, as evident from surviving press reports.[7] Indeed, on occasion films of Gaelic games could take the place of a feature, such were their popularity, with a supporting programme of films and variety acts assembled around them.[8]

The GAA had a close affinity with nationalist Ireland, with many members also volunteering as members of the major nationalist and republican groups that emerged in the late nineteenth and early twentieth centuries. The 1910s in particular was a turbulent and unpredictable decade, and challenging for the association. While members of the association were imprisoned – including its president James Nowlan, who was interned in England after the 1916 Rising – GAA matches were also occasionally included under 'banned public meetings' and the restrictions imposed by the British government on travel during the War of Independence severely impacted the association and its activities. The hostility of the British forces to Gaelic games in this period is depicted in two of the most popular films (discussed further in Chapter Eight) released in Ireland over the past twenty years; in Ken Loach's *The Wind that Shakes the Barley* (2006) a game of hurling is followed by the interrogation of the players by the Black and Tans and the eventual killing of one because he refuses to give his name in English. Neil Jordan's *Michael Collins* (1996) portrays – albeit somewhat inaccurately, as discussed later – the 'Bloody Sunday' massacre of 1920, when British Auxiliaries burst into Croke Park during a game and opened fire, causing the deaths of fourteen civilians, in retaliation for a series of Irish Republican Army (IRA) attacks earlier in the day. Though both films contain much fictionalisation of events during the decade, they also suggest both the importance of Gaelic games in the period concerned and the challenging context in which the association operated.

Films featuring Gaelic games were also received by audiences within a rising tide of nationalist sentiment. As noted by Denis Condon, 'the gathering of a local audience to watch the film of a game prolonged the demonstration of popular nationalist sentiment that the match itself represented'.[9] These films would appear to have appealed particularly outside of Dublin and above all in the two counties competing in major Gaelic games. Indeed, as Condon also observes, it is evident from newspapers of the time that films of Gaelic games in particular 'received the most favourable local press'.[10]

Cinema proprietors were quick to identify the appeal of Gaelic games on film, including Cork-based impresario Alex McEwan. McEwan managed the Assembly Rooms Picturedrome in the city and, when Cork qualified to play Tipperary in the 1912 Munster hurling final (held at Fraher Field, Dungarvan, County Waterford, on Sunday 27 October), he arranged for the match to be filmed. The fact that this screening was the major event on the bill (as indicated in the advertisement for the screening (Fig. 1.1)) suggests the popular appeal of films of Gaelic games at this time. The Cork-based *Evening Echo* also reported the considerable local interest in the film's first showing in Cork (as the advertisement below indicates, the film was subsequently also screened in Limerick's Athenaeum Hall):

[v]iews of every passage of the exciting and scientific contest are shown, and the loud and frequent applause which was heard at intervals during Wednesday night's performance testified to the great enjoyment that was derived by all present.[11]

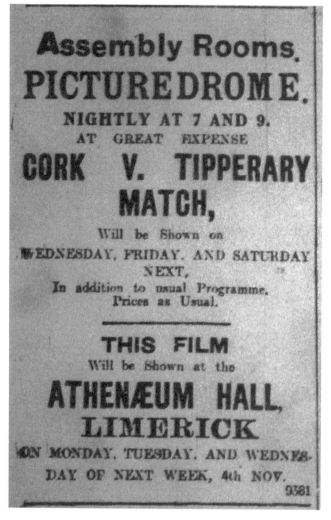

Figure 1.1. Advertisement for the film of the 1912 Munster hurling final between Cork and Tipperary, *Evening Echo*, 28 October 1912[12]

As many provincial towns lacked their own dedicated cinema spaces in the early twentieth century, films were often screened by travelling companies as part of a bill that also included song and music. Jameson's Irish Animated Picture Company were the pioneers in Ireland of this format and occasionally included in their screenings footage of recent Gaelic games. Indeed, such was the appeal of GAA fare that programmes were occasionally changed to accommodate match coverage, as evident in the following report from the *Cork Examiner* of 3 July 1913:

There will be a change of programme at the Opera House tonight, when a most interesting series of films will be shown. The chief feature will be the reproduction of the sensational match for the Dr Croke Memorial at Jones' Road, Dublin, last Sunday, between Kerry and Louth. Gaels were enthused by the mere description of the game, and its presentation through the cinema should attract very large houses to the Opera House for the remainder of the week. It was a great game, and should be well worth watching. The enterprise of the Opera House in securing the films must be highly commended.[13]

The Dr Croke Memorial Tournament was organised by the GAA's Central Council to raise funds for a suitable monument to the association's first patron, Archbishop Thomas Croke. In a much-anticipated game that attracted a then record crowd of 26,000 to Jones' Road (renamed Croke Park shortly thereafter, with much of the proceeds of the game going towards its purchase), Kerry overcame reigning All-Ireland Gaelic football champions Louth. James T. Jameson had arranged for the replay to be filmed and the resulting footage was exhibited in venues managed by Jameson across the country, including in Dublin and Cork; it was met, however, with particular interest in Kerry (where the company held an extended lease at Tralee's Theatre Royal), as evident in the following report from the Cork-based *Evening Echo*:

Large audiences attended this week at the Theatre Royal, Tralee, and there was unbounded enthusiasm when the pictures of the Kerry and Louth match was [sic] thrown on the screen. For three nights the place was packed with enthusiastic people who showed their appreciation of the enterprise of the management in having this splendid picture shown so soon after the contest.[14]

Regrettably, none of the films mentioned so far survive; at the time few appreciated the significance of these films as records of early Gaelic games, while the unstable nitrate-celluloid film stock ensured many failed the test of time. Fortunately, however, damaged extracts from one film from the period have survived, one minute and forty-nine seconds of the Irish Animated Picture Company's film of the 1914 All-Ireland football final replay between Kerry and Wexford. These extracts were rediscovered in the early 1980s in a drawer in New Ross, County Wexford, and were included in Louis Marcus' GAA centenary documentary *Sunday after Sunday* (1985).[15] The game took place on a very windy day, evident in the brief shots of sideline flags. The breeze benefited Wexford in the first half and they scored six points without reply; however, Kerry returned after the break to score an impressive 2-3 – also without reply. The footage includes shots of the solid-silver cup, presented by the Great Southern and Western Railway, which Kerry won outright for claiming their second final in a row. Harry Boland, later a close associate of republican leader Michael Collins, was the referee and he is captured shaking hands with the team captains before the match begins.

The scarcity of surviving footage of Gaelic football from this period is all the more poignant given the fascinating insight into this evolving sport that can be gleaned from this brief piece. The footage (again anticipating a pattern still evident in the coverage of GAA games) places considerable emphasis on the build-up to the game; indeed, this comprises almost one minute of what survives, including shots of the crowd waving to the camera; shots of people entering the ground; panning shots of each team before the game; a shot of the winning trophy (presumably with representatives from the sponsors on each side); a shot of the captains shaking hands as the referee tosses the coin to decide the direction of play for each team; and a final crowd shot before Boland throws in the ball to begin the game.

The footage opens with shots of supporters as the camera scans the crowd, the cameraman already aware of the appeal such shots will have for audiences. Supporters are very aware of the camera, as most raise their hats (ubiquitous in this period) and wave vigorously towards it. Most supporters are dressed formally, probably having attended Mass earlier in the day before travelling to the game. There are no barriers evident between supporters and players; for those early to arrive they had the privilege of sitting right along the side of the pitch. Though men predominate in the crowd, there are a significant number of women also present, with several seated right at the front along the sideline; attending Gaelic games was already a family affair.

There are distinctive early features of the game evident in this film that would soon change: competing counties were still represented by the winning club in the county championship (a practice that would be discontinued the following year), though since 1892 they had been allowed to pick players from other teams in the county also. Wexford was represented in the 1914 All-Ireland by the Blues & Whites club from Wexford town; Kerry by the Killarney Crokes, captained by the legendary Dick Fitzgerald. Fitzgerald published the first GAA coaching manual, *How to Play Gaelic Football*, just over a month before the replay. He is featured prominently in a panning shot of the team early in the footage; a similar shot is included of the Wexford team and anticipates what has become a standard ritual of Gaelic games: the photographing of the teams before the game begins. Wexford captain Seán O'Kennedy is featured prominently here and, though on the losing side in 1914, would lead his team to four All-Irelands in a row in the following years – the first team to do so (though also the last All-Ireland win for Wexford's footballers).

The throw-in was not confined – as now – to players positioned at centre field. Many more competed for the ball at the game's outset. In a feature that would continue into the 1920s (as discussed in the next chapter), much of the play was on the ground – the 'solo run', now a key part of Gaelic football, was still in development and was not perfected in the game for another nine years, when Mayo's Seán Lavin demonstrated the toe-to-hand technique against Dublin in the 1921 All-Ireland final (delayed until June 1923 due to the Civil War).[16] A further distinctive feature of the game at the time, inherited from soccer, was the throwing in (rather than kicking) of the ball from the sideline when it went out of play, and the film includes a shot of Dick Fitzgerald doing so.

Only one camera was used at the game, which was moved from the sideline to the end line as the game developed, capturing play at random intervals; the largely unsatisfactory nature of the coverage of the actual game may also explain why much of the focus is placed on preceding events and crowd shots, including two shots of the young mascots for each team ('Up Kerry,' the Kerry mascot remarks with his arm in the air at one point). Also evident is a ritual that would continue for many decades at Gaelic games (until recent changes at Croke Park): the crowd invading the pitch at full-time to congratulate the victorious Kerry team.

Figure 1.2. A steward admits supporters to the 1914 All-Ireland football final replay while holding an old-style hurling stick (Still from damaged surviving footage, Irish Animated Picture Company, 1914)

A further distinctive feature from the footage is the presence of an old-style hurling stick (Fig. 1.2), held by a steward admitting supporters. It is closer in design to the stick used in hockey, as we will see in the first representation of hurling in fiction film, to which we now turn.

GAELIC GAMES IN EARLY FICTION FILM: *KNOCKNAGOW* (1918)[17]

Cinema became increasingly popular in Ireland in the second decade of the twentieth century; as Kevin Rockett has observed, 'the number of premises where films were being shown regularly increased dramatically during the years 1910 to 1914', with 149 cinemas and halls showing films by 1916.[18] In that year, one of the most important indigenous film production companies was established in Ireland, the Film Company of Ireland (FCOI). The turbulent political context of that year would have a considerable impact on the company, however: its first films were destroyed in the fires that followed the 1916 Rising. Many contributors to the FCOI, though, were quite sympathetic to the republicans involved in the Rising itself, and this was apparent in the themes of the films the company produced. Its co-founder, James Mark Sullivan, was arrested after the Rising and charged with complicity, while a prominent actor and director with the FCOI, John MacDonagh, was a brother of one of the signatories of the 1916 Proclamation, Thomas MacDonagh.

It is understandable, therefore, that its first major feature-length production, *Knocknagow* (1918), should demonstrate these nationalist sympathies. The political resonances of the film could not have been lost on contemporary audiences, based as it was on the hugely popular book *Knocknagow: or, the Homes of Tipperary*[19] by the prominent Fenian Charles Kickham. Indeed, the film had its first public showing on the second anniversary of the 1916 Rising, 22 April 1918, in the Empire Theatre in Dublin.[20] Moreover, while the novel's precise time setting is unclear,[21] though often presumed to be the 1850s,[22] the film is unambiguously set in 1848 – during the Famine and the year of the Young Ireland Rising – adding a further political relevance to the work.

Much of the novel is taken up with a succession of love stories, though there is a noticeable focus on the suffering of the peasantry and the forced depopulation of rural Ireland by unscrupulous land agents in search of bigger rents from larger farmers. As one character (the militant 'old croppy' Phil Morris) remarks in the book: ''Tis the big grass farms that's the ruination uv the counthry' (p. 260). In the film, these relationships with the land are further emphasised through the addition of an emotive scene not present in the book: the eviction of Mick Brien and his family.[23] This scene is also preceded by an incendiary intertitle that might be interpreted as a reference to 1916 or possibly a call to arms on the eve of the War of Independence, as Mat Donovan says to the land agent Pender before the family are evicted, 'There will be a stern reckoning for this one day, Pender, if not in our time, then when other men will know how to deal with this oppression.'

Indeed, the Irish War of Independence began in Tipperary on 21 January 1919, less than a year after the first screening of *Knocknagow*, with an attack by members of the IRA on a police cart carrying gelignite to a local mine.[24] Shots in the film of the innocent Mat Donovan behind bars, wrongly imprisoned in Clonmel jail under a false charge of robbing the corrupt land agent Pender, resonated further with the recent imprisonment of republican prisoners, and their subsequent execution following the 1916 Rising. Mat's eventual release becomes a further call to all Irishmen, as the subsequent intertitle declares (in words again not included in the novel):

FELLOW IRISHMEN: Let us take to heart the lesson in the vindication of Mat Donovan's honour and in the proof of his innocence. We must cultivate under every dire circumstances patience and fortitude to outlive every slander and to rise above every adversity. We are a moral people above crime, and a clean-hearted race must eventually come into its own, no matter how long the journey, no matter how hard the road.

The political significance of the film was also remarked upon in contemporary commentary following its release, with the *Bioscope* reviewer in particular noting that it was 'dangerously tinged with political feeling'.[25]

Knocknagow is particularly significant for followers of sport in Ireland. Firstly, the film includes one of the earliest surviving depictions of hurling on film – and the earliest depiction found in fiction film – when the local hero, Mat 'the Thrasher' Donovan, leads his team in a game. This scene is followed by one of the highlights of both Kickham's novel and the FCOI film, the hammer-throwing contest between Mat and the outsider, the undefeated British officer Captain French. These scenes provide valuable insights into both these sports in this period and, indeed, in an earlier period as the film's producers attempted to capture the way these sports were played in the mid-nineteenth century.

The inclusion of hurling also added to the film's political connotations for contemporary audiences, given (as discussed in the Introduction) the association of hurling with republican figures in the early twentieth century. Indeed, political associations with hurling were already evident in the novel when Mat Donovan lamented – with Captain French, Edmund Kiely and Wat Murphy – the clearance of tenants in the locality to make way for larger farmers' grazing animals, remarking that the 'hurlers are gone' (p. 616), in a passage that includes repeated criticisms of the mistreatment of the people of the area, including the families of those who fought in the British army (pp. 616–17). As will be discussed below, the depiction of the hammer-throw in the film may also have had political resonances for Irish audiences in 1918.

As indicated earlier, sport was among the most popular subjects in early cinema, and its presence in *Knocknagow* reflects this phenomenon. Some journalistic responses to the first screenings of the film in 1918 highlighted its sporting sequences, suggesting that these were particularly appreciated by audiences at the time. After a screening of the film in Cavan town, the *Anglo-Celt* reported:

> The happy peasantry, the prowess of the youth at the hurling match, the hammer-throwing contest, the unexpected 'hunt', the love scenes and the comedy – the life as it was before the agent of the absentee landlord came like a dark shadow on the scene, and with crowbar and torch, laid sweet Knocknagow in ruins – all were depicted by the very perfect actors who made up the cast.[26]

A further contemporary publication, the *Watchword of Labour*, also remarked on the sporting elements in the film, describing 'Mat the Thrasher' as 'always first in the hurling field and other manly sports'.[27]

SPORT AND SOCIAL CLASS IN *KNOCKNAGOW*

In Kickham's novel, the men on each team to play in the hurling game are divided not just by a river but also by their social class, with Mat's men consisting of 'labouring men' while those on the team from the other side of the river are all farmers' sons (p. 389). Though this division is not apparent in the FCOI's adaptation, Mat is clearly marked in the film as a farm labourer from his first appearance ploughing a field, and the similar dress of other hurling players in the film would suggest membership of the same social class. The status of those playing hurling is significant, as one of the central concerns of the GAA when set up was to make athletics accessible to all, at a time when organised sport in Ireland was effectively reserved for members of the upper classes. Michael Cusack, who founded the GAA in 1884, criticised the expansion of the British Amateur Athletic Association (BAAA) into Ireland in the late nineteenth century. As Cronin, Duncan and Rouse outline:

> Cusack was ... irked that officially recognised athletics meetings were held on Saturdays, yet the traditional day for sport in rural Ireland was Sunday, and that the rules of the British AAA narrowed the range

of athletes who could compete. This was sport not for the 'amateur', but for the 'gentleman amateur'. In general, Cusack abhorred the increasing tendency of certain sporting organisations in Victorian Britain to move towards elitism and to seek to preserve their events for people from a certain class.[28]

This issue of social class is particularly significant in both book and film when we consider the representation of sport. In *Knocknagow* the novel, the term 'sport' is primarily associated with the upper and upper-middle classes, while the peasantry engage principally in 'games'. The words 'sport' and 'sportsman/men' are only used in reference to blood sports, in particular hunting (of both fox and hare, as the mention of 'foxhounds or the harriers' (pp. 160, 340, 469, 470, 482–3) suggests)[29] and bird-shooting (pp. 89–93, 608, 610). Though sport is mentioned in relation to a description of bull-baiting (pp. 431–7),[30] its depiction clearly questions its status as a sport, where those in attendance were 'struck with the cruelty of the "sport" they had been watching so eagerly' (p. 436). While bull-baiting is depicted as an activity engaged in by the peasantry and farm labourers, the other blood sports described in the novel are those in which the Protestant upper class and well-off Catholic middle class indulged.

The association of sport solely with blood sports in the novel reflects the view of the period in which it was written. As Ikuo Abe has observed, the description of 'sport' in English and American dictionaries was confined principally to 'skills in the field, like riding and hunting' until the 1880s and 1890s, when this term began to be applied more generally to athletic 'or physically competitive activities'.[31] The changing application of the term also reflected the codification of sports during the mid to late nineteenth century as institutionalisation and bureaucratic organisation, along with 'rational calculation in the pursuit of goals, emphasis on task performance, and seriousness', would come to 'distinguish sport from other types of physical activities such as play, recreation, and games'.[32] Blood sports such as hunting were also affectively denied to the lower classes in the period in which *Knocknagow* (novel and film) was set. It is indicated at one point in Kickham's novel that, as a licence was required for gun ownership, they were effectively unavailable to the peasantry, as noted by local farmer Maurice Kearney's son Hugh:

'Don't you know it is a crime to have arms in Ireland?' said Hugh, sarcastically. 'No one can have arms without a licence, and men like Tom Hogan would not get a licence. So poor Tom has come to look upon never having fired a shot as a proof of his honesty and respectability.' (p. 336)

The lack of gun ownership is also given further political resonance in the film adaptation as Tom Hogan's claim to having never handled a gun provides reassurance to the land agent Pender before he evicts the small farmer and his family. As the intertitle attributes to Pender at one point: 'Did you hear that? He never fired a gun. A safe man – a very safe man to evict.'

The film adaptation depicts the prelude to one of these blood sports, when a hunting party and hounds gather in the background as Barney Broderick attempts to seduce Peg Brady. In this scene we witness the 'blooding of the hounds' as the hunt leader with his bugle throws what appears to be a dead hare to the dogs, who proceed to tear the animal to pieces while being cheered on by Barney and Peg and to the obvious enjoyment of the huntsmen themselves depicted in the background. Though we are spared the full unpleasantness of this sequence due to the black-and-white cinematography, the scene is nonetheless unsettling, including the pleasure that Barney, Peg and the huntsmen get from the evisceration of the hare.

THE DEPICTION OF HURLING IN NOVEL AND FILM

In terms of the depiction of hurling in *Knocknagow*, the Tipperary setting has a particular resonance. The GAA was founded in Thurles, County Tipperary, in 1884, eleven years after the first publication of *Knocknagow*, and the county has gone on to produce some of the greatest players and teams in the history of the sport. Altogether, Tipperary has won the All-Ireland hurling title twenty-seven times (up to 2018) and is part of hurling's 'holy trinity' along with Kilkenny and Cork, the other most successful counties in the sport. Indeed, Tipperary won the first hurling All-Ireland final in 1887, while the first president of the GAA was

Tipperary-born athlete Maurice Davin. Davin was invited by Michael Cusack to take on this role because of his formidable achievements as an athlete – significantly, in view of its depiction in the film, in the weight-throwing disciplines – and he was considered in his lifetime to be one of the greatest athletes in either Great Britain or Ireland.[33]

With regard to the representation of hurling and the hammer-throw in the novel and film, one is struck first by the heroic status bestowed upon the leader of the Knocknagow hurling team Mat Donovan in both texts, a status comparable to that of the legendary hurling-playing warrior figure in Irish mythology, Cúchulainn, and one affirmed by his ability as a sportsman. Described variously in the novel as a 'magnificent specimen of the Irish peasant' (p. 18) and the 'hero of the district' (p. 351), Mat achieves this status despite being 'only a poor labourer' (p. 352). Indeed, fears are expressed in the book about the well-being of the village as a whole if Mat did not perform well in the sledge-throwing contest (transformed into the hammer-throw in the film), such is his importance to the esteem of the community. As Phil Lahy remarks after Mat takes a fall from the top of a large hayrick:

'What I'm afraid uv is that this fall may come against him in throwing the sledge with the captain. I'll advise Mat not to venture. 'Tis too serious a matter. And – and [...] a man should not forget his duty to the public. That's Mat's weak point. He can't be got to see that he's a public character. The people at large are concerned. The credit of Knocknagow is at stake. So I must explain this to Mat. The captain, too, though a good fellow, is an aristocrat. That fact cannot be lost sight of. So I must explain matters to Mat. An' if he's not in condition, he's bound to decline throwing the sledge with Captain French on the present occasion.' (p. 365)

At times there is almost a homoerotic charge to the descriptions of Mat in the novel, as when trainee priest Arthur O'Connor first encounters him:

Mat was greeted as an old acquaintance by both Edmund and Father Carroll, but Arthur O'Connor had never seen him before, and contented himself with admiring the broad shoulders and sinewy limbs of the young peasant. (p. 401)

In the film this heroic depiction continues, with Mat described in an early intertitle as having a heart 'as stout as his arm' and being the 'finest lad in the county' and later by Mary Kearney as 'worth twenty such men', with reference to a British soldier who seeks the affections of Bessy Morris, the woman Mat eventually marries towards the close of the film.

In the novel the hurling game is eagerly anticipated, with repeated references to the upcoming 'long-disputed hurling match' (p. 341) between 'the two sides of the river' (p. 68). However, the novel also reflects on the violence that could be part of such encounters, an aspect entirely missing from the film adaptation. This is particularly apparent in the sermon given by the local curate Father Hannigan, who deplores the violence of previous hurling encounters:

> … then there's the hurling. There's a deal of bad blood when ye hurl the two sides of the river. If there's any more of the work that was carried on at the last match, ye'll be the disgrace of the country, instead of being, as ye are, the pride of the barony. (p. 68)

However, the match itself is eventually cancelled due to the non-appearance of the captain of the opposing team, Tom Cuddehy, and a 'promiscuous match' (p. 448) is played instead, 'wudout any regard to the two sides' (p. 448), which appears to be more for fun than a serious encounter and acts as a prelude to the main event, the throwing of the sledge. In the film, no such qualification for the game is given, though the encounter we witness does seem rather 'promiscuous' insofar as it is difficult to identify opposing teams as all chase after the ball. Even in the eighteenth and nineteenth centuries it was normal for opposing teams to wear distinguishing colours or dress,[34] neither of which are evident in the film, or are impossible to distinguish in the black-and-white photography, with all players dressed similarly in shirts and breeches. Possibly the film's director Fred O'Donovan and those involved in the production may have omitted team colours to denote the 'promiscuous' nature of the game, presuming that audiences would be familiar with its depiction in Kickham's

Figure 1.3. Mat Donovan leads his Knocknagow team in a game of hurling wielding a distinctive long, narrow, sharply curved, heavy-heeled hurling stick (*Knocknagow*, Film Company of Ireland, 1918)

very popular novel. It would appear from the footage that a ball is thrown in among the players, who then fight for possession, but it is very difficult to identify a ball in the clip once the play begins. It seems hurling did not suit the nature of cinematography at the time with its fixed camera position and angles and very limited panning movement, evident in the clip of the sport in the film, which results in players running out of view when the ball is played to the left before returning to the camera's view again. The challenge of trying to film hurling may also have contributed to the decision to only include a very short clip of the game, in total some forty seconds, while the hammer-throwing sequence lasts for over three and a half minutes.

It is noticeable, however, from the shape of the hurling stick (Fig. 1.3), with its longer and narrower boss, and the nature of the brief game featured in the film that this is primarily the ground-based pursuit practised in the eighteenth and nineteenth centuries (when, for example, handling of the *sliotar* was forbidden), rather than the game of today in which the ball is more frequently played in the air. The hurling stick itself is of the earlier form, 'long, narrow, sharply curved, heavy-heeled', as described by Diarmuid O'Flynn, 'which made hitting off the sod that little bit easier'.[35] The shape of the hurley has changed significantly during the twentieth century as the sport has evolved from 'the slower game that emphasised ground hurling, hip-to-hip combat, and encounters of strength' evident in the depiction in *Knocknagow*, to the more possession-focused game of today 'which demanded getting the ball into the hand, and this in turn required a more manageable stick that made it easier to pick up the ball off the ground'.[36] The sequence of play featured in the film also indicates little positional awareness among the players, with all chasing the ball wherever it moves.

DEPICTING 'THROWING THE SLEDGE'/ 'THE THROWING OF THE HAMMER' IN NOVEL AND FILM

'Throwing the sledge' follows the hurling match in both novel and film, and here Captain French, who we are told in the film's intertitle 'had won great honours as an athlete in London', challenges Mat. Incidentally, it is also clear in the novel that the aristocratic captain, possibly reflecting his class and military bias, had little time for hurling:

Captain French was a soldier, and the son of a soldier, and, as one by one the hurlers stepped forward as their names were called, and pulled off their coats, he thought what a sin and a shame it was that such splendid 'material' should be going to waste in that way. (p. 448)

As well as being popular at fairs and athletic gatherings in Ireland throughout the eighteenth and nineteenth centuries, weight-throwing, like hurling, had a much older heritage, as noted by Watterson and Naughton:

The tradition went back as far as Cúchulainn, hero of the Red Branch Knights, who, legend has it, could throw a huge stone, lashed to the wooden beam of a chariot wheel, prodigious distances. This was the era of the Tailteann Games, the oldest of all sporting festivals, which dates from 1829 BC. During the Middle Ages, the makeshift implements thrown by the ancient warriors were replaced by items such as the sledge-hammer used by blacksmiths. Henry VIII was known for his prowess at 'throwing the sledge', as was Mat the Thrasher, who helped redeem the honour of Charles J. Kickham's fictional village of Knocknagow when he challenged and beat the interloper Captain French in a test of strength.[37]

Possibly influenced by the contemporary competitive nature of the hammer-throw in the early part of the twentieth century, particularly at the Olympic Games, where Irish-born athletes were extraordinarily successful and received considerable coverage in the Irish press,[38] the novel's 'throwing the sledge' is retitled 'the throwing of the hammer' in the film. Between 1900 and 1932, Irish-born athletes dominated the weight-throwing events every year the Olympic Games were held, winning gold in the hammer-throw at each Games except for 1924 when Matt McGrath (discussed below) won the silver medal. Before independence, the event was dominated by Irish-born emigrants to the United States, who represented that country and were collectively known as the 'Irish Whales'.[39] The success of Irish-born athletes in international competition was well documented in the Irish press of the time and Mark Quinn has described the 'intense interest in all sections of the Irish Press' in the fortunes of Irish athletes at the 1906 Intercalated Games.[40] In the Olympic Games that directly preceded the release of *Knocknagow*, in Stockholm in 1912 (the 1916 Olympics were cancelled due to the First World War), a drawing of shot-put champion and Clare native Patrick 'Fat Mac' McDonald was prominently featured in the *Irish Independent* under the headline 'Irishman's world record' (Fig. 1.4).

IRISHMAN'S WORLD RECORD.

P. MacDonald, a Southern Irishman, now in the New York Police, who won the weight-putting event in the Olympic Games at Stockholm yesterday, creating a world's record.

Figure 1.4. Olympian Patrick 'Fat Mac' McDonald as featured in the *Irish Independent*, 11 July 1912[41]

Another successful Irish-born athlete at the 1912 Olympics also had a close connection to the place where *Knocknagow* was set. Matt McGrath, who won gold in the hammer-throw event, also representing the United States, was born in Nenagh, County Tipperary, and visited his home town to a great reception after his victory, as reported in the *Nenagh Guardian* of 3 August 1912.[42]

The dominance of the Irish in this discipline reflected the popularity of weight-throwing events at sports meetings and festivals in Ireland throughout the nineteenth century. However, it has also been suggested that the Irish brought a particular style and approach to the event that gave them a distinct advantage over their American and international challengers. In the US, throwers demonstrated limited movement of their feet; however, the movement of the feet in the wind-up to the throw played a crucial role in the success of what became known as the 'Celtic style'.[43] It has been described by Johnny Watterson and Lindie Naughton in their book *Irish Olympians, 1896–1992* with recourse to Kickham's description of Captain French's throw in *Knocknagow*:

> He took the heavy sledge, and placing his foot to the mark, swung it backwards and forwards twice, and then wheeling rapidly full round, brought his foot to the mark again, and flying from his arms as from a catapult, the sledge sailed through the air, and fell at a distance that seemed to startle many of the spectators. (p. 452)

This, however, is not an accurate description of French's throw in the film. Indeed, though French is marked in the novel as a British officer, son of a local landlord and 'aristocrat' (p. 391), he is also clearly identified as a Tipperary native. However, this is never acknowledged in the film and he is presented not just as a British officer but in attire a member of the upper class, an outsider against whom Mat must defend the honour of Knocknagow, further accentuating the political resonances of the encounter. Equally, the captain's throws involve little if any foot movement. It is Mat's final victorious throw that is closest to the style described in Kickham's book, including the characteristic 'wheeling rapidly full round' before releasing the hammer.

Mat's throw is inspired by a concern, as the intertitle tells us, 'for the honour of old Knock-na-gow I must win', a concern also highlighted in the novel, where Mat utters the words 'For the credit of the little village!' (p. 453) before throwing the sledge. This concern would become a defining aspect of the development of sport in Ireland in subsequent decades, particularly those games promoted by the GAA.[44] The GAA's decision in 1887 to use the dividing line of parishes for Gaelic football and hurling clubs ensured that Gaelic games would be defined by place, a crucial factor in their subsequent popularity. The choice of the county boundary for the elite level of the sport would also have far-reaching consequences, not least the increasing importance of counties for Irish people's own sense of identity. However, the precedence afforded club (parish) over county in the early years was evident (as discussed above) in the practice whereby the winning club in each county represented the county in the major national competition (the All-Ireland Championship), a convention that prevailed until 1915. Indeed, in a 2009 obituary for the legendary Wexford hurler Billy Rackard, the *Irish Independent* noted that 'Charles Kickham had produced a blueprint for the GAA when he wrote *Knocknagow* eleven years before the Association was founded. The honour and the glory of the little village was what Kickham espoused. The GAA nursed the concept into being.'[45] This local focus continues to play an important role today, particularly in rural communities, providing, for example, a point of communal association and support in times of trauma.[46] In an *Observer* article in May 2011, Fintan O'Toole stressed the significance of the sentiments expressed by Mat Donovan while reflecting on the killing of Police Service of Northern Ireland officer and GAA player Ronan Kerr and the support provided by the community for the officer's surviving relatives and friends:

The hero of the classic GAA novel, Charles Kickham's *Knocknagow*, published in 1873, is a farm labourer who goes on to the hurling field with the cry: 'For the credit of the little village!' GAA players still take the field for the credit of all the little villages – not just the literal ones like Ronan Kerr's Beragh, but the psychological villages to which we cling in a globalised culture – the idea of a place, of a community, of something that is not yet owned by a TV company or a corporation.[47]

It is often commented upon by the GAA itself, as well as other observers, that its continuing strength lies not in the inter-county game but in the parish-based model, where communities are affirmed and revolve around their local club. At the 2003 GAA annual congress, for example, its then president, Seán Kelly, remarked on 'the importance of the local GAA club to the Association. The GAA club is the cornerstone of the Association and the needs of the GAA club must be addressed.'[48] Indeed, the GAA's mission statement continues to stress this local base, describing the association as 'a community-based volunteer organisation promoting Gaelic games, culture and lifelong participation'.[49]

As was the case internationally, sport was also an important and popular subject matter in early cinema in Ireland. And due to their increasing popularity and political resonance, Gaelic games featured frequently in film and attracted large and appreciative audiences to screenings. While few of the earliest films survive, the brief extracts that do show sports that were rapidly evolving but that still shared similarities with other popular Victorian pursuits, including soccer. They also show that aspects of the indigenous games still familiar today – including the prematch ceremony and its appeal to spectators across genders – were already evident in the 1910s.

As that decade developed, narrative film became increasingly dominant in cinema programmes, and hurling would feature in the first major production of the influential Film Company of Ireland, *Knocknagow*. The depiction of sport in *Knocknagow* is significant, not just for audiences at the time of the film's initial release, but also for viewers today interested in sport. Both sport and film played significant roles in the affirmation and popularisation of national sentiment in Ireland in the late nineteenth and early twentieth centuries and *Knocknagow* provides a relevant example of this process. The film also offers an important record of the sports depicted, indicating the form and style of both hurling and the hammer-throw (considered an important Gaelic sport at the time) in the early twentieth century and, indeed, in an earlier time. This includes the ground-based form of hurling played, and the narrower shape of the hurling stick, as well as the style of the hammer-throw itself, a style that contributed significantly to the success of Irish-born hammer-throwers at international events for much of the early twentieth century. While having important implications for the representation of social class in the period concerned, the depiction of sport in *Knocknagow* also contributed significantly to the political resonances of the film, given the association of hurling with republican politics in the period, but also through the emphasis in the film on the hammer-throw challenge as an international contest between an Irish peasant (Mat Donovan) and a representative of the British establishment (Captain French). Furthermore, in its highlighting of the importance of local identity to Irish people, the film affirmed a central focus that has been crucial to the growth and development of the GAA throughout its history, and continues to be relevant to its role in Irish society today.

The significant indigenous film production of the 1910s, including the work of the Irish Animated Picture Company and particularly the Film Company of Ireland, boded well for Irish film in subsequent decades. However, the promise shown was not to be realised. Regrettably, both companies had disbanded by the end of the decade, and the divided Ireland that emerged at the beginning of the 1920s failed to support or encourage an indigenous film culture. As a result, the filming of Gaelic games in the interwar years would be undertaken primarily by foreign-owned newsreel and production companies, and it is to these we now turn.

2

Gaelic Games
in the Newsreel Era[1]

I
n the years immediately after Irish independence in 1922,
various groups sought to promote indigenous Irish culture while
simultaneously emphasising Ireland's difference to Britain. In this
context, organised sport would play a crucial role. Significantly,
the GAA grew to become the largest and most successful organisation
promoting not just the sports it was responsible for, but also a distinctly
nationalist expression of Irish identity through which the team games
of Gaelic football and hurling were affirmed as *the* definitively Irish
sports. Both the print and broadcast media – in particular radio – had
an important role to play in this process, though cinema newsreels also
contributed to the rising popularity of Gaelic games. Indeed, the very fact
that nationalist Ireland employed both sport and the cinema to promote
its cause in the early to mid-twentieth century is indicative of the cultural
importance and influence of both forms. However, surviving footage of
Gaelic games from the 1920s and 1930s come almost entirely from foreign
newsreel companies such as Pathé and Movietone and these depictions,
while important as records of the evolving games in the period, also
sometimes reveal a foreign eye on sports not entirely comprehended.

The signing of the Anglo-Irish Treaty on 6 December 1921 and the
subsequent establishment of the Irish Free State the following year presented both challenges and opportunities for the GAA. Partition led
to problems for an association operating then, as now, on an all-island
basis, including the hostility of the unionist-dominated parliament that
emerged in Northern Ireland. Furthermore, the Civil War that ensued

in the South between 1922 and 1923 divided clubs and members within the association, much as it divided families throughout the country. Nonetheless, Gaelic games provided one of the few spaces where those divided politically could encounter each other, and the GAA played an important role in helping to repair the divisions that the Civil War wrought.[2]

Despite these challenges, the GAA benefited significantly from the emphasis within the Free State on indigenous culture and quickly set about reorganising the association and its competitions. County boards and clubs were re-established and regular dates were assigned to the All-Ireland finals in both hurling and Gaelic football. A new national competition, the National League, was introduced for both codes in 1925 and the following year the interprovincial Railway Cup competition was established. It was also in this decade that the major trophies, now synonymous with their respective championships, were first presented: the Liam McCarthy Cup for the hurling All-Ireland in 1923 and in 1928 the Sam Maguire Cup for the Gaelic football championship. As will be discussed further in Chapter Three, in the 1920s the GAA introduced annual tours to the United States for the All-Ireland champions in both hurling and football, tours that would eventually be captured on film and inspire Hollywood studios to make films featuring hurling. The GAA also undertook a major development of its main stadium, Croke Park, and two new stands were built: the Hogan Stand in 1924, and what was then a revolutionary double-decker stand, the Cusack, in 1938.[3] These developments contributed to the growing popularity of Gaelic games in Ireland in these decades, with attendances at major games for both codes increasing significantly, rising from (the then record) 37,500 for the 1926 All-Ireland football final to 68,950 for the 1938 final.[4]

Newspapers and radio were undoubtedly the most significant media in the promotion of Gaelic games, though cinema newsreels also played their part. Indeed, the impact of moving-image representations of Gaelic football and hurling players in the 1920s and 1930s should not be underestimated, particularly in the pre-television era. As Ciara Chambers has noted, newsreels in general had an important role to play in both encouraging support for the nationalist movement and shaping views of Ireland – 'the rural, the peasant, the childlike, the feminine'[5] – abroad, and it is likely that depictions of Gaelic games within these newsreels had comparable results. Furthermore, this footage provides us today with a unique insight into both codes as they were played in the early twentieth century, as well as fascinating perspectives on the context in which games were played and how they were received by spectators – and all this despite the sometimes ill-informed commentary in the mainly foreign productions.

NEWSREELS AT HOME AND ABROAD

Newsreels were an important cinematic form that emerged in the early decades of film production. The pioneering film work of the Lumière brothers anticipated the themes of newsreels in later decades in their focus on 'short actuality films [or *actualités*] of factory workers streaming out through … factory gates, members of a photographic convention disembarking from a river trip, princes and heads of state on official visits'.[6] Newsreels were first screened in Britain in June 1910 with *Pathé's Animated Gazette*, less than a year after the first 'specially edited newsfilm' was shown in France by Pathé's then parent company.[7] Newsreels typically included four or five weekly news items, each approximately a minute in length.[8] In Britain, they were exhibited on a circuit that travelled from cinema to cinema every three days, taking around three weeks to reach all cinemas. By 1912, the popularity of newsreels was such that they were issued biweekly following the changes to cinema programmes.[9]

In Ireland, newsreels were part of film programmes by the mid-1910s, though actualities had been screened from the very earliest years of film showings in Ireland, including episodes featuring Gaelic games. As newsreels developed in the 1910s, the Irish experience – unsurprisingly, being part of the United Kingdom – was one with a strongly British emphasis. Apart from a short-lived Irish-produced *Irish Events* newsreel between 1917 and 1920, newsreels exhibited in Ireland in the interwar years came almost entirely from Britain and America, in particular five major international companies: Movietone News (jointly owned by the British press baron Lord Rothermere and the American company Fox Movietone), Paramount (Paramount Pictures, US), Pathé (originally

French-owned but by the mid-1920s jointly owned by Associated British Picture Corporation, UK, and Warner Bros, US), Gaumont British News (also originally French-owned but controlled by Gaumont British, UK, by the 1930s) and Universal (owned by General Distributors, US).[10] These newsreels, while occasionally featuring items of Irish interest, were primarily geared towards British audiences; as Ciara Chambers, in her history of newsreels in Ireland, observes, 'Ultimately, the distribution circuit was a British one – and newsreels were mostly aimed at audiences throughout Britain rather than Ireland.'[11]

The principal concern of newsreels was entertainment. In the words of the *Pathé Pictorial* newsreel editor: 'The Pictorial does not attempt to enforce education upon an audience. Our primary business is to entertain, amuse and interest our audiences.'[12] Consequently, controversial subjects were generally avoided though items on political events did feature, and not always from a neutral perspective. Coming as they did principally from British companies, newsreels tended to be pro-British and conservative, often featuring members of the royal family, all of which occasionally led to protests in Ireland and among Irish nationalists. In 1932, members of the IRA visited cinemas across the country, including in Dublin, Waterford and Sligo, and instructed managers, under the threat of violence, not to screen newsreels of 'an anti-nationalist character' or depicting English royalty.[13] On one occasion an allegedly 'imperialistic' newsreel was removed from a cinema in Dublin and burned in public.[14] In response to this, the Fox Distributing Co. sent an extraordinary letter to a Dublin cinema manager expressing its sorrow that 'Óglaigh na hÉireann [as the IRA referred to its organisation] object to depicting the royal family in the movietone news'. The company also retitled its Irish newsreel editions as *Irish Movietone News*, replaced the Union Jack in its opening caption with an Irish emblem, and omitted items featuring the British royal family from subsequent editions distributed in the Irish Free State.[15]

Apart from objections to film and newsreels on political grounds, the Catholic Church in Ireland also viewed the cinema with considerable suspicion. The passing of the Censorship of Films Act (1923), one of the earliest pieces of legislation to be enacted in the new parliament of the Irish Free State, reflected this suspicion by both Church and state. This particularly restrictive Act was concerned with the censoring of work considered 'indecent, blasphemous, or obscene' and allowed only for a general certificate for releases, such that, as Kevin Rockett has noted, 'for the first four decades of national film censorship in Ireland ... about 3,000 films were banned and some 8,000 films cut as the film censors equated Irish children with adults'.[16] For many in the Church the cinema was a decadent foreign cultural form likely to corrupt those who encountered it. As the Irish bishops declared in a 1927 pastoral:

> The evil one is ever setting his snares for unwary feet. At the moment, his traps for the innocent are chiefly the dance hall, the bad book, the indecent paper, the motion picture, the immodest fashion in female dress – all of which tend to destroy the virtues characteristic of our race.[17]

Newsreels were occasionally the subject of Irish censorship, and in 1936 the distributors of Pathé's cinemagazine *Pathé Pictorial* were instructed by Irish film censor James Montgomery to remove shots of girls 'indecently "clad" in brassieres and trunks' in an item concerning a beauty contest.[18] However, given the generally uncontroversial nature of newsreel content, this was a rare occurrence.

Despite the reservations and evident suspicion among nationalists, film-going was nonetheless a very popular pursuit in Ireland in the 1920s and 1930s. This was apparent in the large numbers of cinemas built in this period, increasing from 149 cinemas and halls showing films in 1916 to 265 cinemas by 1930.[19] In her 1935 paper 'Cinema Statistics in Saorstát Éireann', Thekla J. Beere found one cinema for every 16,000 people in the Free State, with one cinema seat for every twenty-seven persons. Most of these cinemas had screenings at least five days a week.[20] From her findings, Beere estimated 18.25 million admissions per year to cinemas in the state – an average of over 350,000 people, out of a population of nearly three million, attending each week – with most in Dublin and other urban centres. While not among the highest attendances per capita in Europe in the 1930s, Beere's description of the growth of cinema to become a major social institution in Ireland is nonetheless impressive.[21] Furthermore, in a time of considerable social challenges, with unemployment, for instance, increasing alarmingly from 29,000 in 1931 to 138,000 in 1935, film and sport provided Irish people with crucial recreational outlets.[22]

SPORT IN THE NEWSREELS

Given that newsreels tended to feature uncontroversial items, it is not surprising that sport was often among them. Sport also suited the requirements and limitations of early newsreels. In a time when travel and equipment were less developed or sophisticated, newsreel editors preferred staged stories – such as sporting events – 'as they were much easier to plan and coordinate in advance'.[23] Equally, the huge interest in sport – and the excitement that it could engender – meant that such items were among the most popular in newsreels. Studies of British newsreels have revealed that the sales of individual newsreel episodes could increase considerably if particular sporting events were featured.[24] Newsreels depicting sport would also appear to have attracted considerable public interest among Irish audiences. There are limited accounts surviving of responses to newsreel screenings in the interwar period, though the presence of occasional advertisements, particularly in local and regional newspapers, for the screening of All-Ireland games would suggest an expectation of significant audience interest.[25] The fact that these newsreel items are mentioned in advertisements concerned principally with promoting the latest Hollywood releases suggests that there was audience interest in them. With a general lack of information on contemporary responses to such newsreels, we must, as historian Luke McKernan has advised, 'go by what ended up on the screen, and then deduce reasons why'.[26]

British newsreels distributed in Ireland featured an array of sports, including Gaelic games. The depiction of Gaelic games reflected the recognition by British and American newsreel companies of audience interest in local stories. From the 1920s onwards, local editions, with one or two items relating to a specific city or region, were produced. As noted by newsreel historian Linda Kay, exhibitors would occasionally get in touch with a newsreel company and alert them to an important local event 'so that people could see themselves, their friends, or their community on the big screen';[27] it is within this context that depictions of Gaelic games emerged. Gaelic games were featured as late as the 1970s, though less regularly than during the interwar period. Newsreels were on much safer ground, particularly south of the Irish border, when they featured Gaelic games rather than British royalty, and items featuring royalty were on occasion replaced by sporting items in editions distributed in the Free State.[28] The association of these sports with nationalist Ireland and the growing popularity of Gaelic games throughout the interwar period ensured a positive response and considerable interest among audiences. Gaelic games featured in the newsreels of all the major companies distributing in Ireland, including British Movietone and Gaumont British News. However, Pathé newsreels gave the most widespread coverage of both codes and consequently comprise the principal focus of the remainder of this chapter.[29]

THE GAA'S RESPONSE TO THE MEDIA IN IRELAND

In common with the Catholic Church, the GAA also responded post-independence with some alarm to the increasing presence of 'foreign' cultural forms, including non-indigenous sports, in Ireland. The organisation was also sensitive to depictions of its own sports in Irish and foreign media and often found fault with these portrayals. In particular the GAA was concerned about the portrayal of Gaelic games as violent; the considerable coverage given to sports perceived as non-Irish; and the media's role in promoting what it considered un-Irish and un-Christian ideas in Ireland.

Members of the GAA were concerned that a hostile and uninformed media was exaggerating the potential for violence in Gaelic games to affirm prevailing stereotypes of the 'savage Irish'.[30] As indicated later in this chapter and the next, these concerns were at least partly justified based on the evidence of some surviving newsreels and occasional references to Gaelic games in the English print media, including a claim in the *Daily Mail* in October 1921 that 'you cannot have a good hurling match without a fight'.[31] However, Gaelic games were rarely covered in the British media, although some Irish editions of British publications did carry reports of matches from the 1920s. These were viewed with suspicion by members of the GAA, with some contending that such reports existed principally to draw Irish people to generally foreign and decadent content in the publications.[32] The GAA's suspicions of the British media were evident in the decision taken at the association's congress in 1930 to ban members from 'writing Gaelic notes or giving information on Gaelic matters to British newspapers'.[33] For the Belfast-based proposer of this motion, Seán McKeown, British newspapers were 'anti-national and anti-Gaelic', and anyone who assisted in bringing them into Ireland was 'a greater traitor than Dermot McMurrough'.[34] McKeown also objected to 'the smutty English papers in their attempts to demoralise our people' through their inclusion of 'full reports of murders, suicides, divorces and every form of crime'.[35] The ban was eventually lifted in 1937 when the then GAA president Robert O'Keeffe argued that the association needed to be in a position to respond to articles concerning the GAA and its games in British newspapers.[36] The GAA also recognised the importance of the British media in relaying reports and broadcasts of Gaelic games to Irish audiences in Britain; the 1939 congress passed a motion proposed by the London branch to request the assistance of the BBC in relaying radio broadcasts of All-Ireland finals in England.[37]

While the GAA was concerned about the reporting and broadcast of its own games, it also objected to the reporting of what it considered 'foreign' games, including cricket, rugby, soccer and hockey, in the Irish media. In particular, it objected to the interruption of broadcasts of its own games by reports from other games, particularly soccer. At its annual congress in 1936, the association condemned this 'insidious method of introducing non-Gaelic pastimes' to Irish people and threatened non-cooperation with Raidió Éireann, the national radio station, in protest.[38] Furthermore, the association's Central Council contemplated in 1938 ending its practice of advertising in Dublin-based daily newspapers, due to their 'persistent featuring and propaganda of alien pastimes, whilst neglecting, if not ignoring, the historic games of the Gael in the various county competitions'.[39]

Members of the GAA did occasionally express concern regarding the influence of the cinema in Ireland and its potential impact – moral, athletic and commercial – on GAA members and the association. A local Gaelic games columnist in Derry in 1921 remarked that many of his fellow Derry men preferred 'Charlie Chaplin, soccer, and jazzing, [and] filthy English periodicals' to Gaelic games.[40] In Letterkenny at a reorganisation meeting of the GAA in Donegal, held in December 1931, the local Labour Party TD Archie J. Cassidy lamented, in comments that received vocal support from those present, that

> the youth who in the past age passed their idle hours in healthy athletics now chose instead the picture-house, where so many immoral pictures were displayed. These were pictures which were importing the mannerisms and tastes of Hollywood, which were certainly not racy of the soil of Ireland.[41]

The Gaelic games correspondent with the nationalist *Fermanagh Herald* during the 1930s was also particularly scathing of the cinema's influence in Ireland, asking on one occasion 'how many [GAA members] did you see entering those chain-houses of de-nationalising influence and Imperial propaganda, commonly called cinemas?'[42] In an article the following week in the same newspaper by a columnist simply identified as 'Gael', the writer asked whether cinemas were succeeding

> to a greater extent than foreign games in undermining our Christian Nationalism. Cannot our County Board do something about it, or is it helpless in the matter? If we must imitate the foreigner, why not imitate the American and form a 'Legion of Decency'? How could any self-respecting Gael absent himself from such a campaign?[43]

These concerns were echoed in 1940 when the influential Father Michael Hamilton, a County Clare GAA official, lamented the idolisation by Irish people of the 'artificial heroism of filmland'.[44] GAA officials also expressed concerns regarding the perceived emasculating effects of the cinema, with one commentator contending that films were 'wreaking havoc on the physique of the younger generation'.[45] The secretary of the Waterford county GAA attributed his county's poor performance in the 1936 championship to the effeminacy of picture houses and jazz halls.[46] In the same year a Donegal club official contended that young men preferred 'to go and see Greta Garbo and Shirley Temple' than play Gaelic games.[47] Occasionally, the cinema was also viewed as a significant commercial rival to social events, such as *céilithe* (traditional Irish dances), organised by the GAA to raise funds. GAA officials in Dublin in 1933, for instance, expressed alarm that they could not maintain their own social premises as there were 'too many cinemas'.[48]

While the comments above reflect concerns among some GAA members regarding the influence of cinema in Ireland, in general the cinema received less criticism than other 'foreign' cultural forms, including sports, music and dances. Indeed, the GAA occasionally used the cinema to promote its own events and for fundraising purposes. In the 1920s, the association in Belfast succeeded in having announcements in local cinemas of upcoming games,[49] while the GAA board in Derry city ran a comedy matinee in a local cinema to raise funds in 1934.[50] Occasionally, team trips to the cinema were organised, including that of the Cavan team in 1937, to build team morale prior to big games.[51] Moreover, it is evident from the extent of surviving newsreels of Gaelic games in the interwar years that the GAA facilitated newsreel companies in the filming of their games, and valued the footage that was shot and exhibited.

REACTIONS TO NEWSREELS BY THE GAA

There is limited information available with regard to the response of the GAA to newsreels. However, what evidence there is indicates that the association was aware of the impact in Ireland, including on its sports. At its annual congress in 1930, officials discussed what they viewed as disproportionate coverage in newsreels of 'foreign' sports, including Association football and rugby, when compared to Gaelic games.[52] One official – Tom Markham from Dublin – recommended the setting up of 'something in the nature of an intelligence department ... to attend cinemas where foreign games were thrown on the screen. They seldom saw Gaelic games thrown on the screen but they frequently had Soccer and Rugby.'[53] The impulse for such a development followed from the GAA's ban on members participating in or watching such 'foreign' games as soccer and rugby. Markham, along with the Gaelic games columnist of the republican newspaper *An Phoblacht*, 'Cimarron' – likely the same person – were among the most prominent critics of the depiction of 'foreign' sports in newsreels. For 'Cimarron' the GAA congress had a responsibility to promote the inclusion of items featuring more 'national events' in newsreels: 'Why not screen our hurling, and football matches?' he wrote.[54] Markham also argued at the GAA's annual congress in 1933 that the association needed to employ the cinema more effectively in 'the propagation of national games'.[55]

At the same congress, a Wexford delegate remarked on the 'inspiring' experience of viewing a film of the previous week's National Hurling League final (featuring Kilkenny and Limerick) in the cinema.[56] However, GAA officials were less impressed with newsreels produced by Irish Movietone News, the name of which (as indicated above) was changed in the early 1930s in response to complaints from Irish audience members. At the 1933 congress the then GAA president, Seán McCarthy, criticised the screening of foreign games by Irish Movietone News and declared that it was 'nothing less than a scandal' to have 'Irish' associated with items that were 'not Irish'. 'If Movietone News was not going to be Irish, then they should be stopped using the title "Irish"', he continued.[57] McCarthy's remarks reflected the conviction among some GAA officials that the association's responsibilities went further than the administration of its games, including working on behalf of the moral and social well-being of the country.

It is from such concerns that some officials, unhappy with the overwhelming Anglo-American content of cinema programmes and newsreels, sought to employ the substantial membership and moral force of the association to convince cinema owners to exhibit what they considered more fitting material for Irish viewers. As the Antrim delegate Seán McKeown remarked at the 1935 congress, the GAA membership was 'a very effective weapon' for 'hitting the cinema proprietors in the pockets', and convincing them to 'bring the news more in harmony with national feeling'.[58] For one Cork delegate present there was 'nothing Irish about Movietone Pictures', while the GAA president, Seán McCarthy, declared that the majority of the news was of no interest and had little educational or national value to Irish people.[59] Given the questionable content of some Movietone newsreels discussed later in this chapter, it is not surprising that the GAA responded as it did. In the end, however, no decision was taken to launch a national initiative regarding newsreel content, due both to the enormity of the undertaking and the perception of GAA officials that other bodies, including the government, did not support the GAA sufficiently in its attempts to re-Gaelicise the country.[60] However, some local initiatives were taken, including in County Wexford in 1935 when GAA officials complained to proprietors of local cinemas regarding the screening of a newsreel featuring a rugby match, and 'the cinema people afterwards showed a film of a match in Croke Park which the Gaels supported'.[61]

Ultimately, there appears to have been some satisfaction among GAA members regarding newsreel depictions of their games, evident by the continued facilitation of such filming throughout the interwar years. As one of the most popular entertainment forms in Ireland in these years, the cinema offered an important profile for Gaelic games in the formative years of the Free State.

NEWSREEL COVERAGE OF GAELIC GAMES

While a considerable number of newsreel depictions of Gaelic games survive from the interwar years, these sports were by no means the most often filmed by newsreel companies. An examination of the surviving newsreel films of British Pathé, the company responsible for most newsreel depictions of sport in Ireland in this period, indicates that while Gaelic football was the seventh most featured sport, hurling was the thirteenth. As Table 2.1 indicates, the most popular sports featured in Pathé's archive in the 1920–39 period are horse racing (95 newsreels), rugby (77), (men's and women's) hockey (56), equestrianism (44), athletics (43), motorcycling (39), Gaelic football (31), tennis (30), Association football (28), swimming (28),[62] motorcar racing (24), hunting (22), hurling/camogie (20), and golf (12).[63]

As is evident from Table 2.1, sports followed more often by members of the middle and upper classes comprise the majority of those featured. This may reflect the view of the newsreel editors that audiences in Britain were more likely to be interested in coverage of sports they were already familiar with. However, the very fact that Gaelic games do feature prominently indicates that they did attract audiences in Britain, presumably among Irish immigrant communities in particular. There may also be a parallel

Table 2.1. Number of Pathé newsreels of Irish sport, 1920–39[64]

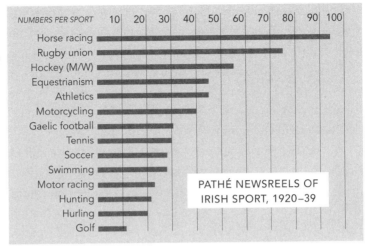

here with the high number of instances of American football featured in British newsreels, despite the sport not being played widely in Britain. As film historian Luke McKernan has noted, this was 'not because anyone in Britain knew or liked the game, but because sporting activity (particularly if vigorous) seems always to have gone down well'.[65] McKernan has also contended that surviving newsreel footage of Gaelic games may not have always been the result of careful planning in advance but rather, in some cases, a newsreel cameraman may have been covering another event nearby and took the opportunity to film a visually exciting event like a hurling or Gaelic football match.[66]

While Gaelic games and Association football would appear to be under-represented in surviving newsreel footage – relative to their popularity more generally in Ireland – this could also be due to concerns among club officials that such coverage may have reduced attendances and the gate money clubs were so dependent on for survival. The lack of an international dimension to Gaelic games – with the exception of occasional exhibition games against teams from the United States – may also have affected the extent of newsreel interest.

The coverage of Gaelic games in newsreels was also confined principally (with a few exceptions) to matches played in Croke Park, while few games other than All-Ireland finals are featured. Pathé did, however, cover a county hurling final in Cork[67] and an All-Ireland final played outside Dublin.[68] Although it featured far fewer games than Pathé, Gaumont did film at least one notable Gaelic games newsreel at a provincial location: 'Gaelic Football at Dungannon'.[69] This 1929 footage – featuring teams from Tyrone and Antrim – is particularly noteworthy as it contains the first example on film of the penalty kick in Gaelic games, some eleven years before the rule was officially confirmed by the GAA. It would appear therefore that in practice the penalty kick was in use much earlier in Gaelic football encounters.[70]

A further point of note regarding newsreel coverage of Gaelic games is that the focus is almost exclusively male; there are only two newsreel items depicting women playing camogie. Despite describing camogie in an intertitle to a 1922 newsreel as the 'Irish Ladies National Game',[71] Pathé, and other newsreel companies, rarely featured women engaged in Gaelic games.

Due to the focus on All-Ireland finals, newsreels give us little sense of the vibrant and important GAA activities at local and regional level across the island. Club, inter-county or provincial rivalries rarely feature, despite their importance to GAA culture and its development. Neither does the GAA's engagement in other non-Gaelic games activities, from céilí dances to athletic events and Irish-language classes. However, despite these gaps in the coverage of GAA activities, Pathé newsreels in particular offer a generally positive portrayal of Gaelic games. Indeed, by featuring international games between Ireland and the USA at the Gaelic Olympiad, the Tailteann Games, in both 1928 and 1932, as well as visits of GAA county teams to the US in the 1930s, Pathé suggested an international dimension to the association that exaggerated the significance of such games. The reality was that teams representing the US, while relying entirely on Irish immigrants to that country, offered little competition to Irish teams. The GAA lacked (then, as now) a significant international dimension in terms of other national teams that could compete against an Irish team; however, the Pathé films nonetheless depicted Gaelic games as international sports, rather than affirming the alleged insularity of which the association was sometimes accused.

NEWSREEL SUPPORT FOR THE STATUS QUO

In a manner comparable to newsreels of Association football in Britain during the interwar period, newsreels of Gaelic games in Ireland also tended to affirm the prevailing political and social establishment in Irish life.[72] Indeed, as Southern Ireland moved towards independence, newsreels adapted to the changing political landscape. For instance, a newsreel from October 1921, filmed and exhibited during the Truce between British and Irish forces during the War of Independence, features 'Commandant [Seán] McKeon' attired in an IRA uniform throwing in the *sliotar* to begin a hurling match.[73] From the perspective of the British administration in Ireland, McKeon had no such military status; however, Pathé's newsreel nonetheless referred to him as a military officer, thereby lending legitimacy to both his position and the army he was part of while also anticipating the emergence of an independent Irish state. However, in a feature typical of newsreels throughout the interwar period, Pathé rarely acknowledged the seriousness of political events in episodes featuring sport, indicating in one newsreel from November 1921 that 'Ireland still has racing despite its little war'[74] – the 'little war' being a rather condescending reference to the Irish War of Independence.[75]

Despite intertitles such as this, Pathé newsreels were generally careful not to offend potential viewers; episodes tended to be neutral politically, if pro-Treaty following the signing of the Anglo-Irish Treaty in December 1921. A newsreel featuring horse racing during the Irish Civil War opens with the title 'Rebel "Spoil-Sports" defied, Mr Tim Healy – Governor General – and Mr Cosgrave – President – attend Punchestown races'.[76] However, newsreels of Gaelic games in the interwar period rarely featured political figures, though individuals such as the president or governor general were often included in episodes about horses and horse races. Their inclusion, as with films of Association football in Britain, affirmed the importance of such figures in Irish life, particularly during periods such as the Civil War when their status was violently contested.[77] In the interwar period, it was Catholic clerics who were the principal dignitaries at Gaelic football and hurling matches, with several newsreels featuring the throwing in of the ball by a bishop to start the game.[78] The Pathé

Figure 2.1. Still from Pathé newsreel item, 'Hurling Final at Killarney', 9 September 1937
© British Pathé

footage of the 1937 All-Ireland hurling final also features players kneeling to kiss the bishop's ring before the game gets under way (Fig. 2.1).[79]

Ceremony and ritual were important parts of major Gaelic games and these are featured prominently within surviving newsreels. This includes the opening parade by the two teams, occasionally behind an individual carrying the Irish tricolour. As Mike Huggins found in his study of newsreels of Association football, theories of ritual illustrate how such practices associated with Gaelic games contributed to the drama of the events featured while also affirming the political and social order.[80] The inclusion of shots of members of An Garda Síochána, the recently established Irish police force, on duty at games also reinforces this impression. Ireland from the mid-1920s may have been a relatively peaceful country, though the legacy of the Civil War is occasionally evident in surviving newsreels, particularly as disillusionment with the

Figure 2.2. Pathé newsreel item, 'Gaelic Football – Kerry defeat Kildare by 9 points to 2 at Croke Park', 20 October 1930 © British Pathé

Cumann na nGaedheal government increased as the decade progressed. In the opening shots of the Pathé newsreel of a 1930 game between Dublin and Kildare, a banner is evident in the background protesting against the imprisonment of 'political prisoners 12 months in solitary confinement without exercise' (Fig. 2.2).[81]

COMMENTARY AND CAMERAWORK IN NEWSREELS

While not always the case with other companies, Pathé's newsreels offered a generally positive perspective on Gaelic games. Indeed, in both captions and commentary, these newsreels often begin by remarking on the popularity of the games featured, with frequent references to 'record'[82] or 'enormous'[83] crowds. This was by no means unique to depictions of

Gaelic games, yet it did nonetheless affirm the importance of such games in Irish life, a feature all the more apparent in references to hurling as 'Ireland's national game' in several newsreels from the 1920s.[84] Such a characterisation of hurling could only have met with the approval of the GAA as it sought in this transformative period to promote its sports as distinctive (and ancient) Irish cultural practices.

When newsreels were silent, audiences had little information about what they were watching, apart from that provided by the opening title card. The footage was often quite limited, as generally only one camera was present at games (most likely operated for Pathé by their chief cameraman in Ireland, Belfast-born John Gordon Lewis),[85] usually positioned at one end line and therefore confined to the action surrounding the nearest goalmouth. This restricted perspective meant that the newsreel viewer got very little sense of how the play flowed, with most episodes comprised principally of what would appear to be random passages of play, presumably included as they were considered the best extracts from the footage captured.

Over time the shooting of Gaelic games in newsreels gradually improved, and by the mid-1930s a discernible advance in both camera angles and the overall standard of images is evident, with more passages of play featured. These advancements also coincided with the addition of spoken commentary, first evident in Pathé newsreels of Gaelic games in 1934. While the commentary provided some increased information, there are significant limitations evident in surviving newsreels. Often commentaries did not follow the play as depicted, sometimes mis-identifying the teams featured. This could partly be accounted for by the limitations on camera positioning, which meant scores were often only captured at one goalmouth. However, limited information was given about the scoring system, tactics or rules of the game, and on occasion commentators appeared to resort, rather erroneously, to other sports to explain the action, for example with county teams being referred to on one occasion as 'clubs'[86] and a reference to the beginning of a Gaelic football game as a 'kick-off' rather than a throw-in.[87] In another episode, the commentator simply allows the footage to roll, with very few remarks, commenting that 'In this game the ball isn't left long in any position –

so sit back and watch the struggle', before the film continues for over a minute accompanied only by the sound of the crowd.[88]

Commentators rarely identified individual players, partly due to the brevity of reports, which rarely last for more than two minutes. Another factor, however, was the seemingly limited knowledge of Gaelic games among newsreel commentators. While standard for British newsreels of the period, the rather contrived, clipped, upper-class 'Oxford' accents evident in newsreel commentary seem rather incongruous for reports of Gaelic games. Such accents may not necessarily have been frowned upon by followers of Gaelic games in the interwar years, however, as they did confer a certain respectability and international recognition on the sports featured, though they may have contributed to the occasional mispronunciation, as in the case of Cavan ('Ca-vinn')[89] in a 1937 newsreel and Laois ('Leese') in footage from the 1936 All-Ireland football final.[90] Occasionally, informed live commentaries were provided in local screenings of newsreels of Gaelic games in Ireland, partly due to the limitations of the official versions.[91]

The commentaries provided by Pathé, while limited in content, nonetheless were generally positive in tone, emphasising the excitement and 'terrific speed' of games, as well as the impressive and enthusiastic attendance. Rarely is criticism evident in the commentary, be that of overcrowding, pitch invasions or rough play, all of which are evident in surviving newsreels. As the commentator observes in the Pathé newsreel of the 1935 football final between Cavan and Kildare, '[t]he tightly packed spectators forget all about their discomfort. But all the same when three big men are crushing you – phew, it's hot!'[92] Similarly we are told in the commentary of the following year's hurling final that 'once the game is on they forget they're packed as tight as sardines'.[93] However, there were instances of serious crushing in finals in this period, as fans attempted to gain admission to an already overcrowded stadium, sometimes forcing the gates open.[94] Other controversial issues off (and on) the pitch were also ignored, such as the refusal of the Kerry football team to participate in the 1923 All-Ireland final until several of its players were released from internment.[95] No mention is made either in the newsreel of the 1926 football final replay of the death, since the drawn game, of one of Kerry's best players, full-back Jack Murphy. Equally, the newsreel of the 1938 football final replay between Galway and Kerry does not depict or refer to the farcical ending when, following a pitch invasion, some players walked off the field and Kerry had to play the final minutes with a number of supporters replacing missing players.[96]

The most obvious example of Pathé's avoidance of controversy is the absence of any reference to violent incidents during games, even where such incidents are apparent in the newsreels. Rather, hurling is characterised as 'no game for weaklings'[97] and a sport of 'hard knocks'.[98] Indeed, footage of a player collapsing following an injury during the 1938 All-Ireland hurling final is accompanied by the jovial commentary, 'It's fast and it's tough. He's down, and he's out!'[99] Physical altercations between players were rarely noted in contemporary commentary in Pathé newsreels, though later cataloguers have identified 'confrontations'.[100] It is possible that a focus on violence during games would have attracted the attention of the Irish film censor as newsreels featuring all-in wrestling were banned up until 1936 due to their perceived brutality.[101]

Despite these omissions, overall Pathé newsreels presented a positive, if at times condescending, depiction of Gaelic games. However, this was not always the case with other British newsreel companies, in particular British Movietone. In its newsreel of the 1937 All-Ireland football final, the following commentary was delivered in an exaggerated Irish accent:

> Now there'll be some ignoramuses who'll be asking, 'What is this game? Is it association or rugby?' Well, it could be the one or the other, if it wasn't both, and sure it's between Kerry and Cavan. You'll recall that when Gaelic football was introduced every footballer felt he had as much right to handle the ball as the goalkeeper, which indeed he has, so it's in the rules ever since.[102]

Apart from remarks such as this, the commentary to this fifty-eight-second clip offers almost no insight into the game itself, focusing instead on the suggested peculiarity of Gaelic football. This episode was by no means unique within British Movietone's output but rather part of a pattern in their productions in this period whereby traditional and condescending long-held British stereotypes of Ireland were seemingly affirmed. A further newsreel featuring an Irish athletics meeting in 1936, at which President Éamon de Valera was present, finds the events 'most peculiar', even though they are the internationally recognised sports of pole vault and hammer-throw.[103] For Movietone, it seems, Irish sport provided a means of poking fun at the Irish while offering comic material for its newsreels. A particularly offensive example is a 1951 item featuring an 'Irish rally' at Sydney Stadium. Irish dancing is included, along with a hurling match between Australian state teams, and the piece begins with the pronounced upper-class commentary typical of the genre. However, when the hurling is shown, an exaggerated Irish accent asks, 'What's hurling?', before offering the following explanation:

It's a game played with a dirty big stick called a hurling. There are fifteen men a side at least to start with. There was only one broken skull, a hurly-burly in the goalmouth with clubs swinging like shillelaghs at a policeman's picnic. Nearly all the players are Irish-born but it's a stone moral certainty they'll be dying right where they stand if they keep this game up. Where's the ball? For now, look, it doesn't matter much, there's Michael O'Flaherty's head we can work on.[104]

Gaumont British was also responsible for occasionally condescending and problematic depictions of Irish sport. In its newsreel coverage of the Cavan-versus-New York exhibition Gaelic football match in 1938, the commentator observes:

It's not quite soccer; it's not quite rugger; it's not quite netball; it's a fight. Call out the marines as well and keep the peace. A team from Ireland beat the New York team, they beat them hollow and they beat them up. In the end there was so much red blood flowing they had to call in their girlfriends to help them paint the town white.[105]

SPECTATORS AT GAELIC GAMES IN NEWSREELS

Pathé newsreels of sporting events often featured spectators prominently, and this was also the case in footage of Gaelic games. These sequences regularly foregrounded the large attendances by panning around the spectator areas, occasionally picking out individual faces for closer shots. While such scenes managed, in the manner of newsreels of Association football in the same period, 'to reflect back to the audience an image of itself',[106] they also provided rare positive and uplifting depictions of Irish life at particularly challenging times, whether in the aftermath of the Civil War or later during the Anglo-Irish Trade War that dominated the 1930s and brought considerable suffering to many. Shots of crowds celebrating, laughing and generally enjoying the atmosphere conveyed a sense of communal joy, complemented, with the arrival of sound, by remarks such as 'Croke Park goes plum crazy'[107] and 'The crowd is wild … except this little fellow.'[108] There was, however, a further rationale for this focus on spectators as it also contributed to a sense of community among cinema audiences, particularly those whose county was depicted on screen. As Nicholas Pronay has observed of the experience of watching newsreels in cinemas, this

> could evoke a greater degree of rapport and emotional involvement from the audience than printed words and pictures could, especially so in the case of the semi-literate majority of the ordinary people … newsfilm could act upon the audience somewhat like a demagogue; it could reduce the individuality of the people in the audience and substitute a mass response for a critical and individual assessment.[109]

Whatever Pathé's motivation, shots of spectators in newsreels offer fascinating insights into the period. Almost without exception, men are dressed in suits, most likely due to their attendance at Catholic Mass prior to games, which were traditionally played on Sundays. Hats or caps are also worn by most spectators, often used as part of celebrations when teams score, as flags and rattles were less a feature of Gaelic games in the interwar years than in later periods. Though men predominate, women and children are also featured in the surviving footage. Pathé focuses in particular on the more enthusiastic spectators as they leap into the air or invade the pitch to celebrate with their team at the end of a match. Surviving newsreels also indicate that some supporters were inclined to leave games early if their county was losing by a large score.

Footage also reveals that there was no segregation of supporters, while crowd trouble would appear to have been non-existent. Indeed, there seems to have been minimal segregation even between supporters and players, with some supporters (as also evident in the Irish Animated Picture Company's footage of the 1914 All-Ireland football-final replay discussed in Chapter One) seated right along the side of the pitch. However, it is apparent that overcrowding existed at games, with fans clearly tightly packed together in possibly dangerous circumstances. However, as indicated above, little reference is made by the commentators to the risks of injury, instead tending to make light of such overcrowding. Furthermore, there is no indication of fights between supporters, despite opposing supporters being packed tightly together. Indeed, the overall impression given of Gaelic games in newsreel coverage is of good-natured contests followed by amiable supporters.

TACTICS AND STYLE OF PLAY

Despite the limited length of surviving newsreels, rarely exceeding two minutes per match, the films do indicate salient aspects of the evolving sports of hurling and Gaelic football. A noteworthy feature is that both codes appear to have been principally *propelling* games, rather than the more possession-orientated sports they are today. In hurling, the faster sport, the *sliotar* was struck principally on the ground, with players only occasionally taking the ball into their hands. However, it is very difficult, due to its small size and the technical limitations of the time, to follow the *sliotar* in surviving newsreels and it is possible therefore that the hurling newsreels may not have had the same appeal as those featuring the more easily followed Gaelic football. Overall, newsreel films indicate that the common perception of Gaelic football in the early twentieth century as being dominated by 'catch and kick' tactics is accurate. Often, players' kicks seem to be largely random in the direction of the opposing goal, with little evidence of a carefully placed pass. There is less evidence, however, of the high overhead catching that has been claimed for the game in this era. Yet even within the two interwar decades considerable change is evident in the style of play, particularly in Gaelic football. In the earliest footage – such as a 1924 Pathé newsreel featuring two university teams[110] – soccer-style dribbling with the ball along the ground is prominently featured, but is less apparent in the newsreels from the 1930s, when the hand-pass becomes more prominent. However, the ball often appears to be thrown (and rarely penalised) rather than struck from the hand as the rules dictated.

An ever-present of cinema schedules from the early to mid-twentieth century were biweekly newsreels, sometimes including footage of Gaelic games. Scholars of newsreels in both the United States[111] and Britain[112] have identified them as an 'invaluable resource'.[113] Newsreels featuring Gaelic games also offer a unique insight into the development of these sports, their form and reception. Though GAA officials occasionally expressed concern and suspicion regarding the influence of the cinema in Ireland, the fact that a considerable amount of newsreel footage of Gaelic games survives, undoubtedly facilitated by the association, indicates that the GAA was aware of the importance of the cinema in the promotion of its games. The recurring focus on the large attendances and the excitement of the games affirmed the position of the GAA as the major sporting organisation in Ireland and its sports as *the* national games.

British Pathé and British Movietone produced newsreels up until the 1970s, when the increasing popularity of television led to their eventual demise. Gaelic games continued to feature occasionally, particularly when matches were played in Britain following the GAA's decision to host an annual Wembley exhibition between 1958 and 1976 – what became known as the annual 'Wembley at Whit'.[114] Short items on these games were produced, though they seem more aimed at a non-Irish audience evident in their tendency to explain Gaelic games rather than focus on how the matches were progressing. In the final film produced, a British Movietone item on the 1976 encounter between Dublin and

Kerry,[115] there is a recurring emphasis on the apparent oddity of the sport, while established Irish stereotypes are also invoked by the commentator:

> In Gaelic football the ball can be thrown, punched, kicked, flung, headed, kneed, carried or pushed towards the goal … Whatever you think of Gaelic football, you've got to admit, it's fast and it's furious … Dublin lead by two points and the Irish are getting their Irish up!

British newsreels of Gaelic games, therefore, reveal sometimes limited understanding of the sports themselves, while offering intriguing examples of the employment of sport to affirm constructions of Irishness abroad. It is these constructions, particularly as they emerged within American cinema between the 1930s and 1960s, to which this study now turns.

3
Hollywood Hurling: representing Gaelic games in American cinema, 1930–60

Fun was in the air. Kilkee talent gave us songs and dances. Kevin Casey cleverly rattled off a sort of 'Irish Calypso', bringing in everybody's name. Mike Duffy sang lovely songs and John Cowley started a dramatic recitation to be broken up by the entrance of Ford, Killanin, Potter and Trubshaw doing a very funny turn in the hurling boys' jerseys.

ANITA SHARP-BOLSTER

The above description appeared in the *Irish Independent*'s report of 30 April 1957 of the wrap party for John Ford's *The Rising of the Moon* (1957). Unfortunately, no photographs survive of Ford outfitted in one of the 'hurling boys' jerseys', though the report does invite speculation as to why the major Hollywood director of the day, along with others involved in the production, should enter the party so attired. While Ford's choice of jersey was no doubt unusual, the description above nonetheless provides a significant pointer to the role of Gaelic games in his work and that of a range of American film-makers between the 1930s and 1960s, a fascinating period when major studios produced films featuring hurling, culminating in the Oscar-nominated short on hurling, *Three Kisses* (Paramount Studios, 1955). These depictions and references to hurling are often brief and could quite rightly be accused of drawing on long-established stereotypes regarding Ireland and Irish people. However, rather than dismiss them entirely, this chapter will place them in the context of the time of their production and contend that they reflect larger processes at work within American society (and internationally) and in particular among the Irish-American community, a process evident in both the life and work of John Ford.

Though sport could not be included among the most prominent themes in his films, John Ford had a considerable personal interest in sport, which was apparent at least from his high-school years. According to Ronald L. Davis in his biography of Ford, when John Feeney (Ford's birth name) entered Portland High School in 1910, 'his consuming interest was football',[1] by which Davis of course refers to the American variety rather than the Irish. Apparently, Ford was a versatile and aggressive footballer (Fig. 3.1), playing half-back, full-back and defensive tackle and earning the nickname 'Bull Feeney – the human battering ram' for his tendency to put 'his head down and charge' while playing.[2] As teammate Oscar Vanier remarked some years later, 'It didn't matter if there was a stone wall there, he'd drive right for it.'[3]

Figure 3.1. Portland High School 1913 state champions football team of which John Ford was the star full-back (pictured on the far right of the back row). Source: Joseph McBride, *Searching for John Ford* (New York: St Martin's Press, 2001). Photo reprinted with the permission of Portland Public Schools, Portland, Maine

Ford also played baseball and, as the fastest runner in his school, earned a place on the track team.[4] American football, however, was always his favourite sport. Ford's reputation on the football field may appear to affirm a prominent stereotype of the Irish in the period – what Joe McBride describes as a 'battling lout'.[5] However, sport simultaneously had an important role for the young aspiring Irish-American – as 'a means', in Davis' words, 'for an Irish youth to win acceptance by the Yankee majority'.[6] This chapter will contend that the references to hurling in Ford's films (and indeed across a range of American films made between the 1930s and 1960s) can be viewed comparably to the role football played for the young Irish-American. On one level, Ford was certainly aware of the stereotypes and prejudices concerning the Irish, and the role that hurling could play in their affirmation. These stereotypes were also key aspects of what John Urry has described as the 'tourist gaze', another factor influencing the depictions of Gaelic games in American film. However, as commentators such as Lee Lourdeaux and Martin McLoone have noted, Irish-American film-makers (including Ford) were engaged in a process of exploiting the performative potential of Irish stereotypes with a view to the ultimate assimilation of Irish-America into mainstream American life, a process also relevant to the references to hurling in Ford's films and other American productions in the mid-twentieth century.[7] Moreover, in a feature noted by Luke Gibbons and others, Ford's films also repeatedly, and cleverly, undermine prevailing stereotypes, as part of a process whereby what might be called 'functional performative violence' is employed to facilitate processes of social cohesion and assimilation.

HURLING AND TOURISM

It is certainly the case that references to Gaelic games in Ford's films seem inevitably to precede (or suggest) an occasion of violence, in line with representations of hurling found generally in American cinema from the 1930s onwards. Informed by stereotypical constructions of Irishness, these depictions also reflect the influence of a 'tourist gaze', an increasingly significant factor in depictions of Ireland as the twentieth century progressed. The term was coined by John Urry in his 1990 book of the same name to describe a culturally constructed manner of perceiving a place which informs tourist expectations. For Urry the tourist gaze was 'constructed through difference' and 'in relationship to its opposite, to non-tourist forms of social experience and consciousness'.[8] Furthermore, much as stereotypes play a central role in commercial cinema by allowing audiences to recognise and identify more easily with characters by 'reducing other landscapes, other peoples, and other values … to a normative paradigm',[9] the tourist gaze is similarly, as Urry continues, 'constructed through signs, and tourism involves the collection of signs'.[10] 'The tourist', Jonathan Culler has also observed, 'is interested in everything as a sign of itself … All over the world the unsung armies of semioticians, the tourists, are fanning out in search of the signs of Frenchness, typical Italian behaviour, exemplary Oriental scenes, typical American thruways, traditional English pubs'[11] or, indeed, typical Irish pastimes, such as Gaelic games. Of course, Gaelic games are not unique in this respect, and John Arundel and Maurice Roche, in their 1998 study of the relationship between British rugby league and Sky TV, found similarly that:

> As with the tourism industry, the media sport industry, in general … tends to promote local identities in a way which transforms them from the unreflected 'ways of life' and traditions of local people, into reflexive and organized cultural productions and stagings for outsiders, whether tourists or TV viewers. [Where] this process does not threaten the very existence of cultural forms and ways of life, it certainly raises the problem of their 'authenticity' in their new touristic or mediated guise.[12]

Ironically, as Gerry Smyth has observed, the search for the 'authentic' has nonetheless been an important determinant of tourism in Ireland, though one 'with a long and troubled career in Irish cultural history'.[13] Hurling in particular, by far the most common Gaelic game portrayed, or alluded to, in American productions, seems to have provided an 'authentic' and 'primitive' contrast to the presumed modernity of American sports such as American football, while also apparently containing the violence so often associated with the Irish. As Rockett, Gibbons and Hill have noted,

'Whether it be rural backwardness or a marked proclivity for violence, the film-producing nations of the metropolitan centre have been able to find in Ireland a set of characteristics which stand in contrast to the assumed virtues of their own particular culture.'[14] Rockett et al. are referring in particular to the nostalgic pastoral emphasis in many American depictions of Ireland, most notably in John Ford's greatest commercial success, *The Quiet Man*.[15] Hurling's association principally with rural Ireland, and the apparent violence of the game, particularly to those unfamiliar with it, provided a shorthand for familiar Irish stereotypes, and it is these traits that are often to the fore in depictions, descriptions and references to the sport in American productions.

HURLING AND HOLLYWOOD SHORTS[16]

Indeed, in the first American productions to focus on hurling in the 1930s we find a recurring emphasis on the alleged violence associated with the game. The GAA organised annual tours to the US in the 1920s, 1930s and 1940s by the All-Ireland winners in both hurling and Gaelic football to promote the games stateside. These visits seem to have inspired some American producers to consider hurling in particular as the subject for their work. Both Pathé and Fox Movietone newsreels covered several of the games during these trips,[17] and hurling also appeared in a number of short films released in cinemas in the early 1930s.

Ted Husing, regarded as the father of sports commentary in the US, 'single handily [sic] establish[ing] the in's and out's, prims and propers of the modern sports broadcaster',[18] introduced and narrated two one-reel series, *Ted Husing's Sports Slants* and *Sports Thrills*, made by the Vitaphone Corporation for Warner Bros. in 1931 and 1932 respectively. The distinctiveness of hurling in particular seems to have appealed to the producers as, unusually, it was featured in both series, episode no. 4 of *Husing's Sports Slants* and no. 5 of *Sports Thrills*.[19] Each item on hurling is approximately three minutes in length. However, what most struck the producers about the game is clear from the rather unusual juxtaposition of hurling and moose hunting in the *Sports Thrills* episode and the description they supplied in the Vitaphone catalogue:

Moose hunting in the mountains of Wyoming, Hunters shown from the time they start off to the time they kill 1200 lb. moose in 10 below weather. Irish game of hurling. One of the roughest competitive games ever played.[20]

The relevant episode of *Ted Husing's Sports Slants* featured the 1930 All-Ireland hurling champions, Tipperary, described in the item as the 'world's champions', who toured the US in 1931. During their tour, Tipperary were presented with a 'World Hurling Champions' trophy engraved with the names of the travelling team members following victories against teams in New York.[21] This was a Tipperary side that included such hurling greats as Martin Kennedy, John Maher, Phil Purcell and Jimmy Lanigan and was captained by John Joe Callanan.

The game depicted is between Tipperary and a New York selection played at the Polo Grounds in New York City, the then home of the Major League Baseball team the New York Giants. However, the moments of the game chosen for inclusion place a heavy emphasis on the alleged violence of the sport, with shots of players lying injured taking up a considerable portion of the short.

In the *Sports Thrills* episode, released the following year, are clips from at least three separate games played in New York and featuring teams with markings of New York, Galway, Clare and Cork, all likely New York-based selections. Here again the moments selected place an emphasis on injured players and violent incidents, exacerbated by Husing's commentary (with similar remarks in the *Sports Slant* item):

Most games start with a bang. Here's one that starts off with a couple of bangs and holds the world's record for sustained thrills and sustained bruises ... we're now watching one of the roughest competitive games ever played. It's when the ball gets close to the goal that hurling becomes a spectacle bordering on massacre. About ten players swing for the ball, at least half of that number get it on the head. The marksmanship is perfect, the idea being to aim at the ball and hit your competitor on the bean. One of the players just made thirteen holes in two, that is thirteen holes in two heads ... It begins to look like Flanders Fields … A great game built for none but the brave but personally I'd prefer war.

Followers of Gaelic games may rightly take offence at this disparaging depiction of hurling. However, as evident here, these episodes are ultimately concerned more with the comic than the violent potential of hurling, a theme returned to shortly.

There are no precise reports of Husing's shorts being screened in cinemas in Ireland, though there are several mentions of Vitaphone Varieties being shown in the early 1930s.[22] As Richard Ward has noted, 'At the beginning of the 1930s, practically all Warner–Vitaphone shorts were grouped under the umbrella title "Vitaphone Varieties"', so it is possible that they were screened in Ireland though they appear (in common with most shorts screened in the period) to have attracted little commentary in the press.[23] This, however, could not be said of the next American production to feature hurling, the Pete Smith Specialty *Hurling*, released in the US in 1936 but not in Ireland until early 1938. After images and comments from the film were circulated in a British periodical, a contributor to the *Fermanagh Herald* remarked:

A more scandalous libel on a game I have seldom seen … This is a most scandalous perversion of the truth. The suggestion is that blood battles with hurleys are quite common, that the players are rough, unsportsmanlike men, who purposely swing for their opponent's head with a stick, with the deliberate intention of causing serious injury, that those attacked often reply in kind, and that battles with hurleys as 'effective weapons' are the result … I urge upon our association to take serious cognisance of this type of anti-Gaelic propaganda. There is a way of dealing with detractors of this kind that will make them, so far as Ireland is concerned at any rate, see the error of their ways.[24]

The anonymous contributor, credited simply as 'Gael' (and identified in Chapter Two as a staunch critic of the cinema), does not specify precisely the nature that such action might take, but, after the film was shown in cinemas in Dublin and London in early 1938,[25] a delegation from the GAA, led by the *ard-rúnaí* (general secretary) Pádraig Ó Caoimh, visited the film censor, James Montgomery, to ask that 'objectionable comments' be removed from the film. In the end, according to the minutes of a meeting of the GAA Central Council held on the matter on 16 March 1938, 'The Censor explained [to the delegation] that he had no power under the Act to cut the film but that the distributors had agreed to cut out the objectionable parts.'[26] The GAA also met a representative from MGM regarding the film, but it is unclear what the outcome of these discussions were.[27]

The director of Hurling, David Miller, was apparently inspired, according to an article in the Connaught Tribune of August 1936, to make the short following his attendance at the Limerick-versus-New York hurling match played in Yankee Stadium in May 1936.[28] The short film was produced by Pete Smith, who also provided the narration, as part of the Pete Smith Specialties series of short films produced for MGM Studios from 1931 to 1955. These black-and-white one-reel novelty shorts were very popular during their run, no more than eleven minutes in length (Hurling is ten minutes long), and characterised by Pete Smith's own humorous and 'rather sarcastic narration'.[29] This ironic comic voice also appears in promotional material relating to the film, where the potential for serious injury for hurling players is most emphasised. In a surviving publicity sheet for Hurling sent out to exhibitors in the US,[30] recipients were advised on how to 'sell the Irish' through the use of 'fake mallets' resembling, we are told, the 'swinging shillalahs [used in hurling apparently] [which] sock every part of the players' anatomy from head to shins'. This feature of the game is suggested to promoters as a great advertising opportunity as 'The remedy calls for all manner of liniments, abrasives, bandages etc. – and here is your perfect opportunity for interesting window and ad tie-up with drug stores!' Indeed, a prominent feature of the publicity sheet is its contrasting of hurling with the implied more civilised games in the US, including ice hockey, la Crosse[31] and football – presumably American – all of which are mentioned. Unlike these games, however, hurling, we are told, 'is perhaps the roughest outdoor sport of them all' where 'Players [...] don't deign to reflect on their Irish manhood by donning padded helmets or similar sissy safeguards' and 'the game does not stop when players are disabled'. The violence of hurling – described as 'Ireland's Athletic Assault and Battery' – is further underlined in the posters and advertising

Figure 3.2. Promotional advertisement for the MGM short *Hurling* (MGM, 1936) included in the publicity sheet distributed to promote the film[32]

materials used to promote the film, which place particular emphasis on the strong possibility of serious physical injury for any would-be players (Fig. 3.2).

Furthermore, 'catchlines' suggested to exhibitors to promote the film include 'Doctor's Delight: the dizziest game since Connor MacNessa reigned as Árd Rí of Ireland', '"Shillalah Swing Time": you'll thrill each time a wild Irishman's skull shatters', and 'Science and Sock: Pete Smith reveals in hurling a scientific form of mass murder'.

Featured in the film, shot at Baker's Field, Columbia University in New York, are Irish-American teams the 'New York Selected' and the 'Cork Fifteen'. The narrative begins inoffensively with a selection of shots demonstrating how hurling is played. It is clear from this opening segment that the players featured are capable hurling players and this section was described by several delegates as 'quite good' at a meeting of the GAA Central Council held on 12 February 1938.[33]

However, it is the depiction of a game itself, where a recurring focus is on the potential for injury, and Smith's own ironic narration, that was no doubt most problematic for GAA members. The only player identified is a certain 'Low Gear' O'Toole, who, as the publicity sheet relates, 'enters the scene as the second half begins' but is the only one to survive the mayhem, for, '[a]s the contest reaches a crashing climax, no member of either team remains to score the winning goal. They are all laid out as Chopin's Funeral March sounds a sad accompaniment.' This scene appears to have been most problematic for members of the GAA executive and was likely deleted by distributors from screenings in Ireland.[34]

As with the Vitaphone shorts, the depiction of hurling in this film leaves much to be desired. However, it is important to place these productions more generally within the context of how Irishness and sport were depicted in American film in the early to mid-twentieth century, which often featured the recurring stereotype of the violent Irish. As Stephanie Rains observes of representations of the Irish-American male:

> His overt masculinity was largely connected to lawlessness and violence, particularly during the 1930s era of gangster films. James Cagney, among other stars, was a vehicle for such representations of urban, modern Irish-American masculinity.[35]

However, these more threatening characters were offset by the equally ubiquitous figures of the Irish priest or policeman (associated in particular with actors like Pat O'Brien or Spencer Tracy) in this period, an example of more positive representations as the Irish-American community moved from the margins to the centre of American life during the twentieth century. In the process, suspicion of, and the threat of violence associated with, the Irish was assuaged through this balancing of established stereotypes of the 'fighting Irish' with more positive characters or placing such violence in a non-threatening or comic context. Indeed, as evident in the use of the 'fighting Irish' as the moniker for sports teams representing the University of Notre Dame today, this term would be transformed over the twentieth century to refer to perseverance and the ability to overcome rather than the pejorative associations of an earlier period.

Sport as featured in American cinema from the 1920s to the 1950s was often exploited for its comic potential. Some of the most famous feature films from this period, including Harold Lloyd's *The Freshman* (1925),

Buster Keaton's *College* (1927), Charlie Chaplin's *City Lights* (1931) and the Marx Brothers' *Horse Feathers* (1932), all employ sport, from American football to boxing and field sports, for primarily comic purposes. This is also reflected in those short films featuring hurling, where the violence depicted is on a par with that found in Charlie Chaplin or Marx Brothers comedies, and indeed *Hurling*'s director, David Miller, had his greatest success as director of the Marx Brothers' 1949 feature *Love Happy*. There are even comic sound effects used in *Hurling* reminiscent of those found throughout the Marx Brothers films. And it is within this context that we find references to hurling appearing in John Ford's films.

THE QUIET MAN (1952)

Irish-America provided the participants and, no doubt, a large segment of the hoped-for audience for films such as *Hurling*. The presence of this huge ethnic community in the United States was an important factor in the popularity, among directors, of Irish-themed subject matter in American productions. As Martin McLoone has noted, Irish-American film-makers, including John Ford, were also engaged in exploiting the performative potential of Irish stereotypes in film while contributing to the assimilation of Irish-America into mainstream American life. McLoone remarks on the 'role of ethnic film-makers in both allaying the fears of the Anglo-American audience and in inducting this audience into the virtues of ethnic culture' and I would contend that this is also relevant to the references to hurling in Ford's films.[36] However, as the reactions of the GAA to *Hurling* suggest, the performative dimension of films such as Ford's *The Quiet Man* or *The Rising of the Moon* was not always recognised by audiences in Ireland. As Arjun Appadurai has noted in his discussion of the increasing 'deterritorialization'[37] of the planet (the process through which such diasporic communities have emerged), while

> deterritorialization creates new markets for film companies ... the homeland is partly invented, existing only in the imagination of the deterritorialized groups, and it can sometimes become so fantastic and one-sided that it provides the fuel for new ethnic conflicts.[38]

This 'fantastic and one-sided' perspective might also be compared to the tourist gaze; both are characterised by their distance from life or culture in Ireland and their concern with contrasting presumptions regarding American culture with exaggerated and traditional depictions of Ireland and Irish people. One is hesitant to compare the work of a film-maker of the stature of John Ford with a film such as *Hurling*; nonetheless it is notable that, where referred to in Ford's films, hurling also seems inevitably to precede or suggest an occasion of violence. We do not actually witness a game of hurling in Ford's biggest commercial success *The Quiet Man*, though, significantly, the mere mention of the game, during a dispute between the engine driver Costello (Eric Gorman), the train guard Molouney (Joseph O'Dea) and the stationmaster Hugh Bailey (Web Overlander), seems to inspire violence in those discussing it:

> Costello (from the train engine): Well, we're off.
> Hugh Bailey (shaking a pocket watch): And might I suggest, Mr Costello, the train already being four and a half hours late ...
> Costello: Is it my fault, Mr Bailey, that there's a hurling match at Ballygar and that the champions of All-Ireland are playing ...
> Molouney (pointing his flag in a threatening manner at Bailey): If you knew your country's history as well as you claim to know it, Mr Bailey, you'd know that the Mayo hurlers haven't been beaten west of the Shannon for the last twenty-two years ...
> [May Craig, described in the credits as 'Fishwoman with basket at station', interjects here and shouts, 'True for you, Mr Molouney', only to be cut off by Bailey.]
> Bailey: That's a lie, that's a lie, Costello!
> [At this point there is silence as Costello removes his hat, followed by Molouney, who also removes his glasses. Bailey responds by removing his hat, and begins to remove his jacket for the impending fight only for proceedings to be interrupted by the arrival of Sean Thornton to bring his wife Mary Kate from the train.]

This scene is a great example of Ford's use of what might be called 'performative acting' in the Brechtian sense of a style that acknowledges the audience and 'thus aims to deconstruct the fourth wall realism of both the Stanislavskian stage and Classical Hollywood film'.[39] The actions and wind-up to the almost-fight here are an elaborate display that cues the audience for the following lengthy performative fight sequence between Sean Thornton (John Wayne) and Red Will Danaher (Victor McLaglen) that facilitates Thornton's eventual acceptance into the Inisfree community. Indeed, Irish audiences in particular are cued to this performance by the dialogue within the scene itself. The suggestion that the Mayo hurlers had not been beaten west of the Shannon for the previous twenty-two years would have been just as ludicrous to followers of Gaelic games in 1952 as it is today. In actual fact, Mayo has not won a senior hurling game west of the Shannon save for one victory over Galway in 1909. Such was Galway's dominance in the province that for twenty-two years prior to *The Quiet Man's* release the county's hurlers were awarded the provincial championship unopposed. As outlined shortly, the performative features apparent here were to be all the more evident in Ford's subsequent Irish-set film, *The Rising of the Moon.*

THREE KISSES (1955)

With regard to the tourist gaze, Ford's own comments (including some referred to below) indicate at least an awareness of the contribution of his work to tourism in Ireland;[40] indeed, as Luke Gibbons has noted, *The Quiet Man* in particular provided a template for the Irish tourist authority Bord Fáilte's (now known as Fáilte Ireland) promotion of Ireland from its establishment in 1952, the year of *The Quiet Man's* release.[41] And with considerable success, evident in the increasing numbers of tourists to Ireland as the 1950s progressed. Four days before the Irish premiere of Paramount Pictures' hurling-themed production *Three Kisses* (Justin Herman, 1955) at the Capitol Theatre in Dublin on 18 July 1956, the *Irish Times* carried a front-page headline declaring 'Tourist Industry has Prospects of Record Year'. 'Since the beginning of the summer', the report continued, '[Aer Lingus, British Railways, and the British and Irish Steam Packet Co.] have been transporting the biggest number of holiday-makers to this country in their history.'[42]

The Oscar-nominated *Three Kisses*, like the Pete Smith Specialty *Hurling*, was released – along with a further Paramount short on the Irish bloodstock industry, *Champion Irish Thoroughbreds* (1955) – as an opener for a main feature, this time as part of the Paramount Topper series, which ran for two weeks in Ireland as support for the Alvin Ganzer-directed boxing film *The Leather Saint* (1955). The Paramount Topper series began in 1951 and lasted for six years, by which time shorts were being phased out by all the majors. Altogether thirty-six were made, with quite a few, such as *The Littlest Expert on Football* (1951), *Touchdown Highlights* (1954) and the final film, *Herman Hickman's Football Review* (1957), taking sport as their theme. All, including *Three Kisses* – released in the US on 7 October 1955 and given an 'Excellent' rating by the *Motion Pictures Exhibitor* trade paper – were directed by Justin Herman, who is also credited as writer of *Three Kisses*. Philadelphia-born Herman, who was also a cartoonist and contributor of short stories to the *New Yorker*, worked as a writer, producer and director of short films at Paramount from the late 1930s until the mid-1950s and altogether made 118 shorts, two of which, *Roller Derby Girl* (1949) and *Three Kisses*, were nominated for Academy Awards.[43]

Three Kisses features a young hurler, Colm Gallagher (narrator of the film), who progresses from playing with his local team in the fictional rural Cork village of Ballykilly to training with the senior Cork team and eventually playing in the Munster Championship final. Gallagher's sporting prowess is partly motivated, the film suggests, by his quest for three kisses from the girl he loves (thus giving the film its title), each a reward for his improving fortunes on the playing field.

Three Kisses is unquestionably a patronising and problematic depiction of Ireland. However, it is a considerably more interesting work than this description might suggest, not least because, though written and directed by an American, it is one of the first examples of the GAA and Bord Fáilte together informing and facilitating a major American studio to produce a fictional work[44] (though one billed as 'documentary') on Gaelic games primarily for international consumption. In terms of the GAA's involvement, as well as featuring several scenes from hurling games in the Munster Championship, including the 1955 semi-final between Cork

Figure 3.3. Cork hurling manager Jim 'Tough' Barry as depicted in *Three Kisses* (Paramount Pictures, 1955)

and Clare, the film also includes appearances by the legendary Cork manager Jim 'Tough' Barry[45] (Fig. 3.3), most of the great All-Ireland-winning Cork team of the 1950s in training (including Vincy Toomey, Paddy Barry, Seánie O'Brien, John Lyons, Joe Hartnett, Mick Cashman, Christy O'Shea and Jimmy Brohan), the GAA general secretary Pádraig Ó Caoimh in attendance at an underage hurling game in Farranferris, and several other prominent hurling figures from Cork in the 1950s.[46] With regard to Bord Fáilte's involvement, newspaper reports of the Irish premiere of *Three Kisses* – which was also the Irish premiere of *Champion Irish Thoroughbreds* – describe the film as having been made with the cooperation of the tourist board and give considerable space to the comments of its then director general, T.J. O'Driscoll, who introduced the film to audiences on the night. According to the *Irish Times*, O'Driscoll 'welcomed the growing interest among foreign film companies in making films in Ireland', pointing out that 'filmmaking was a costly business which the board could not attempt on its slender budget, in the ordinary course of events. For that reason it was more than grateful to Paramount for making these films and distributing them throughout the world.'[47] In the *Irish Independent*, under the headline 'Film and the Irish Tourist Industry', the paper's film correspondent also quoted O'Driscoll's remark that 'Films are one of the best methods of publicising the tourist industry of this country.'[48]

Film reviews also recognised the tourist potential of the work. Benedict Kiely in the *Irish Press*, under a headline 'The Tourists and the Screen', remarked of *Three Kisses* and *Champion Irish Thoroughbreds* that

Even with their defects from our point of view, they could get people interested in Ireland [...] we should always remember that films like these documentaries and 'The Quiet Man', are meant not for us but for an American public. 'The Quiet Man', I'm told, was a great help to the tourist trade; and why not indeed. Who wouldn't like to spend a holiday in a land of green fields, sunshine, horse-racing, singing, fighting, boozing and romance?[49]

Given the differing concerns of each of the organisations involved, however, it is not surprising that the film is of more interest for the tensions that are revealed between its attempt to depict indigenous culture authentically and simultaneously engage a diverse international audience (with preconceived notions of Ireland and the sport of hurling) than for the quality of either the sport depicted or the film overall. It nonetheless features an intriguing encounter between the traditional and the modern – young Gallagher's village of Ballykilly, for example, is depicted as an idyllic pastoral and pre-modern space, complete with familiar horse and cart in the background and village pump for running water. However, Gallagher's – who seems remarkably young for the honour – elevation to the senior hurling team[50] is described as his being picked to represent the 'city' of Cork rather than the county, and the city itself is depicted as 'the mighty metropolis [...] with its busy vehicular traffic and its fine buildings of stone and brick'.

However, there is in all of this quite a patronising tone, including in the film's representation of women and the women's sport of camogie, and where the mere mention of someone having been to 'the United States of America' is considered a remarkable achievement by the narrator, ostensibly young Gallagher himself. Indeed, the film is narrated in an extraordinary accent, which suggests the tension between a wish to present an authentic Irish voice and one that remains accessible to an American audience. And it is an American audience that is the primary concern here, for all involved in the production. A recurring feature of representations of hurling, as seen in the films mentioned already, is the bewilderment of those new to the game in terms of its apparent irrationality and potential for violence. A strong focus is placed in *Three Kisses*, therefore, on illustrating the rationale behind the game, emphasising its rules and downplaying the potential for injury. However, it is a less than convincing riposte to previous representations. As the cinema correspondent of the *Irish Times* remarked, 'The soundtrack informs us that "though you may suffer a fracture of a leg or a concussion of the brain … [hurling] is not considered a rough sport – at least, not by us Irish".' 'This', the indignant correspondent continues, 'is certainly nice to know!'[51]

THE RISING OF THE MOON (1957) AND YOUNG CASSIDY (1965)

A common motif in representations of Ireland, evident throughout *Three Kisses*, is its positioning as a primitive, traditional society. As Gerry Smyth has noted:

> One of the discursive mechanisms through which this effect is realised is the 'chronotope', described by Joep Leerssen (after Bakhtin) as 'a place with an uneven distribution of time-passage, where time is apt to slow down and come to a standstill at the periphery …'. What Leerssen is referring to here is the impression that not only is the island physically removed from 'real' life, but also that time functions differently there.[52]

For John Ford's next Irish-themed film, *The Rising of the Moon* (1957), time did indeed appear to function quite differently in Ireland, not just through the film's depiction of the country as a traditional society – emphasised in the characters and storylines in this three-part work, titled *Three Leaves of a Shamrock* in the US – but equally in the difficulty this society appears to have in adapting to modernity. This includes, in the central segment, 'A Minute's Wait', based on a one-act Abbey Theatre play by Michael J. McHugh, the Irish approach to timekeeping. In rural Ireland, it seems, time – here represented by the Ballyscran-to-Dunfaill train – could wait for everything from prize goats to bishops' dinners, and, in one of the film's most famous scenes, the local victorious hurling team. Though a commercial failure on release in 1957, *The Rising of the*

Moon was important as part of Ford's ongoing attempts to promote the establishment of an Irish film industry that would partly encourage others to set up Ireland's first designated film studios at Ardmore the following year. In terms of representations of hurling, however, the film included one of the most controversial depictions of hurling players that resulted in considerable press coverage during the film's production and a staunch defence of the film and Ford's work by *Irish Times* columnist Myles na Gopaleen.

'A Minute's Wait' was shot in Kilkee, County Clare. As Joseph McBride has observed, the segment

> reinforces the insidious notion of Ireland as a backward island filled with lovable incompetents who haven't yet made it into the twentieth century. Ford's use of an old-fashioned train with an engine built in 1886 was deliberately anachronistic, provoking a complaint from the director of the West Cork Railway who could not understand why Ford refused a modern train with a diesel engine. 'He'll find out when the tourists come over next summer,' Ford grumbled in what [Frank S.] Nugent [the film's scriptwriter] took as an allusion to the tourist craze for jaunting carts provoked by *The Quiet Man*.[53]

Myles na Gopaleen – perhaps better known today as Flann O'Brien, the acclaimed author of the novels *At Swim-Two-Birds* (1939) and *The Third Policeman* (1967) – was an occasional commentator on cinema and was particularly upset by reactions to *The Rising of the Moon* among members of the GAA, even before the shooting of the film was complete. On 1 May 1956, both the *Irish Press* and *Irish Independent* reported the shooting of a scene of hurlers returning victorious from a game, with some 'on stretchers', after an encounter which, the *Independent* correspondent related, 'from the appearance of the players, must have been bloody and very rough, and hardly played according to the rules of the Gaelic Athletic Association'.[54] Unsurprisingly, the GAA responded with some alarm the following day with a statement, published in both papers, from the general secretary Pádraig Ó Caoimh declaring that he was 'deeply concerned lest there should be any substance in this report'. The statement went on to note that Ó Caoimh had been in touch with Lord Killanin, one of the directors of Four Provinces Productions [the production company behind the film]. He has assured me that the report referred to is exaggerated and completely out of context; that there are no stretcher-carrying scenes, and that in fact there is nothing offensive to our national tradition in this film.[55]

The controversy rumbled on nonetheless and by Friday of that week it was on the front page of the *Irish Times*, where it was announced that the shooting of the scenes 'resulted in an official deputation [consisting of Rev. John Corry, CC, chairman, and Mr Seán O'Connor, treasurer] from the Clare County Board of the GAA making a strong protest yesterday in Kilkee to Lord Killanin'. A statement was issued by the board which said it was a matter of

> grave concern to the GAA that the national game of hurling should, or would, appear to be held up to ridicule … the matter of 15 players returning home all suffering injuries would be calculated to give the impression that instead of a national sporting game that they were casualties returning to a clearing station at a battlefield.[56]

While noting that such violent incidents and injuries were extremely rare in GAA games,

> Father Corry pointed out that the scene as depicted was completely derogatory to the Gaels of Ireland and to the hurlers in particular. The scene if placed on the screen as filmed would bring the association into disrepute and would be calculated to hold up the national game to ridicule both at home and abroad.[57]

These final remarks were quoted at length by Myles na Gopaleen some weeks later while referring to what he called the 'farcical drool emitted by the GAA'. Na Gopaleen, apparently at that time a regular reader of the provincial papers, 'the only true mirrors', he observed 'of Ireland as she is', was quoting the Clare County Board's statement not from the *Irish Times* but from the *Clare Champion*. Na Gopaleen went on to note a report on the same page of the *Champion* of a local game between Ruan and St Joseph's which was described as 'probably one of the worst exhibitions of bad sportsmanship ever seen on a Gaelic field'. There was 'literally a procession to the Co. hospital from the match', the report continued, while 'One, a spectator from Ennis, had survived the war in Korea but he almost met his waterloo in Cusack Park.'[58] Na Gopaleen was dismissive of the GAA's criticisms of the film and, while extolling the virtues of Ford (apparently a close friend, the article suggests), remarked that

> To many people, the possibility of vital injury is part of the attraction of hard games ... The non-belligerent spectators regard absence of such occurrences as an attempt to defraud them. They have paid their two bobs to see melia murdher. Failure to present it is, they feel, low trickery.[59]

Whether or not one agrees with na Gopaleen's interpretation of supporters' expectations at hurling matches, and despite Lord Killanin's assurances, the scenes remained in the film, including images of several hurlers being carried on stretchers to the train after successfully winning their match. Indeed, it seems the concerns of the GAA were not taken seriously by those involved in the production. Records of correspondence with Lord Killanin, held in the Lord Killanin Collection at the Irish Film Institute, reveal that the film's producers collected newspaper clippings and correspondence, both for and against the depiction, and appear more amused than alarmed by the concerns raised (see Fig. 3.4).

Figure 3.4. Cartoon commenting on the *Rising of the Moon* (1957) controversy published in the June edition of *Dublin Opinion* magazine, 1956. Included in the Lord Killanin Collection in the Irish Film Institute[60]

" *Go easy with the skullduggery, lads—Ford and Killanin may be on the sideline!* "

As referred to above, Anita Sharp-Bolster, who appears in 'A Minute's Wait' as the recently wed English wife, could recall the arrival at the wrap party of 'John Ford, [and] [Lord] Killanin … doing a very funny turn in the hurling boys' jerseys'.[61] Furthermore, Ford had a small role in an Abbey Theatre Irish-language play shortly after the film's production in which a short passage of dialogue in Irish was improvised for him. When asked if 'he was going back to Spiddal' (the birthplace of his parents), he said he was not as he was 'afraid of the GAA'.[62]

However, as with *The Quiet Man*, these scenes of injured players are ultimately not primarily about hurling. It would appear that na Gopaleen, whose own contributions to the *Irish Times* were often tour de force performances in themselves, including his celebrated moniker,[63] admired the performative elements within Ford's work while also being highly critical of the hypocrisy he sensed in the reactions of the GAA. Indeed, na Gopaleen may also have recognised the 'self-interrogation' Luke Gibbons has identified in Ford's *The Quiet Man* in the later film, which seems more concerned with ridiculing tourists' reactions to hurling than with any perceived violence in the sport itself. As the recently wed English lady remarks to her husband when the hurlers pass her train window, 'Charles, is it another of their rebellions?', an observation that pokes fun at the tourist rather than the hurler.

John Ford co-directed one more film that features hurlers, *Young Cassidy*, an adaptation of Seán O'Casey's autobiography. Though Ford started out as sole director, British cinematographer Jack Cardiff took over early in the production when Ford fell ill. Among the scenes Ford directed was one in which Cassidy meets a group of hurlers.[64] Cassidy, with his brothers Archie and Tom, is in a pub celebrating Tom's recent return on leave from the British army when they encounter the local hurling team returning victorious after a game. The hurlers initially take offence at Tom's uniform; however, the scene ends with all engaging together in a fistfight with members of the Royal Irish Constabulary.

The violence in this scene could be described as what Lewis Coser terms 'functional conflict'[65] – 'conflict that takes place within the clearly defined parameters of traditional and populist community values and that ultimately works in the interest of social cohesion'.[66] This type of conflict is also found in other work of Ford's, including the lengthy fight sequence referred to above in *The Quiet Man*. In *Young Cassidy*, the hurlers quickly get over their argument with Cassidy and his brothers and join forces in fighting the police. So what may at first appear to be a stereotype regarding the reputed violence of hurling and hurlers functions ultimately within the narrative to bring hurlers, Cassidy and his brothers together as they head off merrily together on the back of a cart as the scene closes.

What is remarkable for those who follow hurling is not so much the potential for injury but rather the sophistication and skill levels involved in a game in which injuries are no more common than in many other field sports, aspects almost entirely absent from the American productions discussed in this chapter. Even in a film such as *Three Kisses*, which appears to be, at least partly, an attempt to correct these perceptions, the complicated attempt to address both hurling aficionados and an international audience ultimately compromises the veracity of its portrayal. Colm Gallagher is clearly the local guide who is bringing the uninitiated into the world of hurling, remarking along the way on the incorrect preconceptions regarding the sport. However, all of this is very much framed within a context understandable to the would-be visitor to Ireland, a fact commented on by local observers of the film. In this respect, a film such as *Three Kisses* anticipates Dean MacCannell's observation in the late 1970s that the 'structural development of industrial society is marked by the appearance everywhere of touristic space'. Indeed, *Three Kisses* might be regarded, again with reference to MacCannell, as an example of 'staged authenticity' lending the film an 'aura of superficiality, albeit a superficiality that is not always perceived as such by the tourist, who is usually forgiving about these matters'.[67] Local commentators tend, however, to be less forgiving. As the *Cork Examiner* reviewer remarked on *Three Kisses*' release in Ireland, while comparing it to other films that depict hurling, including Ford's *The Rising of the Moon*:

> That more Americans are likely to come here looking for the 'traditional' Ireland is evident from [the] film ... It is in line with other productions of the type ... 'Three Kisses' ... accurately describes the game itself, but the film company have gone to a great deal of trouble

with the insertion of the 'Blarney'. Result, the picture becomes a farce and hardly a true representation of the Irish scene.[68]

However, American-made films in the mid-twentieth century featuring hurling were also responding to developments within American society and culture. This chapter opened with a description of John Ford, along with others involved in the production of *The Rising of the Moon*, doing 'a very funny turn' in hurling jerseys at the film's wrap party – which is a significant pointer to the role of hurling in the great director's work and that of other American film-makers. On the one hand, hurling provided a useful motif for these directors as it encapsulated prevailing stereotypes of the Irish, including their alleged proclivity for violence. However, as commentators such as Lee Lourdeaux and Martin McLoone have noted, Irish-American film-makers, including Ford, were also engaged in exploiting the performative potential of these Irish stereotypes while contributing to the assimilation of Irish-America into mainstream American life.[69] Much as Sharp-Bolster clearly describes a performance by Ford and others, Ford employed Irish stereotypes – including through references to hurling – to diffuse anxieties regarding the Irish while facil-itating their assimilation and acceptance as a central part of American society and culture. A further relevant film in this context is the 1959 short documentary *Foreign Sports in the US*, produced by the Motion Picture Section of the New York Field Office, a branch of the United States Citizenship and Immigration Services. This government-sponsored film focuses on the lesser-played sports in the US – beginning with Gaelic football and hurling – though an overriding theme is the encouragement of tolerance for the many ethnicities (including Irish) that make up the United States through a focus on their distinctive sports. This does not preclude, however, the inclusion of problematic stereotypes within the depictions concerned; Gaelic football, we are told by the narrator over footage of games played in New York's Gaelic Park (misleadingly called 'Croke Park' in the commentary), is a game of football which '800 years ago the Irish borrowed … from the English and turned into something called "rough and tumble"'. And, unsurprisingly, the narration emphasises both the 'rough' and the 'tumble' of Gaelic football, described as 'the roughest version of the game', with shots of robust encounters between players, including one with his head heavily bandaged. Ultimately, however, the ten-minute production, as mentioned, is concerned with encouraging tolerance and understanding, evident in the narrator's concluding remarks:

> We have learned to play the games of many nations … like millions of other boys throughout the country, these youngsters are taking a first-hand lesson in sportsmanship and fair play. They are learning to respect each other's ways, to build mutual strength out of individual difference. These young Americans are learning what it means to live in a country where people of many tongues work together and play together in peace. Where a man's individual ways are welcomed and encouraged. For they enrich our life, strengthen our culture, and build a new tradition based on freedom.[70]

Followers of Gaelic games may rightfully question these American representations of their sports, and particularly the recurring association of hurling and Gaelic football with violence. Ultimately, however, the depictions have little to do with either hurling or Irish life per se; instead they are concerned with engaging with aspects of an emerging and evolving Irish-American identity, and international tourist industry, in the mid-twentieth century.

4

'Keep the mummers off the green ground of Croke Park': remembering *Rooney* (1958)

I n Chapter Three, we considered depictions of Gaelic games in American productions between the 1930s and 1960s. Given the dominance and influence of Hollywood film internationally, it is understandable that parallels can be found between their representations of sport and those in films from other countries. This chapter considers one such example, the film *Rooney* (1958), an adaptation of a novel of the same name by popular English writer Catherine Cookson and produced by the British production company the Rank Organisation. *Rooney* is one of the few films that features a hurling-playing lead protagonist. However, as with the films considered in Chapter Three, the focus of *Rooney*'s producer on an international audience has consequences for the manner through which hurling and Irish culture more generally are depicted, and it is these consequences that are the concern of this chapter. Nonetheless, the film was a considerable popular success in Ireland – it was widely distributed across the country on release and bucked a trend of declining cinema-going in the country in the late 1950s. As Kevin and Emer Rockett note in their study of film exhibition and distribution in Ireland, when *Rooney* was screened in March 1958 in the Savoy, Dublin, 'it had 30,000 admissions in its first four days following its world premiere at the cinema and broke the Savoy's one-day house record with 10,000 admissions'.[1]

Indeed, on release nationwide the film was repeatedly marketed as 'breaking all box office records'.[2] While it would be wrong to simplistically equate commercial success with general popular approval, *Rooney* would appear nonetheless to have struck a chord with a sizeable Irish audience, partly, I will contend, due to its similarities with John Ford's *The Quiet Man* earlier in the decade, but more generally through its evocation of the appealing predominant trajectory of the American sports film.

ROONEY'S PRODUCTION CONTEXT

Though not a Hollywood production, in its style, content and humour *Rooney* is clearly indebted to previous Hollywood depictions of Ireland and went to considerable lengths in promotional materials such as its poster (Fig. 4.1) to stress the 'Oirishness' (as defined largely in Hollywood) of the production, through an emphasis on recognisable Irish stereotypes.

However, in reality there was little Irish involvement in the production of *Rooney*. In fact, one could contend that the film in most respects was a quintessentially British production, lacking any strong connection with Irish society and culture, and therefore relying almost entirely on recognisable stereotypes to justify its claim to Irishness. Though the film is set in Dublin city, it had an English director, George Pollock, probably best known for directing the Miss Marple film series in the 1960s.[3] The film was produced by George H. Brown, who had enjoyed a minor success two years previously with another Catherine Cookson adaptation, *Jacqueline*, a film that also saw the transfer of a Cookson story from its original English setting to an Irish locale, albeit in the North rather than South of Ireland.[4] The initial story for *Rooney* also had a British origin: Cookson's novel was set in the English coastal town of South Shields (not a renowned hurling stronghold), where Cookson was born and where much of her work is set. Indeed, an important aspect of her work was her ability to capture the distinctive accent of the north-east of England, and her contribution towards the representation of the region and its people was recognised in later life when she was awarded the Freedom of the Borough of South Tyneside (known today as Catherine Cookson Country).

Figure 4.1. *Rooney* (Rank Organisation, 1958) poster

However, in its transference to the Dublin milieu, considerations of accent were far from the producers' minds, reflected in the choice of non-Irish actors (such as Liverpool-born John Gregson as the eponymous Dublin binman James Ignatius Rooney) for the leading roles, who make largely unconvincing attempts to approximate an Irish accent in the film. Kevin Rockett has noted the significant effect of this:

One distinguishing feature of the local is the importance of textures of speech and voice, essential elements of identity in national cinema. One of the reasons why there is little or no cinema tradition in Ireland is that pressure of market has determined that foreign stars with so-called proper diction should play Irish roles ... In this process as we know from listening to these actors on the screen in Irish roles we may lose local textures of speech and voice.[5]

A number of prominent Irish actors do feature, however, including the ubiquitous Barry Fitzgerald as the querulous grandfather in one of his final moments on film. Pollock would direct Fitzgerald in his final film, *Broth of a Boy* (1959), later in 1958, where Fitzgerald plays the oldest man in the world, found in an Irish village by a British TV presenter. Reviews of that film, in common with those of most Irish-themed films of the period, were complimentary of the performances of the actors, particularly the Abbey Players, though were less impressed by Pollock's direction, which was not, according to the *Sunday Review*, 'up to the standard of his *Rooney*'.[6] *Broth of a Boy* is arguably more significant for being one of the first films produced by Emmet Dalton's production company at the recently opened Ardmore Studios in Wicklow, Ireland's first designated film studios, though a facility that almost immediately became primarily a low-cost premises for hire by American and British production companies rather than a facilitator of indigenous productions. The impetus for Ardmore coming into existence was the adaptation of popular Irish plays – *Broth of a Boy* was an adaptation of Hugh Leonard's *The Big Birthday* – for the growing television market in the United States and Britain. *Rooney*, though made primarily at Pinewood in London (with obvious landmark exteriors shot in Dublin, including Croke Park), was similarly inspired by the hope of capturing some of this TV market and building on the success earlier in the decade of *The Quiet Man*. The *Irish Press* newspaper on the day of *Rooney*'s premiere, 13 March 1958 (the film would go on general release on St Patrick's Day), includes an article celebrating the imminent opening of 'Ireland's first film studio' at Ardmore.[7] *Rooney*'s release became part of this discourse as the producer George H. Brown, in an address to the Publicity Club of Ireland luncheon in the Metropole Hotel on the same day, declared 'that he could see no reason for the absence of a thriving film industry in Ireland'.[8]

'THE MOST STAGE-IRISH FILM OF ALL TIME ...'

Described by Eamonn Sweeney as maybe 'the most stage-Irish film of all time ... [making] *Darby O'Gill and the Little People* look like a documentary',[9] the rudiments of stage Irishry are apparent in *Rooney* from the opening shots of the Guinness brewery, which we are told (in a narration provided by Barry Fitzgerald) is 'essential to the life of a great city'. Indeed, humour based around alcohol or drunkenness is a recurring feature of the film, while whiskey and pints of porter feature prominently throughout, from Rooney's dinner table to recurring scenes in the local pub. From early on faces familiar from *The Quiet Man* appear; apart from Fitzgerald, Jack MacGowran plays one of Rooney's closest friends, and co-worker, Joe O'Connor. *Rooney* also takes from *The Quiet Man* not just the whimsical depictions but also the almost musical quality of the film, in this case workers without notice breaking into song, in particular the rather risible theme tune 'Rooney-Oh'. This song was itself entirely the product of the British music scene in the late 1950s; the music was composed by London-born composer Philip Green (resident musical director of the Rank Organisation at the time) with lyrics by English songwriter Tommie Connor (possibly best known for composing the Christmas hit 'I Saw Mommy Kissing Santa Claus') sung in a faux-Irish accent by popular Liverpool-born crooner Michael Holliday. It was a minor hit in the UK for Holliday, reaching number 26 in the charts in February 1958 as the B-side of the single 'In Love'.

HURLING IN *ROONEY*

It is in this context that *Rooney* includes sport as a significant part of the narrative. However, hurling is not evident in advertisements for the film (including Fig. 4.1), possibly due to concerns that it might have alienated potential British and international viewers unfamiliar with the sport. Perhaps unsurprisingly, the depiction of sport in the film is less than convincing, particularly for followers of hurling. The central protagonist, James Ignatius Rooney, is a Dublin binman whose real talents (apart from being much sought after by a succession of landladies) are on show with his local hurling club – the fictitious Sons of Erin. The club where Rooney plays early on in the film is actually Dublin club St Vincent's, whose dual county star and twice All-Ireland-medal winner in football in 1958 and 1963, Dessie 'Snitchy' Ferguson, attempted valiantly, though with little success, to educate Gregson in his use of the *camán* (hurley).[10] With regard to the skills of rubbish collection, Gregson was introduced to this world, according to a *Cork Examiner* report, by retired Dublin Corporation binman Patrick O'Reilly, who had another notable connection with the world of the arts as a friend of George Bernard Shaw.[11] These reports reflected the considerable press interest in *Rooney*, and the *Irish Press* also reported that the film's leads were given an official reception at the Mansion House in Dublin, where Gregson and Muriel Pavlow, the English actress who plays Rooney's love interest Maire Hogan, received (rather appropriately, given the stereotypical depictions found in the film) figurines of a leprechaun and an Irish colleen from Dublin's lord mayor, James Carroll.[12]

In the film, Rooney's hurling talents are eventually spotted by a county selector, leading to a place on the Dublin county team playing in the All-Ireland final. A Dublin team in an All-Ireland hurling final in the late 1950s is not as surprising as it might sound: Dublin won a hurling All-Ireland in 1938 and lost to Cork in the final only five years before the production of *Rooney*; they were in the final again in 1961, losing by just a point to Tipperary, the last hurling championship final in which they competed (as of 2018).

However, *Rooney* is little concerned with providing an authentic or sophisticated depiction of hurling, evident in its portrayal of a Dublin team wearing the black and amber colours of Kilkenny rather than their usual sky and navy blue. This was necessary as Kilkenny played in the 1957 hurling final, the game used for the scenes in Croke Park in which our hero is depicted playing. Kilkenny's opposition in that game – Waterford – were offered first option of having Gregson togged out in one of their jerseys. However, conscious perhaps that this was the county's first final appearance since their victory over Dublin in 1948, 'and not wishing to add to the team's nervousness – the Waterford mentors refused permission'.[13] Former Waterford player and president of the GAA from 1970 to 1973 Padraig Ó Fainín recalls cycling over to see Pádraig Ó Caoimh (then general secretary of the GAA) at his accommodation in Ranelagh, Dublin, at one o'clock in the morning to inform him that Waterford were refusing the honour of having Rooney 'play' with them in the final.[14]

As David Rowe has summarised, in Hollywood sports films customarily 'all manner of social, structural, and cultural conflicts and divisions are resolved through the fantastic agency of sports'.[15] These films are indebted to a key ideology in American life: the American dream, which maintains that, regardless of one's position in life or disadvantage, the opportunity still exists to be successful through hard work. This trajectory was also present in British popular culture, including in comic-book sporting characters such as Alf Tupper.[16] It is a trajectory also present in *Rooney*, as the eponymous Dublin binman rises to heroic status through his hurling prowess. Along the way, his sporting connections ensure more salubrious accommodation and the attentions of a wide array of women, before he eventually settles for the much put-upon Maire, seducing her with the inspired chat-up line, 'I never rightly thanked you for doing me curtains.'

However, despite sharing this trajectory with sports films internationally, the actual footage of hurling offers little insight into the game or how it is played, with the scenes of Gregson running with the *sliotar* particularly unconvincing. Indeed, there is a strange lack of dramatic tension (usually a key aspect of the sports-film genre) evident in the hurling footage, partly due to Gregson's own very limited sporting ability. As the *Strabane Chronicle* of 21 September 1957 reported:

> For three weeks past Gregson has been inducted into the mysteries of hurling by a well-known County Dublin hurler. The pupil did not find it an easy job. As he said himself, hurling is a game for youth, and he did not learn his lesson in time. So it was that the Kilkenny and Waterford hurling teams were kept at Croke Park for many hours, until finally John Gregson scored his point.[17]

In fact, the Kilkenny and Waterford teams were kept for over six hours in Croke Park to film the hurling scenes.[18] The Kilkenny captain on the day, Mickey Kelly, also recalls the occasion:

> He [Gregson] stepped into the pre-match parade, tucked in behind Sean Clohessy, the left full-forward. A lot of people, especially Waterford people, wondered at the time who was Kilkenny's extra man![19]

RECEPTION

The premiere of *Rooney* was a major event for Dublin (held in aid of the Theatre and Cinema Benevolent Fund), including in the audience the president of Ireland Sean T. O'Kelly, members of the government and diplomatic corps, and receiving considerable coverage in the press the following day.[20] Critical reaction to the film was also generally positive, though concerns were raised by the *Cork Examiner* (a publication with a discerning interest in the sport) that the hurling scenes were 'not well faked'.[21] Indeed, the challenges of trying (and ultimately failing) to integrate a non-hurling-playing lead protagonist convincingly into a hurling match may account for why these match scenes (again unlike the conventional sports film) do not provide the film's climax; instead, the climax is based around an unconvincing subplot involving the alleged theft of jewellery by Maire, with Rooney racing to bring the evidence together to secure her release from a local police station following the game.

The footage included of the hurling final features shots of Rooney intercut with Waterford legends Philly Grimes and Frankie Walsh, and Kilkenny stars Dick Rockett (wearing number 13 and who seems to 'double' for Rooney in several scenes) and Paddy Buggy, who would later be elected president of the GAA in 1982. Unfortunately, we have only ten minutes of actual footage (filmed by the National Film Institute of Ireland, discussed in the next chapter) of the match, the 1957 All-Ireland hurling final. Indeed, that final is viewed today as one of the best ever – leaving *Irish Independent* reporter John D. Hickey 'groping for words to describe it all' in his match report – with Kilkenny winning (similar to the depiction in *Rooney*) through a dramatic late score by left wing-forward Mickey Kelly.[22] Followers of Gaelic games will also notice the involvement of legendary Irish sports commentator Michael O'Hehir (to whom we will also return in the next chapter) providing commentary on radio in one scene, which no doubt added to *Rooney*'s appeal in Ireland.

It is noteworthy, however, that the footage of the hurling final included in *Rooney* foregrounds the more robust encounters during the game; indeed, the *New York Times* reviewer was moved to describe hurling as 'a murderous game' following his viewing of *Rooney*, and Irish reviews regretted this emphasis in the film.[23] The *Irish Independent* reviewer lamented, 'Why Pollock wanted to introduce a bit of Donnybrook Fair stuff at another hurling game is his own affair, but he could have left it out.'[24] Benedict Kiely was particularly critical in his *Irish Press* review, remarking that 'if you expect nothing from "Rooney" you will not be disappointed'. 'Mr Gregson is not … Christy Ring', Kiely reminds readers (in case there was any doubt), and 'The Croke Park scenes … I found embarrassing. The preliminary hurling game, with Noel Purcell et cie in grips on the green sward, I found offensive.' Kiely also recalled in his review angry reactions to the depiction of battered and bruised hurlers returning from a game in *The Rising of the Moon*. Furthermore, he makes the astute observation that we have in *Rooney* a depiction of a national sport unlikely to be found in films concerning English national pastimes. 'Nor do I recollect', he declares,

> any occasion on which a Wembley Cup Final, or say, Twickenham, on the day of a Wales–England game (or Lords on the day of a Test match) was used thus as a stage-setting for mediocre comedy. Here was one excellent case for the application of the ban. Keep the mummers off the green ground of Croke Park. It was meant for higher things.[25]

Given the overall dependence on Irish stereotypes throughout the film, the emphasis on violence in the hurling scenes is not surprising. As noted previously, where depicted or referred to in international productions, this emphasis is often apparent, and hurling would seem to provide a shorthand for one of the most familiar and problematic representations of Irishness.

Rooney was not the only British production featuring Gaelic games to appear in the 1950s; possibly inspired by the moderate success the film enjoyed (particularly in Ireland and the UK), another British production featuring both hurling and Gaelic football (as well as an array of other popular sports played in Ireland) was produced a year later, *Ireland, Isle of Sport*. This promotional documentary film, produced by the British company Rayant Pictures and financed by the Caltex oil company, used sport and Ireland to promote Caltex, its products and activities. Caltex began sponsoring the annual Irish Sportstars Awards the previous year, including awards for the leading Gaelic footballer and hurler. *Ireland, Isle of Sport* emphasises the centrality of sport to Irish life, with the Irish narrator, Eamonn Andrews, remarking, 'Any way you can think of to put man or beast to the test and have a bet on the result, you can be sure we've thought of it too and made a game of it.' Directed by Kenneth Fairbairn, the film provides an upbeat and at times humorous account of sport in Ireland, with Gaelic games featured prominently. However, as with *Rooney*, the depiction is placed clearly within established constructions of Irishness, including foregrounding the importance of alcohol ('What need could be greater than this?' the narrator asks over shots of barrels of porter and the Guinness brewery) and beginning and ending with images of a church. Even before the initial credits roll, a priest emerges from a rural church to be met by a young boy playing hurling. 'In Ireland', Andrews tells us, 'the village priest is a figure of considerable power and influence and certainly not to be taken lightly by any as insignificant as a small boy with a hurley stick', upon which the boy plays the *sliotar* towards the priest, who reveals some sporting ability himself as he ably catches it. 'But in Ireland', Andrews continues, 'his reverence is as likely as not a player too.' Though the film features an array of other sports played in Ireland, including rugby, equestrian sports, greyhound racing, athletics, cycling, soccer, handball, water sports and golf, Gaelic games are celebrated above all with lengthy sequences of both Gaelic football and particularly hurling. Our narrator continues, 'The boy with the hurling stick is one of thousands up and down the land to whom all the cricket, the baseball, the hockey and even international football itself are mere pastimes against the mighty sport of hurling and the mighty men who play it.' *Ireland, Isle of Sport* reflected the growing international focus on Ireland, and aspects of Irish life and culture such as Gaelic games, in a context where tourism became increasingly important as a global industry and as a key component of the Irish economy.

However, as revealed in *Rooney* – a British production of an English novel transferred to an Irish locale and employing recognisable and distinctive tropes of Irish culture – this tension between the national and the international has consequences for the manner in which distinctive cultural practices are depicted. Despite the rather unengaging scenes of hurling, in other respects *Rooney* follows the conventions of the American sports film in depicting a marginalised individual rising from humble beginnings (here a binman) to sporting success and glory. However, with minimal input from Irish creative personnel – beyond supporting cast or internationally recognised acting figures – the film depends largely on a perception of Irish life and culture informed by previous Hollywood depictions. It is worth returning to the film's poster (Fig. 4.1) to conclude, and note the tagline therein: 'As <u>Irish</u> as the blarney and as funny as they come.' This underlining of 'Irish' may well reveal the real anxiety among the British producers and promoters about how Irish the film actually was, or rather was not.

5

'Ar son an náisiúin': the National Film Institute of Ireland's All-Ireland-final films[1]

On 4 September 1948, the *Irish Independent* carried a small announcement on page ten indicating that the Gaelic Athletic Association had authorised the filming of the All-Ireland hurling and football finals of that year. They were to be filmed by the National Film Institute of Ireland (NFI), set up three years earlier, and this marked the beginning of the first sustained period of indigenous filming of Gaelic games in Ireland. As discussed earlier, the first two decades of independence saw little indigenous film work produced in Ireland, with coverage of Gaelic games left primarily to foreign newsreel and production companies. These representations, found in Pathé, Movietone and British Gaumont newsreels and less often in some American major-studio shorts, while important as among the only moving-image representations of players of the period we have, nonetheless sometimes presented these games in a less than flattering and sometimes condescending manner. The development of indigenous film-making was hampered by the failure of the state to support film production and the Catholic Church's suspicion of what they viewed as a decadent cultural form.

However, the Church's position mellowed as the 1930s developed, particularly following the publication in 1936 of Pope Pius XI's encyclical *Vigilanti Cura*, which recognised the potential 'great advantage to learning and to education' of the cinema.[2] Pope Pius' words inspired members

of the clergy to become more involved in film production in Ireland, culminating with the setting up of the National Film Institute of Ireland in
1945 under the patronage of Dr John Charles McQuaid, archbishop of
Dublin. The institute was initially established to import and distribute
educational films to Irish schools and parish halls but soon set about making films of its own. Significantly, from the beginning these films placed
a strong emphasis on affirming and celebrating the relatively new independent state of Ireland, apparent in one of its first documentary films, *A
Nation Once Again* (Brendan Stafford, 1946), made to mark the centenary
of the death of Thomas Davis, the leader of the nationalist Young Ireland
organisation of the 1840s. Described by Ruth Barton as 'a classic instance
of the use of history as a legitimising discourse',[3] as the title suggests the
film provided a nationalist and uncontested account of Irish history and
identity. While exploring Davis' legacy and celebrating his political ideals, it featured prominently Éamon de Valera, the then Taoiseach (prime
minister), as well as aspects of Irish society and culture, including Gaelic
games. In one sequence, over images of Gaelic football and Irish dancing,
the narrator Dan O'Herlihy reminds us that Davis' teaching is 'the sure
basis on which to plan a united nation free from shore to shore and the
hope of all true Irishmen is that in this as in most things else this man
was prophet as well as leader'. In these words O'Herlihy connects Gaelic
games, a sport that operated then, as now, on an all-Ireland basis, with
Irish nationalism and its ambition of a united Ireland, a theme that was
maintained in the institute's highlights films of All-Ireland finals.

Among the first directors of the institute was Pádraig Ó Caoimh,
the then general secretary of the GAA. Following the playing of the
1947 All-Ireland football final between Cavan and Kerry in New York,
Ó Caoimh realised the importance of and demand in Ireland for quality
moving-image representations of Gaelic games. The highlights footage
of this match, shot by New York-based Winik Films under Ó Caoimh's
supervision, was a major attraction to Irish cinemas and parish halls,
particularly in the counties featured. This is evident, for example, in
the film's prominence in advertisements from the period where it was
frequently billed above popular Hollywood fare (Fig. 5.1). Inspired by
this success, Ó Caoimh set about facilitating, through the institute, the
filming of highlights of all subsequent All-Ireland finals. This chapter will

Figure 5.1. A rather misleading advertisement (given the ten-minute length of the actual film) for a screening of the 1947 All-Ireland football final, *Anglo-Celt*, 11 October 1947

examine the films produced and their employment of Gaelic games to promote their conception of Irish identity in the period.

JOHN GRIERSON

O'Caoimh's efforts, and those of the institute as a whole, were encouraged by a lecture given in the Gresham Hotel, Dublin, on 11 May 1948 under the auspices of the National Film Institute of Ireland by the seminal Scottish documentarian John Grierson. Grierson was a pioneering director and producer of films during his time working for the Empire Marketing Board and the General Post Office in Britain and subsequently as commissioner of the National Film Board of Canada. In these roles he promoted his firm belief in the important role film could play in promoting the national interest, as he noted in his lecture in Dublin, entitled 'A Film Policy for Ireland', using film 'internally and externally as a full-fledged instrument of national purpose'.[4] For Grierson, film was 'a most valuable aid not only in maintaining the morale of a country but also in securing that higher measure of understanding and co-operation which no modern country can do without'.[5] Towards this, Grierson emphasised the importance of preserving 'what we had of our own traditions, our own culture, our own way of looking at things', and the crucial role film could play in this process.[6] The focus on nation-building through film was already evident in the institute's previous work, including the film *A Nation Once Again*; however, Grierson further supported their efforts in this respect while also encouraging a focus on a particular part of Irish culture, sport. Among those aspects of Irish culture that Grierson identified as important 'to preserve and foster', he included Ireland's 'games of its own played on a nation-wide scale'.[7] Though only mentioned briefly, it is noteworthy that the Scottish film-maker should have noted the distinctive role that sport played in Irish culture in a paper focused primarily on 'the use of the film for national purposes'.[8] Significantly, within four months of Grierson's lecture, the institute began the first sustained period of indigenous filming of Gaelic games in Ireland, a process that involved not just the preservation and promotion of these games, but also the promotion of the national project itself in the post-war era.

THE NATIONAL FILM INSTITUTE'S ALL-IRELAND-FINAL FILMS

The National Film Institute's All-Ireland-final films are each approximately ten minutes in length, following the pattern of the popular film of the 1947 final. This was also the approximate length of the one-reel short films that preceded features in Irish cinemas in this period, including sport-themed shorts such as *Hurling* (1936) discussed in Chapter Three. Though the short length was criticised in the press at the time,[9] these highlights packages were nonetheless a considerable improvement on previous newsreel depictions of Gaelic games, rarely longer than two and a half minutes, and offered more detailed accounts of the build-up and the role of these games in national life. Though limited by the length of each production and the technology of the time, the institute's films nonetheless include rare footage from the pre-television era of legendary hurling players such as John Keane (Waterford), John Doyle (Tipperary), Bobby Rackard (Wexford) and Cork's celebrated Christy Ring. The films feature moments of superb hurling technique from these and other players, including a point scored from the ground by Ring in the 1952 final and an impressive palmed point from the same player in the 1956 final.

In football, the institute's films provide almost the only footage we have today of leading players such as Dan O'Keeffe and Seán Murphy (Kerry), John Joe O'Reilly (Cavan), Kevin Heffernan (Dublin) and Seán Purcell (Galway). In some instances, as in the highlights of both the

1949 All-Ireland football and hurling finals, footage of teams in training before the match is featured. Some of the highlights packages, such as the film of the 1948 hurling All-Ireland-final also feature the arrival of supporters from all over the country to Dublin for the match, while many also include scenes outside Croke Park prior to the throw-in. The parade of supporters to the stadium is also featured in some films, as in the shots of Dublin followers processing from Fairview and Marino behind a horse-drawn carriage prior to the 1958 football final. In these shots we find sometimes fascinating renderings of the urban space prior to games – with crowds arriving at Kingsbridge Station (renamed Heuston in 1966) and gathering on O'Connell Street – as well as an insight into the various means of transport to games in the period, including bicycle, horse and cart, car, bus and, in one shot from the 1948 football-final highlights, the back of an open-top cattle lorry packed with standing supporters. Most of the packages also include highlights of the minor final that preceded the senior game.

In terms of the games themselves, as these productions now involved two cameras rather than the one used previously for newsreel footage, they also provided considerably fuller coverage (though by no means comprehensive), including a more detailed depiction of play where prominent players were now identified, a rare occurrence in earlier newsreel footage. Given the stature of the players featured in these highlights packages, including nine from the hurling and eleven from the football teams of the millennium,[10] it is not surprising that they became both popular cinema attractions in the pre-television era (discussed further below) and vital instructional tools for GAA clubs across the country throughout the 1950s, 1960s and 1970s.[11] The *Irish Independent* of 2 March 1965 announced that

Ten-minute 16mm films on each of the All-Ireland senior hurling finals from 1948–'64 inclusive can be hired from the National Film Institute of Ireland, 65 Harcourt St., Dublin 2. The films of the 1960, '62, '63 and '64 finals are in colour. The hirage charge is 6/- plus 2/6 per day for each black-and-white film and 7/6, plus 2/6 per day for the films that are in colour.[12]

The *Kerryman* of 27 March 1965 reported that the Coiste Iomána (hurling committee) in Kerry had procured 'films on All-Ireland hurling finals from 1948 to '64' from the National Film Institute, which were to be 'shown throughout the county'.[13] By the 1970s, these films were also being screened to schoolchildren after school hours as part of mobile film screenings organised by the institute on behalf of the Department of Health.

However, correspondence between the NFI and the GAA indicates that the institute had some difficulties receiving payment for films hired, while not all films loaned were returned. As the institute's secretary G.J. McCanny remarked in one letter to the association's development director, 'The attached Invoice has been treated as if it were a hurling ball having been pucked to and fro between here and Croke Park and I'm anxious it should come to rest.'[14] It would appear that the NFI had particular problems in reacquiring films loaned to clubs across the border, as is evident in another letter from McCanny to the GAA:

We cannot agree to supply Six-County residents with films. We have experienced too much difficulty in the past even in cases where the film has been collected here and too many films which we know were definitely posted to us failed to reach us.[15]

PRODUCTION, DISTRIBUTION AND RECEPTION OF THE NFI'S ALL-IRELAND-FINAL FILMS

The All-Ireland-final films were initially shot on two cameras, each positioned on the Hogan Stand side of the field, and the rushes then sent on Sunday evening to London for development. The next morning Seán O'Sullivan, the first secretary of the NFI, accompanied by Michael O'Hehir (who provided the commentary until the late 1950s), travelled by plane to the Carlton Hill Studios in London where the sound and commentary were added.[16] These films, distributed initially by Abbey Films, were screened in cinemas around the country by the following Friday as short attractions before the main feature, and proved popular

Figure 5.2.
Cameramen
preparing to film
the 1957 All-Ireland
football final © Irish
Film Archive/Irish
Film Institute

above all in the counties taking part in the All-Irelands, particularly before the advent of live television coverage with the establishment of Telefís Éireann in 1961.

The footage was initially filmed from 1948 by George Fleischmann (Fig. 5.4), who was assisted by the English-born sound technician Peter Hunt. From 1953 onwards, Brendan Stafford, assisted by Robert Monks, took on the filming responsibilities, with Monks, supported by various other cameramen including Vincent Corcoran, Tommy Hayde and Pádraig Thornton, continuing in the role into the mid-1960s. In a significant piece of self-reflexive footage, the build-up to the 1957 football final includes the cameramen climbing to their elevated position before the game (Fig. 5.2).

Particularly in the early years, the footage is clearly the work of cameramen learning the art of filming Gaelic games and challenged above all by the speed of play and the size of the ball in hurling as well as the limitations of the technology of the time that necessitated the reloading of film stock at short regular intervals. During the period of Monks' involvement, the games were shot on Newman Sinclair 35mm cameras, hired from London. These were clockwork cameras that could hold a maximum of 200 feet of film – equivalent to approximately two minutes of footage – before the magazines had to be reloaded.[17] As a result it is sometimes difficult to follow individual passages of play and many of the scores are missed, though the commentary of Michael O'Hehir in particular nonetheless manages to communicate some of the excitement and significance of the occasion. Another commentator who featured regularly in the packages by the late 1950s was Frank Ryan, who spent a period as secretary of the NFI.

As with the 1947 All-Ireland football-final film, announcements for these films featured prominently, sometimes above popular Hollywood releases, particularly in local newspapers (Fig. 5.3), while newspaper reports indicate considerable interest among local audiences in the screenings. The film of the 1954 Meath v Kerry All-Ireland football final, for instance, is described by the *Meath Chronicle* of 9 October 1954 as one audiences 'should not miss', after being screened to 'enthusiastic audiences' in the Lyric and Palace cinemas, Navan, and in the Savoy, Kells.[18] The *Tuam Herald* of 3 November 1956 also described the

great interest taken in the National Film Institute's film of the All-Ireland football final shown at the Mall and Odeon Cinemas this week. Sean Purcell and Frank Stockwell [two of Galway's star players at the time] were guests at the Mall on Monday night, and the two Tuam men heard the Croke Park plaudits re-echo in the cinema when they flashed on the screen.[19]

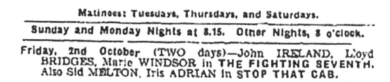

Showing at THE COLISEUM, WATERFORD, on FRIDAY and SATURDAY, 2nd & 3rd OCTOBER.   First - Run Presentation Film.

EXTRA—The All-Ireland Hurling Final, 1953—CORK v. GALWAY—Friday, Saturday and Sunday.

Watch Out for FOOTBALL FINAL—Kerry v. ARMAGH.

Matinees: Tuesdays, Thursdays, and Saturdays.

Sunday and Monday Nights at 8.15. Other Nights, 8 o'clock.

Friday, 2nd October (TWO days)—John IRELAND, Lloyd BRIDGES, Marie WINDSOR in THE FIGHTING SEVENTH. Also Sid MELTON, Iris ADRIAN in STOP THAT CAB.

Figure 5.3. Announcement for showing of the All-Ireland hurling final in 1953, *Munster Express*, 2 October 1953

As well as the 35mm prints sent to cinemas until the late 1950s, there were also 16mm prints produced from the mid-1950s onwards which were exhibited in clubs and parish halls around the country using mobile projectors from the National Film Institute. By 1958, the institute was filming the games on 16mm rather than 35mm and would continue with this format in subsequent years. Prints of the finals were also occasionally screened abroad, including to Irish soldiers in the Congo in 1960,[20] and to viewers in London, New York and Cyprus.[21] At the request of the Italian National Olympic Committee, a special screening was held in Rome during the 1960 Olympics of the institute's films of the football and hurling finals from the previous year.[22] Footage from the 1962 hurling final was also incorporated into an episode of the popular series *Irish Diary* broadcast on twenty USA channels in the mid-1960s,[23] while the BBC showed highlights from the institute's football film in 1957 before filming highlights from some finals themselves from 1959.[24] The films also enjoyed some critical success at film festivals, winning awards in 1956 and 1958 at the Festival of Sports Pictures at Cortina d'Ampezzo in Italy.[25] Indeed, by the end of the 1950s the films had become a crucial source of revenue for the institute, with a minute from its finance and general purposes committee meeting of 3 January 1958 noting that 'the estimated profit on the GAA films in 1957 would be between £180 and £200', a not inconsiderable sum at the time.[26]

Initially filmed in black and white, from the football All-Ireland in 1958 the footage was in colour, partly in response to competing newsreels of All-Irelands from Universal Irish News in that year and subsequently from Gael Linn's *Amharc Éireann* series (discussed in the next chapter).[27] The colour footage also distinguished the institute's films from the black-and-white televised images broadcast by Telefís Éireann, beginning with the All-Ireland football semi-final between Kerry and Dublin in 1962.

PARALLELS WITH *OLYMPIA* (1938)

Of the cameramen who filmed All-Irelands for the National Film Institute, George Fleischmann (Fig. 5.4) had both the most colourful history and arguably the greatest influence on the initial style and focus of the films

Figure 5.4.
George
Fleischmann
(*Memories in
Focus*, 1995)

themselves, a focus that continued after Fleischmann's departure in 1953. He was a *sonderführer* (specialist leader) with the Luftwaffe during the Second World War and after his plane was shot down over Ireland in 1941 was subsequently interned in the Curragh until the end of the war.[28]

Fleischmann's specialism was as a cameraman, having trained at the Berlin Film Academy and worked previously for the largest film studio in Germany during the 1930s and 1940s, UFA.[29] His camera was confiscated on his internment, though at the end of the war, following receipt of a statement from the German authorities indicating that it was his, it was returned to him.[30] As a sign of the scarcity of such equipment in Ireland in the post-war period, Fleischmann quickly became a much sought-after cameraman.[31]

Fleischmann's arrival in Ireland would prove fortunate for the development of sports filming in the country. During his time with UFA, he had worked as a camera operator on Leni Riefenstahl's sports documentary *Olympia* (1938), the seminal depiction of the 1936 Berlin Summer Olympics.[32] While it would be wrong to overstate the similarities, particularly given the fascist context of 1930s Germany and the vastly superior resources available to Riefenstahl, there are nonetheless intriguing parallels to be found between *Olympia* and the early NFI films of All-Irelands. First, there are similarities in the filming of the games themselves. This is most evident when one compares the filming of

Association football in the second part of Riefenstahl's film of the 1936 Olympics, *Olympia 2. Teil – Fest der Schönheit* (1938) with the NFI's All-Ireland-final films in the late 1940s, where both adopt similar principal camera positions – one elevated camera from the stand at midfield and one roving camera to the right of this position behind the goal (Figs 5.5 & 5.6 and Figs 5.7 & 5.8).

Figures 5.5 & 5.6. Screen grabs from the NFI footage of the 1949 (top) and 1948 (bottom) All-Ireland hurling finals © Irish Film Archive/Irish Film Institute

Figures 5.7 & 5.8. Screen grabs from the 1936 Olympic Games Association-football final, *Olympia 2* (Olympia-Film, 1938)

Over the years that the All-Irelands were filmed the cameras moved to more elevated positions closer to both goals in an attempt to capture more scores. Another feature of *Olympia* that is also apparent in the NFI films is the prominence of radio commentators. In the original version of *Olympia*, Germany's leading radio commentator, Dr Paul Laven,[33]

Figures 5.9 & 5.10. Some of the commentators featured in *Olympia* (Olympia-Film, 1938)

introduces events, describes athletes and provides running commentary on the various competitions. Indeed, radio commentators feature prominently in the film itself, apparently (their language and appearance would suggest) from Italy, France, Japan, Spain, the US and Germany, with all seemingly broadcasting the games live from Berlin, though the images were actually recorded after the event (Figs 5.9 & 5.10).

Figures 5.11 & 5.12. Screen grabs from NFI films of Michael O'Hehir at work in footage of the 1948 All-Ireland hurling final, and of a family listening to their radio, presumably to his commentary, in the footage of the 1948 All-Ireland Gaelic-football final © Irish Film Archive/Irish Film Institute

In similar fashion, Pádraig Ó Caoimh arranged for the leading Irish radio sports commentator of the time, Michael O'Hehir, to provide the commentary to the NFI All-Ireland-final films up until the late 1950s. As noted earlier, since the establishment of 2RN in 1926 radio played a central role in the popularisation of Gaelic games via live coverage of matches, most famously through the distinctive and thrilling voice of O'Hehir, who began broadcasting in 1938.[34] Indeed, O'Hehir is often shown on screen (Fig. 5.11), and it is clear the producers were attempting to build on his huge radio following as we watch him relay the action to 'wirelesses' across the nation during the game. Some of the highlights packages also include images of families gathered around the radio listening (it would appear) to O'Hehir's commentary (Fig. 5.12).

However, the most significant parallel between both productions is their attempts to celebrate and affirm the nations in which the sports depicted take place. The filming of the Berlin Olympics in 1936 – often referred to as the 'Nazi Olympics'[35] – by Riefenstahl was centrally concerned with celebrating the achievements of Nazi Germany and affirming the German nation. As Taylor Downing in her study of the film has observed:

It's clear that it was decided at the highest level in the Reich, probably by Hitler himself, that the Games should be used as an opportunity to promote the achievements of Nazi Germany before the war. Hitler decided that money would be no problem in creating a national spectacle to show off Germany to the world ... the Nazis intended the games to promote the 'new order' in Germany.[36]

While the international context is less evident (apart from occasional references to Irish-America) in the institute's All-Ireland-final films, at least until the 1960s, the post-Second World War milieu after the 'Emergency' nonetheless provided the perfect arena for the popularisation of national spectacle through film. Southern Ireland's neutrality during the war reinforced the country's independence against heavy criticism by Winston Churchill and other world leaders, and as the institute's films of Gaelic games indicate, the nation and its celebration is a recurring theme of the coverage, particularly until the end of the 1950s.

This is evident in the films' focus on the prematch ceremony, including the national anthem and national flag and the attendance of dignitaries such as the president of Ireland, the Taoiseach and various bishops, including at the 1952 football final the papal nuncio, Dr Gerald O'Hara (Fig. 5.13). In particular, the recurring shots of religious in attendance

Figure 5.13. The Cavan captain, Mick Higgins, is captured kissing the papal nuncio's (Dr Gerald O'Hara) ring prior to the 1952 Gaelic-football final © Irish Film Archive/Irish Film Institute

is striking, as in the build-up to the 1951 football final where O'Hehir comments on the 'many personalities of the political, ecclesiastical, and diplomatic world [who] view the colourful scene below'. Particularly in the case of the football finals, it would appear that bishops from the competing counties were often invited, as in 1955 when Dr Denis Moynihan of Kerry and Dr Fitzpatrick of the Dublin diocese participated in the prematch ceremony. In a sign of the Church's prominent role more generally in Irish society in the 1940s and 1950s, it was these bishops who got proceedings under way by throwing either the ball (Gaelic football) or *sliotar* (hurling) in amongst the players, following the singing of the hymn 'Faith of Our Fathers' and the ceremonial kissing of the bishop's ring by the team captains (Fig. 5.13).[37] Significantly, in the 1959 football final it was GAA president Dr Joseph Stuart, and not a bishop, who threw the ball in, and the practice of having bishops begin games was discontinued by the mid-1960s.

These images provide a further parallel with *Olympia*, which also focused on the presence of political leaders, particularly Hitler, and dignitaries present at the games. The dignitaries in the NFI films do not, however, dominate proceedings quite in the manner of Hitler, who appears to preside over events, particularly in the Olympic Stadium, from his opening address, and to whom the camera returns repeatedly. Yet as with British newsreel depictions of Gaelic games in the interwar years, explored earlier, the NFI films were also concerned with supporting the status quo in Irish politics and society. Indeed, their foregrounding of political and religious figures had an analogous effect to that identified by Mike Huggins with regard to the prominent depiction of members of the British royal family in English soccer newsreels: it reinforced the significance of both the sport and the dignitaries featured in national life.[38] While the focus on the clergy in particular was already evident, if to a lesser extent, in surviving foreign newsreels of Gaelic games, Irish political figures featured less often in such footage. Furthermore, the NFI productions give a much more detailed portrayal of the prematch ceremony, thereby confirming its importance.[39]

CONTAINING DISSENT

This focus in the institute's films on maintaining the status quo is also evident in the manner through which they contain dissent or downplay controversy. Whether wading through the canal next to the stadium to gain access to games (the 1958 football-final footage) or seated precariously on the walls surrounding the stadium or on the roof of the Hogan Stand (recurring images found throughout the 1950s footage), spectators took increasing risks to watch All-Ireland finals as the 1950s progressed and attendances soared. However, little is said in the commentary of the obvious dangers involved for such spectators. Attendances at All-Ireland finals by the 1950s and 1960s reached record-breaking levels, exceeding 90,000 by 1961.[40] This was well above the capacity of Croke Park and led to serious overcrowding, including the 1953 All-Ireland football final, which attracted a then record attendance of 86,155 (exaggerated somewhat by O'Hehir to 90,000 in his commentary). However, the dangers are downplayed by O'Hehir in his commentary ('even the spacious and ever-improving Croke Park seems to burst at the seams'), despite the fact that we see in the footage that a large portion of the crowd had to be allowed onto the pitch just prior to the game to relieve the pressure on the terraces.

All-Ireland finals in these years were also occasionally marred by moments of foul play or violence on the pitch, though such moments, too, are rarely evident in the NFI footage. A case in point is the 1953 hurling final between Cork and Galway, regarded as one of the most unsporting ever.[41] Unfancied Galway set out to disrupt reigning champions Cork's game, particularly the much-feared Christy Ring. Ring was marked by Galway captain Mickey Burke, who followed the Corkman closely throughout, frustrating his attempts to get into the game. Eventually, it has been alleged, Ring snapped and, as Breandán Ó hEithir has described it, 'hit him [Burke] a belt in the face'.[42] Whether in response to Ring's actions or not, reports of the game also indicate that Ring was subject to abuse from a sizeable segment of the crowd, who booed him whenever he got possession, though this abuse is not evident in the highlights.[43] Though O'Hehir makes reference to 'Mickey Burke subduing the immortal Christy Ring', he is quiet on the unsportsmanlike behaviour reported in the press at the time.[44] However, despite attempts to downplay the violence, the NFI footage nonetheless inadvertently captures, approximately seven and a half minutes into the highlights package, an attack by Ring on Burke in the background as Galway equalise in the second half through Hubert Gordon.

'AR SON AN NÁISIÚIN' (ON BEHALF OF THE NATION)

Centrally in these films there is an emphasis on All-Ireland-final day as a national occasion for the entire island, 'north, south, east and west', as O'Hehir remarks in his commentary prior to the 1948 football final. The 1954 football final also includes a pageant for Irish unity at half-time – 'one Ireland, Ireland one, Éire gan roinnt (Ireland without division)', O'Hehir comments. Irish-nationalist history and culture are foregrounded repeatedly, including in the music chosen to accompany the opening credits on most of the packages from the 1950s, the air from the eighteenth-century politically charged *aisling* poem, 'Fáinne Geal an Lae' (The Dawning of the Day).[45] In one of the earliest films, that of the 1948 football final between Cavan and Mayo, there is a strongly nationalist tone evident, particularly in the build-up sequence, which recalls Bloody Sunday (21 November 1920) and the shooting of Tipperary footballer Michael Hogan by British soldiers when they fired upon players and supporters in Croke Park. The 1916 Rising is also remembered in the commentary, accompanied by shots of the General Post Office (GPO) on O'Connell Street, and O'Hehir refers to the alleged use of the ruins of that street after the Rising to build Hill 16, the famous terrace behind one of the goals.[46]

Furthermore, the banner 'Ar Son an Náisiúin' (On Behalf of the Nation) (Fig. 5.14) is prominently captured in a long take during the parade preceding the 1957 hurling final, while the footage of the 1954 hurling final also includes the prematch parade by thirty-two Irish-speaking flag-bearing boys representing, as O'Hehir remarks, 'the counties of our country and each carrying a hurley depicting the aim of the GAA to put a hurley in the hand of every boy in the country'. The Irish language,

Figure 5.14. Parade prior to the 1957 hurling final with the banner 'Ar Son an Náisiúin' visible in the background © Irish Film Archive/Irish Film Institute

too, features prominently, not only in the credit sequences but also in O'Hehir's commentary, which is peppered with passages in Irish, while the 1955 and 1956 senior games are also preceded by exhibitions of Irish dancing. In all of this, these films repeatedly affirm the Irish nation and its culture as well as its leading political and social figures while downplaying controversy and dissent.

The televising of the All-Ireland football final in 1962 is mentioned in the commentary to the NFI's highlights that year. With the arrival of live television coverage, the demand for the institute's filming of All-Irelands reduced considerably. Initially it responded by improving its own coverage of the games, partly informed by requests from the GAA itself to focus more on continuous play rather than scores.[47] Consequently there is more focus on the games and less on the build-up, and a third cameraman was employed by the mid-1960s to get better close-up shots. However, while finals continued to be filmed intermittently until the mid-1970s, interest in viewing the highlights decreased to such an extent that by 1968 General Film Distributors Ltd (which had distributed the films in Ireland from the late 1950s) informed the institute that they

would prefer not to participate in their distribution as indeed very little interest had been evidenced by any of our exhibitors in the finals over the past few years, due no doubt to the very extensive coverage by Telefis Eireann.[48]

In addition, the GAA, which had since 1948 given £500 a year to the NFI for the production of the final films, discontinued this funding in 1968.[49] As a result, the institute became increasingly dependent as the 1960s progressed on orders from Bord Fáilte and Aer Lingus for its films – as the institute's Tom Hyde remarked in his response to General Film Distributors' letter quoted above: 'Thank God for Bord Fáilte and Aer Lingus.'[50] The highlights packages of both the 1961 hurling final and the 1962 football final begin with an Aer Lingus plane landing at Dublin airport, while the packages in the 1960s seem increasingly to be aimed at an international audience, with the nationalist overtones evident in the earlier films, particularly in the build-up to games, less a feature. This development partly reflected a changing Ireland in this period, though it also revealed the institute's increased dependence on Aer Lingus and Bord Fáilte for funding, as both organisations screened the films for their employees and customers, and for promotional purposes as tourism became an ever more important part of the Irish economy.[51] This dependence is

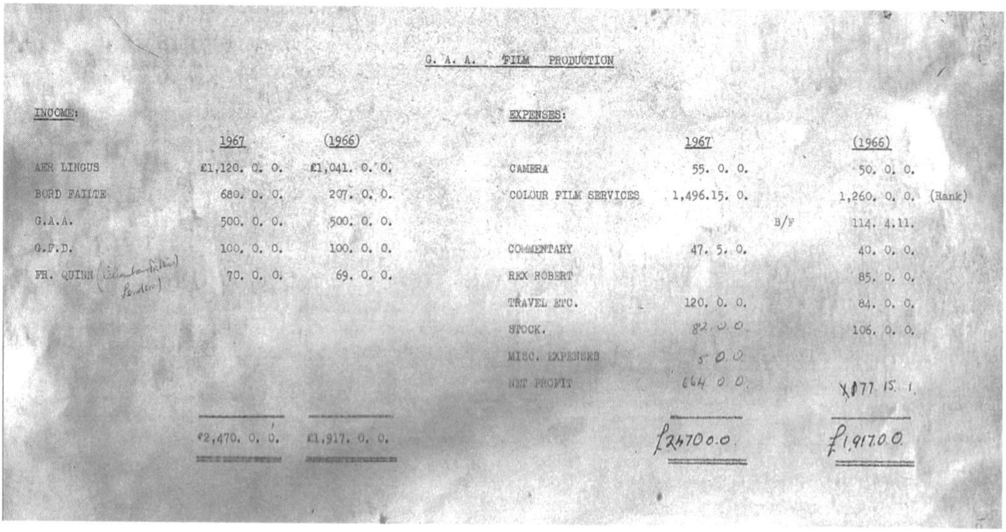

G. A. A. FILM PRODUCTION

INCOME:

	1967	(1966)
AER LINGUS	£1,120. 0. 0.	£1,041. 0. 0.
BORD FAILTE	680. 0. 0.	207. 0. 0.
G.A.A.	500. 0. 0.	500. 0. 0.
G.F.D.	100. 0. 0.	100. 0. 0.
FR. QUINN	70. 0. 0.	69. 0. 0.
	£2,470. 0. 0.	£1,917. 0. 0.

EXPENSES:

	1967		(1966)	
CAMERA	55. 0. 0.		50. 0. 0.	
COLOUR FILM SERVICES	1,496.15. 0.		1,260. 0. 0.	(Rank)
		B/F	114. 4.11.	
COMMENTARY	47. 5. 0.		40. 0. 0.	
REX ROBERT			85. 0. 0.	
TRAVEL ETC.	120. 0. 0.		84. 0. 0.	
STOCK.	82. 0. 0.		106. 0. 0.	
MISC. EXPENSES	5. 0. 0.			
NET PROFIT	664. 0. 0.		177. 15. 1.	
	£2470. 0. 0.		£1,917. 0. 0.	

Figure 5.15. National Film Institute GAA Film Production accounts, 1966 and 1967. IFI, item number 16238, box 317 © Irish Film Archive/Irish Film Institute

evident in the institute's accounts from 1966 and 1967 (Fig. 5.15), which show that most of the funding generated by the films came from these two sources.

The NFI's All-Ireland-finals highlights films represented a crucial step in the evolution of indigenous sports filming in Ireland and were an important part of an emerging and distinctive film culture in the country in the post-war period. These productions, particularly until the end of the 1950s, foreground repeatedly the Irish nation, its language, culture and political and religious leaders. Featuring some of the most acclaimed sporting heroes of the time, the productions enjoyed considerable popularity when screened in cinemas across Ireland, particularly until the arrival of television. Live television coverage of All-Ireland finals would eventually lead to the ending of the institute's filming of finals, though the films already produced continued to offer a significant instructional tool for GAA clubs across the island in the 1960s and 1970s as well as providing Aer Lingus and Bord Fáilte with important viewing and promotional material. Their most important period was unquestionably the late 1940s and 1950s, a time from which little other footage of Gaelic games survives and in which these films provided rare positive portrayals of Irish society and culture in a particularly challenging decade characterised, as Terence Brown has noted, by 'stagnation and crisis'.[52] While sharing some formal similarities with Leni Riefenstahl's *Olympia*, the most significant parallel is in how both projects ultimately affirmed the status quo and the position of the political and social leaders in public life. In Ireland this was at a time when popular protest might well have been warranted with the country experiencing a severe depression and many enduring considerable poverty and hardship as employment fell by 12 per cent between 1951 and 1958 and emigration passed well over the 400,000 mark by the end of the decade.[53] Yet, in the same period, attendances at Gaelic games increased dramatically, reaching over 85,000 for the All-Ireland hurling final in the mid-1950s and over 90,000 for the football final by 1961.[54] The institute's footage of these All-Irelands constitute distinctly Irish sports films that played an important role in affirming the Irish nation in a time of crisis.

6

Coaching Irishness Through Film: Gaelic games in the film work of Gael Linn

---

As the 1950s drew to a close, the National Film Institute of Ireland was joined by another indigenous organisation engaged in the regular filming of Gaelic games. The decision of the Irish-language cultural organisation Gael Linn to undertake this project is inseparable from the group's overall concerns. As its title indicates – a play on words between 'Irish pool' and 'Irish with us' – Irishness was indeed a defining characteristic of Gael Linn from its inception.[1] Above all, for Gael Linn's founders the Irish language, its preservation and promotion was a central concern. However, the beginnings of Gael Linn were also inseparable from Gaelic games; the organisation began as a fundraising project to support initiatives to promote the Irish language and culture, organising a weekly betting 'pool' based on predicting the outcome of matches in hurling and Gaelic football on the model set by the football pools in England.[2] Within a few years of its formation, Gael Linn was sponsoring several Gaelic-games competitions including a Gaelic-football senior tournament,[3] while a major provincial competition for elite-level players of camogie – the female equivalent of hurling – has been the Gael Linn Cup since 1956. This chapter will consider newsreel and coaching-film depictions of hurling and Gaelic football produced by Gael Linn between 1959 and 1964, examining in particular the manner by which these films configure Irishness in a transitional period in Irish society.

FOUNDING GAEL LINN AND *AMHARC ÉIREANN*

Gael Linn was founded in 1952 by Dónal Ó Móráin, under whose guidance the organisation recognised that film could be an important tool in the promotion of the Irish language. In the 1950s, Irish cinemas were dominated by foreign films, in particular from the United States. Even films that featured Ireland – such as John Ford's popular success *The Quiet Man* (discussed in Chapter Three) – were American in origin and had American audiences as their primary concern. The newsreels that preceded the main features in Irish cinemas were also produced abroad and included few items on Ireland – with the exception of occasional footage of All-Ireland finals (discussed in Chapter Two) or items on major political events. Ó Móráin contacted film-maker Colm Ó Laoghaire, who he had known from his university days, in early 1956 and they decided to produce a monthly newsreel series about Irish subjects and with Irish commentary.

Ó Laoghaire was assisted initially by Vincent Corcoran, who had recently procured an Arriflex 35mm camera and was also gaining experience from working on the All-Irelands filmed by the NFI. The magazine-style series, entitled *Amharc Éireann* (which translates as either 'A Look at Ireland' or 'A View of Ireland'), focused initially on one subject in each four-minute episode, with Ó Laoghaire given editorial control over the choice of topic. The first monthly *eagrán*, or edition, appeared in June 1956 and a total of thirty-six episodes were produced, reaching an estimated audience of a quarter of a million each month.[4] In 1959, the series increased to weekly multi-item editions, and 160 episodes were produced before its eventual discontinuation in July 1964, due to declining cinema attendances and the arrival of television in Ireland with the opening of Telefís Éireann on New Year's Eve 1961.

The series was shot on 35mm and distributed by the British Rank Film Distributors, as they were the only company willing to distribute the series for free. Initially Rank attached the monthly *Amharc Éireann* newsreels to the *Universal Newsreel* screened in all Rank-owned cinemas. However, when Rank discontinued its newsreels in Irish cinemas in 1959, largely due to the increased prominence of television in Britain, *Amharc Éireann* became the main weekly newsreel screened in Rank cinemas in Ireland, which at that times accounted for some 75 per cent of cinemas in the Republic.[5] The increased number of episodes required a larger production team and Gael Linn hired Jim Mulkerns and Val Ennis to collaborate with Ó Laoghaire. The eight to ten prints made of each episode premiered first in Dublin city centre cinemas before circulating around the country. Publicity for the series was managed by Gael Linn, who produced a poster for every episode.

The weekly episodes usually consisted of four items, each approximately one minute in length. Occasionally longer items were included or dedicated episodes were produced focusing on a single major event, and it was typically in this form that coverage of Gaelic games such as the All-Ireland final featured, though the series also included shorter items on games that preceded the final. Gaelic games were not featured in the monthly series but did appear with the arrival of the weekly series in 1959 and would remain there until the hurling final in September 1963, the final Gaelic-games newsreel produced by Gael Linn.[6]

The NFI had been filming All-Ireland finals since 1948, and with longer segments than Gael Linn provided in *Amharc Éireann*. Nonetheless, Gael Linn's newsreel provides a much wider focus on Gaelic games in the 1950s and 1960s, by including games played in the National League, the Railway Cup, and at provincial and semi-final stages of the GAA championships in both hurling and football. This means that teams such as Offaly, Roscommon and Derry, for example, that rarely reached the latter stages of the All-Ireland series in this era, were featured in the *Amharc Éireann* items. Furthermore, while previous films of Gaelic games focused almost exclusively – with rare exceptions – on matches held in Dublin, the *Amharc Éireann* series featured games held in other parts of the country rarely captured on film in this period, including Thurles, Navan, Tullamore, Drogheda, Kilkenny and Cork. Similarly, the Railway Cup inter-provincial tournament – very popular in these years though not held since 2016 – also featured players from counties that rarely enjoyed All-Ireland or provincial glory and therefore are an important record from this time.

The surviving newsreels undoubtedly provide an important (if brief) record of Gaelic games in the period concerned, but they also constitute fascinating depictions of Irishness at a challenging time in Irish society.

Indeed, one could argue that the utopian configuration of the Irish nation is a recurring theme of the Gaelic-games coverage in the series. The choice of Gaelic games, and the exclusion of so-called English games such as soccer, cricket and rugby, in the *Amharc Éireann* series is significant in this respect, as is the decision to provide a commentary only in the Irish language. Opening titles are provided in English to give a time and place for the events to an audience that was primarily English-speaking (and with little Irish); however, no allowance is given for this in the commentary. Subtitles were not included on the initial release of the series and were only added when the Gaelic-games footage was rereleased by Gael Linn on DVD in 2008.

Furthermore, the focus in many of the films on the attendance of major political figures (almost always accompanied by senior Catholic clerics) is significant. As already noted with regard to earlier newsreel and NFI depictions of Gaelic games, the *Amharc Éireann* items would also appear to support the status quo in Irish politics and society in this period.[7]

While the series featured much less of the prematch ceremony than the NFI footage did (presumably because of the much shorter duration of *Amharc Éireann* episodes), it was by no means absent. This is particularly evident in footage of All-Ireland finals, where prominent figures in attendance are often shown, as per Figure 6.1, a still from the opening of the *Amharc Éireann* footage of the 1959 All-Ireland football final between Galway and Kerry in which President Éamon de Valera, Taoiseach Seán Lemass and a senior Catholic cleric appear.

Figure 6.1. Still from *Amharc Éireann* footage of the 1959 All-Ireland Gaelic-football final between Galway and Kerry © Gael Linn

Figure 6.2. '1962 Hurling Final: close win for Tipp', *Amharc Éireann* (eagrán 170), © Gael Linn

Figure 6.3. 1962 'Football – National League Final: Down are champions', *Amharc Éireann* (eagrán 154), © Gael Linn

As seen with regard to the NFI footage, the prominent involvement of Catholic hierarchy at games is also captured in the *Amharc Éireann* series, including the 1962 hurling final where we see a religious figure – probably the then patron of the GAA archbishop of Cashel and Emly Dr Thomas Morris – throw in the *sliotar* to start the match (Fig. 6.2).

We also saw in Chapter Five how the NFI films of Gaelic games focused in on such dignitaries as well as the prematch ceremony, including the playing of the national anthem and the flying of the Irish tricolour. These latter two are less apparent in the *Amharc Éireann* films, again presumably because of the much shorter length (on average around two minutes, compared to ten minutes for the NFI films). Significantly, however, the only time we do get shots of the Irish flag (Fig. 6.3) is when Down (or

Ulster in the Railway Cup) feature, a county then, as now, within the contested jurisdiction of the United Kingdom. So it could be argued that this was not just the recording of the prematch ceremony, but rather a larger political statement on the Irish nation – a feature also evident in the longer Gaelic-games coaching films Gael Linn made in the 1960s.

This focus on the united nation is evident in the first Gaelic-games footage in the *Amharc Éireann* series from St Patrick's Day 1959. The footage features the opening of the Hogan Stand in Croke Park – including a religious ceremony, blessing of the stand, and extracts from speeches – and the subsequent Railway Cup provincial hurling final between Munster (featuring the legendary Christy Ring) and Connacht. The episode is particularly interesting for the manner in which it combines issues of Church and state, and it appears to affirm a conservative nationalist interpretation of Irishness while simultaneously celebrating the increasing modernity of Irish society. This is evident in the opening of what is described in commentary as 'the best stand in Europe'; yet there is a curious emphasis on one aspect of the speech by the GAA's then president Dr Joseph Stuart. The commentator highlights in particular Stuart's remark that the GAA 'always stood for a united Ireland', an emphasis also evident elsewhere in the series.

The series' concern to promote a largely positive and uncontested rendering of Irishness in sport did not prevent, nonetheless, occasional signs of protest being apparent, though they are never directly referred to by the commentator. A curious sight during the prematch parade at the 1963 All-Ireland football final between Dublin and Galway is what appears to be a woman marching behind the teams holding a banner over her head (Fig. 6.4).

Figure 6.4. 1963, 'Football: Dublin are champions', *Amharc Éireann* (eagrán 225), © Gael Linn

While it is not possible to identify exactly what is written on the banner, 1963 saw the introduction of what was known as the 'turnover tax', a controversial piece of legislation (and a precursor to what would eventually become VAT in Ireland) that led to protests throughout the year, many of which featured women prominently.[8] As the still indicates, the plan to depict a utopian configuration of Irishness is of course never wholly achieved, something that is again evident in the longer Gaelic-games coaching films produced by Gael Linn in the 1960s, to which we now turn.

PEIL (1962) AND CHRISTY RING (1964)[9]

The sports-coaching film has a long history, dating from at least 1932 with the production of Paulette McDonagh's *How I Play Cricket*, which featured the legendary Don Bradman. However, coaching films dedicated to Gaelic games took longer to emerge, not doing so until the late 1950s. As Hills and Kennedy have noted, representations of coaching in film do more than provide us with an opportunity to examine the various masculinities (the predominant focus) constructed in particular sporting contexts; they also offer a means 'to understand the ways that, as an audience, we are being asked to make sense of the relationships between them'.[10] The remainder of this chapter will consider the manner through which both *Peil* and *Christy Ring* configure Irishness and the role they play not only in coaching young people in how to play Gaelic games but also 'coaching' viewers – and particularly impressionable children and young adults who would have been a principal target audience for these films – on the nature of Irishness itself as an identity construct, including in terms of language, geography, politics and religion. In line with Hills and Kennedy, we similarly wish to 'understand the ways that, as an audience, we are being asked to make sense of' Irish identity as constructed in these films. Such representations, of course, cannot be separated from larger social processes and, indeed, are part of a process which (in Susan Hayward's term) 'textualises the nation'.[11] Film has a crucial role here in how cultural identity is framed and depicted for popular consumption. Coaching films in particular provide fascinating texts, as much for the manner in which they locate and contextualise a particular sport within a given society as for the instructions they provide for the sport itself. With respect to *Peil* and *Christy Ring*, this is particularly evident in the way they reflect the position of the Catholic Church as the moral authority (with considerable political influence) in Irish society in the mid-twentieth century.

Peil and *Christy Ring* can be viewed in common with the NFI films as part of what has been described as a second cultural revival that began in the immediate post-war era.[12] This revival was evident in the increased engagement by the Irish public with indigenous aspects of Irish culture, including sport. As discussed earlier, Gaelic games experienced record attendances in this period, increasing dramatically to over 85,000 for the All-Ireland hurling final in the mid-1950s and over 90,000 for the football final by 1961.[13] This engagement with indigenous culture happened at a time of serious challenges and ultimately great change in Irish society, change that prompted considerable debate about Irish identity, explored in more detail in the next chapter. However, simultaneously a growing engagement with traditional culture, including sport, was evident in the 1960s. 'Tradition', as Simon J. Bronner has noted, 'guides and safeguards continuity in a world of change'.[14] Gael Linn's coaching films were produced and distributed, therefore, at a time when Irish identity was a recurring concern. This ensured that the films would ultimately constitute much more than just coaching guides for Gaelic-games enthusiasts – they were also important affirmations of Irish identity.

COACHING GAELIC GAMES

The importance of films such as *Peil* and *Christy Ring* was underscored by the scarcity of coaching material for Gaelic games in the early twentieth century. With the exception of former Kerry captain Dick Fitzgerald's *How to Play Gaelic Football* (1914) and an instructional manual by former Kildare footballer Larry Stanley (circulated only among fellow Garda Síochána members in the 1940s), limited instructional material existed prior to the 1960s.[15] In 1958, the legendary Kerry coach Dr Éamonn O'Sullivan authored the influential work *The Art and Science of Gaelic*

Football and the following year the first film work dedicated to coaching Gaelic games, Father Moran's *Skills of Gaelic Football* (1959), was produced. *Peil* and *Christy Ring*, therefore, came at a time of increased focus on the importance of instructional material for Gaelic games.

The films were produced by Gael Linn in 1962 and 1964 respectively and each was directed by Louis Marcus. Initially Gael Linn planned to produce two coaching films each on Gaelic football and hurling on 16mm that could be used in schools, but eventually it was decided to produce the two works on 35mm and in colour for cinema distribution, due to the interest in Gaelic games across Ireland;[16] 16mm copies were also produced for circulation to schools and colleges across the country.[17] The premieres of both films were major national events attended by political leaders and given wide coverage in the national media. President Éamon de Valera attended the premiere of *Peil* on 24 November 1962 at the Metropole Cinema on O'Connell Street, Dublin.[18] Also present were the minister for social welfare, Kevin Boland TD, the leader of the Irish Senate, Thomas Ó Maoláin, and the chief of staff of the Irish army, Lieutenant General John McKeown.[19] *Christy Ring* had its premiere at the Savoy Cinema in Cork city on 16 October 1964 and in attendance was the minister for industry and commerce (and future Taoiseach), Jack Lynch TD, who was a former teammate of Ring's on the Cork hurling team.[20] Also present were the lord mayor of Cork, A.A. Healy, as well as members of the Dáil (Irish parliament, lower house) and Seanad (upper house), including Senators T.T. O'Sullivan and S. Dooge, Fine Gael TD Seán Collins, and leading members of the Cork business community.[21] These premieres were also described in the media as more than just the launch of coaching films; they were events of national importance in the promotion of Irish culture. D.R. Mott (general manager of the films' sponsor, tobacco company W.D. and H.O. Wills) congratulated Gael Linn at the premiere of *Christy Ring*, not just for producing the films but also for 'the progress they are making in supporting all things Irish'.[22] In Christy Ring, around whom the hurling film is based, commentators saw a figure not just exemplary as a sportsman ('the very personification of hurling'[23]) but as an Irishman. The remarks of Pádraig Puirséal in the *Irish Press* following *Christy Ring*'s premiere are indicative of the response in the Irish media generally to both Ring and the film:

To those of us who remember the decades when 'Ringey' bestrode the whole hurling world a Colossus poised on a flashing ashen blade it is truly amazing how, through brief flashbacks to matches, to newspaper headlines, to 'still' pictures, Louis Marcus recaptures the aura not along [sic] of greatness but almost of invincibility that the Maestro from Cloyne carried with him onto so many fields through so many years … To me, as to most of those present in the Cork Savoy last Friday and who had, like myself, been reared on the hurling fields, those instructional sequences were nothing short of sensational for, in them, Christy Ring goes far beyond the basic skills of hurling. Here the sorcerer goes near to revealing the very sources of his own magic, the Maestro lays bare, to a remarkable extent, the secrets of his own success.[24]

FOREGROUNDING THE IRISH PUBLIC

A significant feature of both *Peil* and *Christy Ring* is the focus on the crowds attending matches. Following the opening credits, *Peil* begins not with a shot of a game, players or even a playing pitch, but of the crowd attending a Gaelic-football match. Indeed, the majority of the opening scenes consist of crowd shots rather than play. While foregrounding the popularity of the sport featured, these images also indicate that what is depicted in this film has resonance beyond the game itself; resonance for an entire culture and society. As the commentator remarks in Irish, 'The crowd is gathered, the stands are full, every eye directed on the playing field.' *Peil* and *Christy Ring* each foreground repeatedly the social and cultural life around Gaelic games as much as the games themselves. In *Peil* we are brought into the bars and the conversations of men (and only men are depicted here): we are told that the games live on in argument, memory and folklore. This is the field of memories and opinions; here the players of old take on the men of today. This contention is made in an expository style as the narrator's words are confirmed in footage of players from previous decades superimposed over middle-aged suit-wearing men talking in a bar. The footage includes All-Ireland-winning teams from the past parading and playing in Croke Park, taken from highlights produced by the NFI. Here the film places considerable stress on the reception of Gaelic games, on memory and, indeed, on the role that film can play in this regard, in recalling and preserving.

Christy Ring also focuses on the social context of hurling, moving from a survey of Irish legend and history (and hurling's role in it) to its contemporary importance. The film begins with an introduction to hurling, as the narrator (over shots of inter-county encounters) highlights the game's distinctiveness, reputed antiquity and its centrality to Irish history and identity. It is, we are told through Irish, 'the fastest field sport in the world, a game played on the fields of Tara and in Eamhain Mhacha … the games of the Fianna and Cúchulainn', referring to the seats of kings of Ireland and Ulster in medieval times, as well as legendary figures in Irish mythology. The narrator also draws parallels between the history of hurling and that of the Irish people themselves under colonialism, underlining hurling's political significance as a sport banned by the Normans (who invaded Ireland in the twelfth century, conquering large parts of the country) but reflecting 'the resilience of the people that almost perished before the spirit of the country revived'. Hurling is therefore presented as much more than a popular Irish pastime; it is a sport that represents the Irish people, their turbulent past and challenging present.

Christy Ring then moves on to the build-up to a hurling match featuring Ring, at the Athletic Grounds in Cork between Cork and Tipperary – two counties, as the legendary broadcaster and commentator Michael O'Hehir remarks on the soundtrack, 'famed in history, famed in song and famed in story as the greats of hurling'. A strong emphasis is placed on Irish people's engagement with hurling as an important part of their life. As with *Peil*, considerable time is given to the build-up to the game featured, including the arrival of crowds, foregrounded repeatedly as the credit sequence rolls, and the prematch ceremony. We watch supporters making their way to the match, stopping occasionally for cups of tea as they travel by car, van, bus, on foot and by boat (crossing the River Lee to the stadium).

As an important point of identification, these crowd scenes engage viewers still further with sports they are already familiar with and enthusiastic about. However, this focusing on the crowd ultimately involves more than just identification with the sport itself, as very quickly becomes clear in *Peil*. Within the first minute of the film we are presented not just with footage of the crowd but with a prominent shot of their moral and political leaders. While the commentary (in Irish) reminds us that every age and class is present, 'clergy, politicians, teenagers, farmers, housewives', we are presented with a shot of the president, Taoiseach and a senior Catholic cleric in the VIP section of the Hogan Stand at Croke Park (see Fig. 6.1), taken from an *Amharc Éireann* episode. In one image, the film renders the political and moral establishment of the country and affirms the significance of what we are to encounter beyond the field of sport.

DEMONSTRATING THE SKILLS

Once the context and social importance of both Gaelic football and hurling are established in both films, the focus moves to the distinctive skills of each sport. In *Peil*, these are presented by leading players from counties across Ireland, and significantly for a Gael Linn film, this section was available with both English and Irish narration (as well as subtitles in both languages), indicating that the Irish-language organisation was cognisant of the need to have English available to ensure people could understand the coaching. Each individual skill is demonstrated in an empty Croke Park but accompanied by footage from matches to show the skill in action.

While *Peil* features footballers from across the island (including several from County Down, the All-Ireland champions at the time of production) demonstrating the skills of the game, *Christy Ring* focuses primarily on the life and skills of the eponymous hurler. It is Ring who demonstrates the skills of the game (each skill being introduced with wide shots of its occurrence during hurling games in Croke Park), and the film is an important record in this respect of one of the finest exponents of hurling. As the narration continues in Irish, Ring's own introduction and comments on each skill are delivered in English, while the titles are also provided in both English and Irish. In common with the introduction to the film, this skills demonstration is not without political resonance; it is accompanied by a marching instrumental version of the popular nationalist song 'Clare's Dragoons', also featured in the opening credit sequence of *Peil*. 'Clare's Dragoons' was composed by Thomas Osborne Davis (1814–45), a poet and the principal organiser of the nationalist Young Ireland movement in the mid-nineteenth century. The song itself is an ode to a battalion that fought during the Williamite War in Ireland (1688–91) with the Catholic forces under King James II against the army of William III of England.

In addition, the films adopt an instructional approach throughout, even where skills may not be presented. Admonitions such as 'if done correctly', 'should be made only', 'it is vital', 'should be reserved', 'should be kept', 'never think in terms' and 'should be practised' continue to inform viewers even when the focus is on other aspects of Irish society and culture, including the respect and status accorded to markers of Irishness depicted in the films, as well as social and religious leaders in Irish society. All the more so given the impressionable young audience that was the principal target of these films, and the legendary status of the players (including Christy Ring) featured.

UNITING THE NATION

Following the demonstration of skills, both films return to match action. *Peil* features the 1960 All-Ireland football final between Kerry and Down, and once again the focus is as much on the social occasion and the supporters as on the game itself. This includes several minutes of build-up outside the stadium, including supporters arriving by foot, car and match-day buses, with the narrator informing us (in Irish) that 'today more than ever this is the centre of Ireland, they are here from every place, from north and south, crowds from the west and the midlands'.

When we finally enter Croke Park the commentary changes to a combination of Irish and English by Michael O'Hehir. Again, the attention is on the 'huge crowd' (as O'Hehir describes it) and its responses to the events unfolding. The attendance at this All-Ireland was indeed 'huge', exceeding all previous finals with almost 90,000 people present.

Considerable attention is given in both films to the prematch ceremony, including the arrival of the players onto the pitch, the photographing of

Figure 6.5. *Peil* (1962). Black and white reproduction (from original colour still) of VIP section at 1960 All-Ireland football final with President Éamon de Valera to the foreground surrounded by senior religious figures including the then patron of the GAA, archbishop of Cashel and Emly, Dr Thomas Morris (to de Valera's right). Dir. Louis Marcus © Gael Linn

the teams, and the attendance of senior figures in Irish society. In *Peil*, this sequence features a further shot of the VIP section, which includes President Éamon de Valera and then patron of the GAA, archbishop of Cashel and Emly, Dr Thomas Morris. A striking feature of this extra-ordinary shot is not just the prominence of red velvet furnishings (red also being the colour of non-liturgical dress of cardinals in the Catholic Church) but the large number of religious present in the VIP area (evident by their white collars) (Fig. 6.5). In microcosm, this captures a crucial aspect of Irish society in a powerfully suggestive manner: such was the authority and influence of the Catholic Church in early 1960s Ireland that few questions would have been asked of the position accorded them at such games.

The moral authority of the Church is also foregrounded in *Christy Ring*. In addition to the commentary (in Irish), the review of Ring's career in the early part of the film is relayed via photographs, newspaper cuttings, and short extracts from films produced by the NFI. Included is a photo of the hurler kissing the ring of a Catholic bishop prior to a game (Fig. 6.6),

Figure 6.6. *Christy Ring* (1964). Still of Christy Ring kissing the ring of a Catholic bishop prior to the start of a game. Dir. Louis Marcus © Gael Linn

135

a practice that continued before major Gaelic games in Croke Park until the end of the 1960s.

Peil's depiction of the prematch ceremony includes the parade of the teams behind the Artane Boys Band (a regular feature of All-Ireland-final days) and the singing of the national anthem, with all players standing to attention and facing the Irish tricolour, captured flying over the Hogan Stand. This foregrounding of the anthem (a particularly nationalistic and militaristic piece) and the flag also has important political connotations. This final in 1960 was only the second in which a county from 'across the border' in the disputed North participated, then as now a part of the United Kingdom and subject to a different flag and anthem. Whether intentional or not, this depiction affirms a nationalist reading of the Irish nation (contributed to by O'Hehir's earlier commentary regarding the nation encompassing people from north, south, etc.), ignoring the political realities on the ground while promoting a utopian vision of a thirty-two-county Ireland. While foregrounding this utopian political narrative, the depiction simultaneously reaffirms the place of the Catholic Church as the moral arbiter of Irish society, as it is the patron of the GAA 'the most reverend Dr Morris' (O'Hehir's commentary) who gets proceedings under way by throwing in the ball, the customary beginning to All-Irelands until the late 1960s.

The footage of the game is also notable for its focus on the crowd and, frequently, members of the clergy in attendance. Many of the crowd shots at half-time also feature children. Their inclusion no doubt again reflects the intended audience – children learning the skills of Gaelic football – and the hope that such footage might provide a point of further identification. Most of those featured in crowd shots are men and boys. And while women do appear, girls are noticeably absent. For a contemporary audience, the inclusion of children and adults, and the focus on clergy, affirms the centrality and (given the elevated authority of the Catholic Church in Ireland in this period) the status of the sport, as well as the hierarchical structure of Irish society in the period. Here again the audience is being coached not just in the skills of the game but in the structures and functioning of authority within their society.

Similarly in *Christy Ring*, the demonstration of skills is followed by more footage of the featured hurling match between Cork and Tipperary.

Figure 6.7. Closing still from *Peil* (1962) featuring the presentation of the All-Ireland trophy to the Down captain by President Éamon de Valera. In the centre of the still is the then patron of the GAA, archbishop of Cashel and Emly, Dr Thomas Morris. Dir. Louis Marcus

Again, considerable attention is given to the prematch events and the crowd. As commentator Michael O'Hehir remarks, 'Whoever wins, whoever loses, thousands have come to see Christy Ring.' And as with *Peil*, the playing of the national anthem also features prominently, with players and supporters standing to respect both it and the flag.

Peil ends with the presentation of the trophy, the Sam Maguire Cup, to the captain of the winning team, Down. In this ceremony, Church and state come together (in the form of Archbishop Morris and President de Valera) to affirm the role of Gaelic games in Irish life while simultaneously confirming the political and moral order in Irish society, as evident in Figure 6.7.

Gael Linn played a key role in Irish society in the 1950s, promoting and preserving distinctive aspects of Irish culture, including Gaelic games. As part of this project, the organisation employed film effectively, first via its regular newsreel *Amharc Éireann* and subsequently through longer coaching films. Though much shorter than the contemporaneous Gaelic-games films of the NFI, the *Amharc Éireann* items nonetheless give a broader perspective on these sports in the period concerned. By focusing on other competitions and earlier rounds of the championship and not just the All-Ireland final (the almost exclusive focus of the NFI films), *Amharc Éireann* includes teams, players and places rarely captured on film in the 1950s and 1960s. Gael Linn's longer coaching films, *Peil* and *Christy Ring*, offer an important record of the skills of Gaelic football and hurling respectively, as demonstrated by leading exponents of both sports in the mid-twentieth century. However, these films function as much more than football and hurling coaching guides for the country's youth; they are crucial tools for teaching these same children about Irishness itself, and about Ireland's political and moral leaders – all of which were also evident in the *Amharc Éireann* items on Gaelic games. *Peil* and *Christy Ring* present uplifting visions of Irish culture and society, foregrounding repeatedly the nation, its language and culture, and social, political and religious hierarchies within a utopian configuration of a thirty-two-county Ireland. The role assigned to the Catholic Church within such a configuration is substantial and unquestioned. These films were arguably all the more effective due to the fact that they are not didactic (with the exception of those passages instructing viewers in the skills of each sport) but instead present these features as natural, established and unquestionable aspects of Irish identity and society, thereby providing crucial affirmations at a time of considerable change and transition.

The changing nature of Irish society would eventually lead to more critical analysis of Gaelic games and the Church, and their role in Irish society. The next chapter will consider a number of productions that reflected this development.

7

The Critical Turn: Gaelic games in film between the 1960s and 1980s[1]

U p to this point in our examination of filmic depictions of Gaelic games, these sports have provided either a shorthand – in foreign productions – for prevailing stereotypes regarding the Irish or an important cultural resource in affirming Irish identity and established conceptions of the Irish nation. However, Ireland was rapidly modernising in the 1960s and commentators took an increasingly critical view of the Irish state and traditional constructions of Irish identity. The role played by Gaelic games, and the GAA, in these processes would be part of this critical re-examination, including in film. This chapter will chart the movement towards what might be called, following from Richard Kearney's 1995 study, a postnationalist approach to representing Gaelic games, which became evident from the 1960s onwards. However much Gaelic games were part of the construction of Irish identity before and immediately after independence, the depiction of these games in films such as *Rocky Road to Dublin* (1968) and *Clash of the Ash* (1987) – films which reflected the emergence of a critically engaged indigenous cinema in Ireland – would also be part of the deconstruction of such an identity and a critique of the failures of the state. Significantly, each of these films employs Gaelic games to interrogate and critically engage with certain mythologised and narrow-minded understandings of Irishness, including those associated with Irish nationalism and masculinity.

CRITICAL REGIONALISM IN A CHANGING IRELAND

The appointment of Seán Lemass as Taoiseach in 1959 heralded a new era of economic expansion and cultural change in Ireland, inspired by the fiscal plans of the secretary of the Department of Finance T.K. Whitaker. This change of focus, moving away from the economic nationalism associated with Éamon de Valera, would also accelerate the transformation of Ireland from a primarily rural society to an increasingly urban one while opening the country to new economic, political and cultural influences. Telefís Éireann, Ireland's first indigenous television channel, began broadcasting on 31 December 1961 and, as noted earlier, television would soon become the main medium for moving images of Gaelic games. In 1965 Ireland applied for membership of the European Economic Community and would finally be admitted in 1973. In 1967 the minister for education, Donogh O'Malley, introduced free secondary education for all. In the same year, Ireland's strict Censorship of Publications Act was amended significantly so that books which had been banned as 'indecent or obscene' could now be resubmitted for reconsideration after twelve years. A similar amendment was made to the Censorship of Films Act in 1970, permitting the resubmission of films which had been banned over seven years previously.

While Lemass' policies brought some economic success in the 1960s, Terence Brown has documented the 'much concerned, even heated, discussion' which the rapid changes in Irish society prompted. Central to this debate was the issue of national identity, 'in circumstances', as Brown observes, 'where many of the traditional essentialist definitions – language, tradition, culture and distinctive ideology – were widely felt to fly in the face of social reality'.[2] To some degree, these questions anticipated concerns that have increasingly marked contemporary Ireland over the past thirty years, leading Richard Kearney to call for a postnationalist approach to the country that would reassess nationalism in light of postmodernity. In *Postnationalist Ireland* Kearney examines the development of the 'postmodern critique of the centre, established power, whether totalitarianism, colonialism or nationalism'.[3] Drawing from Derrida, Foucault and Lyotard, he argues that:

The postmodern turn seeks to deconstruct the Official story (which presents itself as Official History) into the open plurality of stories that make it up. Modern imperialism and modern nationalism are two sides of the Official Story. Genuine internationalism (working at a global level) and critical regionalism (working at a local level) represent the two sides of a postmodern alternative.[4]

Kearney takes this concept of 'critical regionalism' from the work of Kenneth Frampton, who argues for it, Kearney surmises, as 'the most appropriate response to our contemporary predicament'.[5] While for Frampton critical regionalism is 'an attempt to mediate the impact of universalised civilisation with elements derived from the peculiarities of a particular place',[6] it can also provide a bulwark against the more universalising tendencies of nationalism within the national context itself, offering a critique and commentary on the excesses to which a narrow and insular nationalism, and notion of communal identity, may lead. As Kearney continues, quoting from Frampton:

> Whereas modernism, in architecture at least, tended to represent the 'victory of universal culture over locally inflected culture', the post-modern paradigm of critical regionalism opposes 'the cultural domination of hegemonic power' – a domination which seeks to sacrifice local concerns to abstract ones.[7]

In one of the most important studies of contemporary Irish cinema, Martin McLoone also borrowed from Frampton this notion of critical regionalism to describe the films of Irish directors who emerged in the 1970s, 1980s and 1990s, including Bob Quinn, Joe Comerford, Kieran Hickey and Pat Murphy.[8] A further relevant example considered in this chapter is Fergus Tighe's 1987 drama *Clash of the Ash*. For McLoone these directors, for the first time in indigenous cinema, drew on the established forms of narrative film to cast a critical eye on Irish society. However, the work of these directors was anticipated in the late 1960s by a documentary that has in more recent years been rereleased to wide acclaim. Peter Lennon's *Rocky Road to Dublin*, in its highly critical approach to the Irish state on the cusp of huge change in the late 1960s, anticipated the work of the fiction film-makers McLoone identifies. Indeed, Lennon's decision to make the film was partly inspired, he has acknowledged, by a concern with the lack of a film culture in Ireland. He has referred to his 'wild idea as an Irishman that although we were great film fans we had no film culture'[9] – the importance of which is also emphasised by the seminal Irish-American director John Huston in *Rocky Road to Dublin* itself when he asserts on the Ardmore Studios set of his 1969 film *Sinful Davey*, that

> … a film made by Ireland and Irishmen would be of infinitely greater importance to the country than this foreign film that we are making … it's true that it's ploughing some million dollars into the economy of the country but in the long run that wouldn't mean half as much as a native film made by Irishmen.[10]

ROCKY ROAD TO DUBLIN AND POSTNATIONALISM

Rocky Road to Dublin may seem to precede the postnationalist moment in Irish culture; however, such a moment did not just develop in recent times but rather was anticipated much earlier. In his 1998 essay 'Postmodernism and Consumer Society', Fredric Jameson observed that rather than postmodernism being a movement or an impulse emerging in the recent past and characteristic of contemporary society, aspects of what might today be described as the postmodern were manifest at a much earlier period and apparent within modernism itself. For Jameson:

> … radical breaks between periods do not generally involve complete changes of content but rather the restructuring of a certain number of elements already given: features that in an earlier period or system were subordinate now become dominant, and features that had been dominant again become secondary … My point is that until the present day those things have been secondary or minor features of modernist art, marginal rather than central, and that we have something new when they become the central features of cultural production.[11]

As evident in *Rocky Road to Dublin*, the postnationalist impulse similarly, while more characteristic of Irish society in the contemporary era, has existed as a 'secondary element' in periods in which nationalism continued as a dominant force in Irish life. Indeed, within *Rocky Road to Dublin* both impulses are apparent. Lennon's film from the beginning, when he reflects on the noble ideals of the 1916 revolutionaries and the failure of the state to live up to them, would seem, as Luke Gibbons has contended, to be 'a requiem for a revolution … it is not the hopes and energies of the revolutionaries that are mocked, but the traducing of these ideals through the alliance of church and state in the new independent Ireland'.[12] Yet Lennon's critique of this new state seeks an alternative arrangement, never clearly articulated, but one that may lie in a postnationalist Ireland, in which the complexities of identity are no longer predetermined or delimited according to strict parameters but open to all the possibilities of cultural creativity and encounter.

Given the extent of its criticism of Irish society, Lennon insisted on sitting in with the then deputy censor, Gabriel Fallon, when the film was being censored as he was concerned the documentary might be banned before any Irish people could see it. In the end, Fallon allowed the film without cuts, making the memorable remark that 'Since there is no sex in the film, Peter, there is nothing I can do against you.'[13]

Despite getting the clearance of the censor, Lennon still faced considerable obstacles in trying to get the film screened in Ireland. Even the leading indigenous film festival at the time, the Cork Film Festival, refused to show it in competition, allegedly because it had already been screened to eighteen people in Dublin, mostly journalists, prior to the festival.[14] However, the film was accepted at the Cannes Film Festival in 1968, and featured in the prestigious Critics' Week. Indeed, the film was the last screened at Cannes that year before the festival was cancelled in solidarity with the protesting students on the streets of Paris. *Rocky Road to Dublin*'s central question 'What do you do with your revolution once you've got it?' struck a chord with the protesting groups and was screened many times over the summer of 1968, while receiving rave reviews in the international press, including the seminal French film journal *Cahiers du Cinéma*, which described it as 'One of the most beautiful documentaries the cinema has given us'.[15] Cork eventually relented but screened the film at lunchtime on the same day as the media were invited out of town to a free oyster-and-Guinness reception.[16] Lennon also had great difficulty getting what he has described as 'priest-fearing' cinema managers[17] in Ireland to accept the film, and it was eventually only screened by one cinema, the International Film Theatre, at Earlsfort Terrace in Dublin, where it ran for seven weeks to strong audiences.[18]

The criticisms of the film included the suggestion on the popular RTÉ chat show *The Late Late Show* that it was made with communist money.[19] *Rocky Road to Dublin* was actually funded by an American millionaire friend of Lennon in Paris, Victor Herbert, who agreed to finance the film when Lennon promised he could get the legendary *nouvelle vague* cameraman Raoul Coutard – whose work with Jean-Luc Godard and François Truffaut had established him as one of the pre-eminent cameramen in the world – to shoot it.

The reactions to Lennon's film are to some degree understandable given the prevailing depiction of Irish nationalism, and the GAA, in Irish film prior to *Rocky Road to Dublin*. Indeed, unlike in Lennon's film, the position of nationalism in Irish life had been reaffirmed just two years previously in several works commemorating the fiftieth anniversary of the 1916 Rising. Unsurprisingly, given the centrality of the GAA to the nationalist movement that culminated in this Rising, Gaelic games featured prominently. Louis Marcus' 1916 commemorative documentary *An Tine Beo* (The Living Flame), for example, includes a central piece on the GAA in which emphasis is placed, in a non-questioning manner, on the GAA's role in providing volunteers for the Rising.

However, within two years Lennon would provide the first critical engagement with the association. His film reveals the influence of the counter-establishment and almost voyeuristic new wave aesthetic to which Lennon was exposed while living in Paris as a reporter for the *Guardian* newspaper. However, he received little support in his enterprise from fellow Irish people, with even his friend in Paris, Samuel Beckett, 'declaring, somewhat grandly, that it would never work because the Irish "were not a serious people"'.[20] The film was completed in 1968, and features, as Lennon has said, 'Irish society condemn[ing] itself out of its own mouth'.[21] Though shot in colour, the film was printed in black and white, which contributes further to the bleak tone of the work. As Carol

Figure 7.1. GAA executive officer Brendan Mac Lua in *Rocky Road to Dublin* (Peter Lennon, 1968) © Thunderbird Releasing

Murphy has observed, the film raises 'a collection of questions about the state of a repressed and religiously indoctrinated Ireland in the late sixties'.[22]

Structurally, *Rocky Road to Dublin* is built around interviews with well-known figures in Irish life including Seán Ó Faoláin, Conor Cruise O'Brien, John Huston, theatre director Jim Fitzgerald and Professor Liam Ó Briain, a member of the Censorship of Publications Appeal Board. Lennon also followed the trendy young priest Michael Cleary around for a day in one of the film's most revelatory sequences.

The film chose as the main target in its critical engagement the central institutions in Irish life, primarily the Church, but the GAA is also featured. Its spokesman, Brendan Mac Lua[23] (Fig. 7.1), then executive officer of the association, provides a stout defence of the GAA's continuing ban on members attending or participating in so-called English games, such as soccer, rugby, cricket or hockey. The previous year Mac Lua had developed these ideas when his history of the ban, *The Steadfast Rule*, was published: in it he asserted that 'it is almost entirely to the Ban that the GAA owes what is truly significant in its past'. Furthermore, Mac Lua made a clear link between the ban, nationalism and masculinity, remarking:

The Ban, nationalism and G.A.A. prosperity have … gone hand in hand, constantly complementing each other. The Ban has been the

Figure 7.2. *Rocky Road to Dublin* (Peter Lennon, 1968) © Thunderbird Releasing

symbol of nationalism – the ensign aloft which declared aloud that the Association was still committed to the objective of a decisive victory over all that was alien. It was an open declaration of patriotism which attracted into its ranks young men who sought in it a means of national service and it has been these same young men of nationalistic motivation who have led and developed the G.A.A. down the years. Without them and their sense of commitment to a cause, the G.A.A. could not have reached its present proportions.[24]

Indeed, when Mac Lua asserts that the ban had 'attracted the best of Irish manhood',[25] he was but reiterating long-held beliefs within the association. In *Rocky Road to Dublin*, Mac Lua restates these beliefs, describing the GAA as central to the rise of Irish nationalism and the 'reservoir of Irish manhood', remarks complemented, if in an ironic manner, by Lennon's intercutting of these comments with images of a hurling game in Croke Park. His choice of moments from the game, including tussles between a number of players (Fig. 7.2) and the ominously shot walled and barbed-wire surroundings, offers a bleak depiction and little of the excitement one associates with major games in Croke Park today. Indeed, Lennon's emphasis in this sequence is almost as much on the small attendance, including the foreboding presence of the clergy, as the game itself, a relatively unimportant encounter between two unidentified teams. One could justifiably criticise Lennon for failing to acknowledge in this section the sophistication of hurling, or the important role the GAA played then, as now, in Irish life, particularly at the local level. However, the director was seeking a metaphor for a larger critique, throughout the film as a whole, of Irish society and its continuing oppression by the Church and a narrow-minded conformist nationalist thought that had seen the work of most major writers banned (many listed elsewhere in the documentary) and opportunities for free debate and critical engagement – as was apparent in the response to Lennon's film by the media – limited. Though Lennon's own narration is minimal in this largely observational section, it is clear that the director's critical engagement with the ideas expressed, and his representation of them, marked a ground breaking moment in the re-evaluation of the GAA and what it represented.

THE CHALLENGING 1980s

While the 1960s represented a tumultuous period for Irish society, the 1980s were no less so, if for different reasons. Ireland in the mid-1980s was experiencing considerable change which resulted in a deeply divided society with contrasting positions on how to move forward. This was reflected in successive referenda on abortion and divorce and the continuing debate surrounding the escalating conflict in Northern Ireland, which had reignited in the late 1960s. Unemployment and emigration also reached levels not seen since the 1950s. 'Ireland was confronting', as Cheryl Herr has noted, 'not only economic turmoil and the onslaught of modernization but also widespread civil rights agitation, paramilitary violence, the oil crisis, increasing unemployment, feminist activism and a growing understanding of postcolonial trauma'.[26]

Much as had occurred in the 1960s, the significant changes and subsequent challenges that Irish society was experiencing prompted considerable cultural debate about Irishness itself in this period, much of which became focused around the journal the *Crane Bag*, edited by Mark Patrick Hederman and Richard Kearney. Indeed, one of the journal's frequent contributors, Desmond Fennell, contended in a 1983 article that Ireland lacked in the 1980s a 'serviceable national image', arguing that

> Our first self-definition as a nation began to crumble in the '50s, was assaulted throughout the '60s, and faded away in the '70s. All that is left in its place, as a public image of Irish identity, is the factual 26-county state, without any cultural or ideological overtones other than 'democratic'. We haven't chosen it as our national image: we would prefer to have no image, to be quite invisible to ourselves and others.[27]

Irish film-makers would bring their own critical perspectives to bear on Irish society in this period, with directors including Joe Comerford, Cathal Black and Pat Murphy examining themes such as nationalism, religion and women's place within established understandings of Irishness. One of the most important directors in this period was Bob Quinn, both a fiction and documentary film-maker. While Quinn's fictional work, including *Caoineadh Airt Uí Laoghaire* (1975) and *Poitín* (1978, but rereleased in 2007), problematised previous constructions and representations of Irishness and Ireland, his seminal three-part documentary series *Atlantean* (1983) would raise questions about the established narrative concerning the history of the Irish people. For Quinn, the received notion that the Irish were of Celtic origin was too simplistic for a people, particularly on the west coast, long dependent on maritime trade and cultural exchange. Within his reappraisal of the development of culture in Ireland, Quinn also raised other possibilities for the origin of what had long been regarded as the most ancient and authentic of Irish sports, hurling. In one sequence, in the second episode of the series, the suggestion is made that there may be a connection between a sport played by Berber tribes of North Africa and hurling through the shared Atlantic heritage of both cultures.

'ONE OF THE BEST IRISH MOVIES IN A LONG TIME' THE SUNDAY TRIBUNE

CIRCUS FILMS presents

CLASH OF THE ASH

William Heffernan
Vincent Murphy
Gina Moxley
Alan Devlin

Figure 7.3. *Clash of the Ash* (1987). Permission to reproduce image granted by director Fergus Tighe

CLASH OF THE ASH (1987)

Gaelic games provide a still more important prism through which Fergus Tighe would explore contemporary Irish society in his drama *Clash of the Ash*. Indeed, if there is one indigenous drama that deserves the title of Gaelic-games 'sports film', it is Tighe's partly autobiographical debut work filmed in his home town of Fermoy, County Cork, in August 1986. The film was over four years in production and shot on a shoestring budget of £112,000 – funded by Bord Scannán na hÉireann/the Irish Film Board, the Arts Council and RTÉ. *Clash of the Ash* was one of the final films to receive funding from the Irish Film Board before it was discontinued in the round of cutbacks that followed the return of Fianna Fáil to government in February 1987. Indeed, the film became the subject of the debate that followed the board's demise in the Seanad, where Senator David Norris called for the government to reverse its decision in the interests of the Irish film industry. Norris picked out *Clash of the Ash* in particular as an example of the finest work funded by the board and drew attention to a letter from Tighe published in the *Irish Press* on 3 July 1987 where the director remarked that the film was only made 'because the crew worked for nothing, the equipment was mostly borrowed and I went into debt of £700'.[28] The demise of the first board was to be catastrophic for Tighe, who would not make another fiction film for over twenty years. By 1991, according to an interview with Gina Moxley (who plays the exotic returned emigrant Mary in the film), he was working in a 'pub in the States'. '[A]t least in New York', she continued 'people are willing to believe you're really a film maker working as a bar man.'[29]

Some commentators have argued that the board was shut down because of the unflattering depictions of 1980s Ireland in the films it funded. While the authors of *Cinema and Ireland* suggest that 'many of the films financially aided by the Board were perceived as undermining the image of contemporary Ireland which the state itself wished to project',[30] *Film West* journal contributor Anthony O'Neil 'became convinced that government antipathy to indigenous films was due to what they saw as the disturbing image of Ireland coming through'.[31] Indeed, when the board was reactivated film-makers from the first incarnation revealed a concern not to produce work that might undermine the board's continuing existence. Director Cathal Black in 1996 noted a sense among board members and film-makers to 'let's try and make something feel-good so that we won't be accused of the kinds of things that caused the shutting down of the first Film Board'.[32]

Clash of the Ash has been described as 'one of the key Irish films of the 1980s'.[33] 'This 50-minute drama', the *Irish Times* reviewer continues, 'offers a portrait of a still largely uncharted part of contemporary Irish society – small town life and the struggle of the young to resist its stifling conformity.'[34] Director Fergus Tighe had initially hoped to make the film feature-length but 'surrendered to the Film Board's demand that it should be reduced to a "television hour"'.[35] This requirement (and RTÉ's involvement in the production as a co-funder) reflects the increasing importance of television to depictions of Gaelic games since the 1960s, an issue explored in our Introduction and revisited in the chapters to come. Nonetheless, the film was well received and won several awards including the Starting Out Award at the Eighth Celtic Film and Television Festival, the fiction prize at the Interceltic Festival in 1987, and the Gus Healy Award for Best Irish Short at the Cork Film Festival in the same year.[36] It was also the first film work of cinematographer Declan Quinn, who subsequently established a reputation as one of the world's leading cameramen, with his credits including Mike Figgis' *Leaving Las Vegas* (1995), Mira Nair's *Monsoon Wedding* (2001), Jim Sheridan's *In America* (2003) and Neil Jordan's *Breakfast on Pluto* (2006). Indeed, as regards Quinn's work on *Clash of the Ash*, as noted by Kevin Rockett

> While the themes of emigration and personal angst are common to generations of young Irish people, it is the visual treatment which these themes receive in *Clash of the Ash* which makes the film distinctive. Using a self-conscious 'art' form and photographic style, the film succeeds in evoking an atmosphere which contrasts sharply with the way in which so much realist writing has traditionally dealt with the Irish Provincial town.[37]

The GAA played an important role, as noted earlier, in the articulation and promotion of a singular nationalist identity in the formative years of the Irish state. However, the locally based nature of the association also meant that there were, and continues to be, what Kearney calls a 'plurality of stories' that make up the association.[38] In Chapter 1, we noted that a key component to the GAA's development and success has been the centrality of the parish-based club to local communities.[39] Tighe's focus on one such club, in Fermoy, County Cork, allowed for the distinctive specificities of region, accent and local culture – features a simplistic nationalist reading of Irish identity may elide – to be brought to the fore.

Described by Eamonn Sweeney as one of the few films with a 'real feel for the GAA',[40] *Clash of the Ash* is greatly informed by Tighe's own background as a hurler, winning an All-Ireland senior colleges hurling medal with St Colman's in Fermoy. Indeed, the violent climax to the film's final hurling game re-enacts an event Tighe has recalled from his own playing days.[41] As Lennon did in *Rocky Road to Dublin*, Tighe used his depiction of Gaelic games to draw attention to his own concerns regarding the state of the nation in the mid-1980s. Phil Kelly (Liam Heffernan) is the star player with the Fermoy hurling team and is tipped to make the county minors, but his application is found wanting, at least in the eyes of the team's foul-mouthed and two-faced trainer, Mick Barry (Alan Devlin). His mother meanwhile is more concerned with Kelly's lack of application to his Leaving Certificate studies, but Kelly's interests lie further afield than the modest plans his parents have for him in the local garage, particularly after he meets the glamorous Mary (Gina Moxley) returned from London. While the GAA had promoted for much of the century an ideal notion of Ireland as Irish (Irish-speaking, if possible) and ancient and celebrated the bravery, masculinity and high ideals of its members, Tighe's film reveals its central protagonist, Phil Kelly, the star player of the local team, to be a poor student, temperamental, violent and prone to binge drinking and drug abuse. This includes a scene of Kelly and Mary smoking a joint brazenly in the local coffee shop, where Kelly boasts of smoking joints 'all the time'.

Indeed, such is its depiction of Ireland in the mid-1980s that the film was lucky to be made at all, once the local bishop got his hands on the script. Tipped off by the president of St Colman's College, where Tighe, as former student, had hoped to make the film, the script was condemned as blasphemous and resulted in a call to the local GAA club in Fermoy by the bishop asking that they would have nothing to do with the production.[42] In a sign of changing times in Ireland, the club declined the bishop's advice and continued to facilitate the production while the local technical school provided teams and permitted Tighe to use its grounds for the film.

St Colman's president and the local bishop may have been partly concerned for the reputation of a school whose first president was

Archbishop Thomas Croke, a cleric with a particular concern for Irish culture and its representation (as indicated earlier in this work).[43] The bishop's ire was no doubt further inflamed by aspects of the script which may have offended religious sensibilities but are absent from the finished film, including a shot early on (shot 17) described as 'THE FACE OF CHRIST, crucified on a hilltop shrine, the RAIN TEEMING down as a DROP OF BIRDSHIT splatters on his forehead',[44] and a scene also left out of the finished film of the young protagonist play-acting outside a church and choosing to head for a pint rather than go to Mass.[45]

Overall, in both script and film, we are presented with a town characterised by unemployment, drug abuse and emigration, where hurling offers one of the few outlets for youths to unleash the frustrations and disappointments of their everyday life. Unsurprisingly, these frustrations spill over into violence on the field of play, in the film's climactic encounter in the county final between Fermoy and Mitchelstown. When Kelly is hit over the head with a hurley by an opposing player he retaliates in a similar fashion while running from the pitch, with his trainer's shouts of 'There'll be no job in the bank for you' ringing in his ears.

The depiction of violence in hurling in *Clash of the Ash* may recall the more stereotypical depictions discussed earlier in this work (in Hollywood productions such as *Hurling* (1936)); critically, however, *Clash of the Ash* provides context for the actions depicted (here the economically and socially challenging circumstances of Ireland in the mid-1980s) rather than employing hurling primarily for its opportunities for violent interactions. This distinction is important and will be revisited in the next chapter, examining hurling in contemporary film.

With the launch of Telefís Éireann in 1961, Gaelic games became less a feature of cinematic productions as television provided the main forum for moving-image depictions of these sports. Nonetheless, they continued to feature in fiction and documentary productions, with a notable critical turn apparent in representations from the 1960s onwards, as part of a larger re-examination of Ireland and constructions of Irish identity. A pioneering text in this respect was Peter Lennon's *Rocky Road to Dublin*, a work that in its interrogation of Irish nationalism anticipated the emergence of a critically engaged Irish cinema in the 1970s. For Lennon, Gaelic games, and particularly their promotion, provided an important metaphor for narrower essentialist notions of Irishness that resisted and feared foreign cultural influence, apparent in the continuing ban in 1967 on members of the GAA attending or participating in 'foreign' games such as soccer, rugby or cricket. In this respect Lennon's film also anticipates a postnationalist approach to Gaelic games and Irish society that would continue to develop in subsequent work such as Bob Quinn's *Atlantean* and Fergus Tighe's *Clash of the Ash*, a work that focuses significantly on the local GAA context while providing an important critique of Ireland in the mid-1980s. Its depiction of Gaelic games and their practitioners continued the demythologising of the sport which Lennon's film had begun. Each of these films problematise previous narrow conceptions of Irishness and celebrate the potential for cultural change, encounter and new possibilities. The direction suggested in these works, however, was not necessarily followed in subsequent cinematic works featuring Gaelic games, the subject of the next chapter. As will soon be apparent, the appeal of established stereotypes continues to have a strong influence on contemporary cinematic depictions of Ireland's indigenous games.

8

'The hurley is the new chainsaw': Gaelic games in contemporary cinema

Chapter Seven closed with a consideration of the last film funded by the first incarnation of the Irish Film Board, *Clash of the Ash* (1987), before it was shut down in the round of cutbacks that followed the return of Fianna Fáil to government in February 1987. The years immediately following were bleak indeed for Irish cinema, with very few films made in the country. Ironically, individual films emerged in this period that were to enjoy unprecedented international success, including the Oscar-winning *My Left Foot* (1989) and *The Crying Game* (1992). The success of the latter would encourage the recently appointed minister for arts, culture and the Gaeltacht (and subsequently president of Ireland), Michael D. Higgins, to re-establish the Irish Film Board on 30 March 1993, the morning after director Neil Jordan won the Academy Award for Best Original Screenplay. Though not depicted, Gaelic games (in particular hurling) has a significant presence in Jordan's film, providing an opportunity for the IRA man Fergus to bond with his British-soldier prisoner Jody as they compare the Irish game ('That game where a bunch of Paddies whack sticks at each other?' as Jody calls it) with cricket. Jordan appears alert to the misconceptions regarding hurling here, misconceptions we have explored earlier; Jody's comments suggest how hurling in particular can be used to affirm prevailing stereotypes regarding Irish people. As cinema moved from the twentieth into the twenty-first century, established traditions of representing Gaelic games in film continued, though within a context where an indigenous film industry and culture was finally maturing, if increasingly associated with television. Within the representations that emerged, we find ongoing tensions between the appeal of the stereotype and an attempt to provide more sophisticated depictions of Gaelic games, while the critical turn that emerged in the 1960s continues to be apparent.

FILM AND TELEVISION: *A YEAR 'TIL SUNDAY* (1998)

Television coverage of Gaelic games has expanded significantly over the past twenty years. While soccer and rugby have enjoyed considerable coverage and popularity on Irish television, with horse racing, athletics and boxing also receiving significant exposure, Gaelic games still typically attract the biggest television audiences each year for sporting events.[1] This coverage, for the first thirty years or so of RTÉ's existence, focused primarily on the All-Ireland semi-finals and finals, but the arrival of British satellite channel Sky Sports and the increased number of live soccer games encouraged the expansion of television coverage of Gaelic games in Ireland, helped also by the emergence of two more national television channels over the past fifteen years, TG4 and TV3 (recently rebranded as Virgin Media 1), and one Irish-based cable sports channel, Setanta Sports (also recently rebranded as Eir Sport), all of which have given considerable coverage to sport, including Gaelic games, particularly the Irish-language broadcaster TG4, which has specialised in Gaelic games programming. Since 2014, Sky Sports has also broadcast live a number of GAA championship games, though (as was the case with soccer coverage in the UK) television audiences decreased considerably for these games, available only to Sky subscribers. In Northern Ireland, BBC Northern Ireland and Ulster Television were slower to broadcast Gaelic games, focusing primarily on soccer, in particular the domestic Irish League. However, the success of teams from Northern Ireland in the All-Ireland football championship since the early 1990s and, indeed, the development of the peace process, has seen increased coverage of Gaelic football, particularly on BBC Northern Ireland.

A detailed consideration of depictions of Gaelic games on television is beyond the scope of this study, given the very large number of relevant works involved. However, it should be acknowledged that the dividing line in the contemporary era between television and cinematic depictions has become increasingly fluid; this fluidity is evident in one of the most important depictions of Gaelic games to be made over the past twenty years, Pat Comer's *A Year 'Til Sunday* (1999). Comer's documentary, though introduced in the opening credits as a Comer & Co./Power Pictures Production for RTÉ, owes its origins to developments in the world of film in particular. It is also a work which resists and rejects both the dominant stereotypes in international productions featuring Gaelic games and the national mythologising of earlier indigenous productions. Comer's focus is primarily on revealing the local energies that drive and sustain the popularity of Gaelic games and their distinctiveness.

From the 1980s onwards, developments in video technology have facilitated a substantial increase in low-budget film production while also offering further possibilities with regard to what could be filmed, and how, due to the increased flexibility video facilitated. These possibilities were perhaps most famously celebrated by the influential Danish Dogme movement founded in 1995 by directors Lars von Trier and Thomas Vinterberg.[2] For sports documentarians, the advent of video (with smaller and more versatile cameras and an ability to adapt more easily than film to natural lighting conditions) allowed them to capture aspects of the sporting experience rarely seen on film previously. It also enabled the type of observational filming associated with both Direct Cinema (in the US) and *cinéma-vérité* (in France) in the 1960s to be further developed.

The production of *A Year 'Til Sunday* benefited considerably from these developments and director Pat Comer has acknowledged the influence of Direct Cinema exponent Frederick Wiseman in particular on this work;[3] however, the production had the added ingredient of a director who was a member of the team featured in the film, the Galway senior team competing in the 1998 All-Ireland football championship. As well as being a practising film-maker, Comer was the substitute goalkeeper on the Galway panel and this gave him unique access to the team's unexpected journey to All-Ireland glory that year. As described by Tom Humphries in his *Irish Times* review, *A Year 'Til Sunday* 'is a film which comes from the

Figure 8.1. Pat Comer takes us into the Galway football team's dressing room in *A Year 'Till Sunday* (1998). Permission to reproduce image granted by Pat Comer

inside looking out, rather than a document made by outsiders looking in'.[4]

This insider perspective is perhaps most evident in the fascinating dressing-room scenes included in the documentary (Fig. 8.1). The sight of often undressed and emotionally overwrought players within the confined space of the dressing room has long provided film-makers with the perfect arena to evoke intense and intimate moments of high drama within sport cinema; indeed, inspirational 'locker room' scenes have now become a standard element within the fictional American sports-film genre, evident in a wide range of films including *Slap Shot* (1977), *Hoosiers* (1986), *The Program* (1993) and *Any Given Sunday* (1999). However, this was rarely a feature of Gaelic-games coverage and Comer provides some of the first shots revealing the intensity and sacrifice involved at the elite level of Gaelic games. A recurring theme throughout the film is the huge efforts made by the amateur players featured, whether in the dark, wet days of winter training or the ongoing huge commitment to preparation and playing that is required of an inter-county player. This extends beyond the individual players themselves and Comer brings us into their local communities (including following Ja Fallon on his rounds as a postman) and families, and shows the engagement and supports that are crucial elements for a successful inter-county player and team in the contemporary era.

Tom Humphries in his review also described the documentary in terms of *cinéma-vérité* and as 'the first great GAA film', alluding to the cinematic precursors to Comer's work; however, *A Year 'Til Sunday* is also greatly indebted to other media, including radio, newspapers and above all television. The importance of television to Gaelic-games coverage today is evident throughout the documentary; most of the footage of Galway matches on their way to (and including) the All-Ireland final is comprised of extracts from RTÉ's coverage of the championship. The remarks of TV pundits – including Pat Spillane – are also integrated into the work, which cuts from TV coverage to interviews with players and behind-the-scenes footage from the training ground, the dressing room and along the sideline during games. Television is not the only medium foregrounded within the film, however; radio reports (by RTÉ sportscasters Seán Óg Ó Ceallacháin and Brian Carthy) are also integrated into the documentary's storytelling style, while the print-media coverage of Galway games is referred to repeatedly, including as part of manager John O'Mahony's attempts to inspire his team. Indeed, television and radio are also integrated into the climax of the film, the 1998 All-Ireland final which combines RTÉ television coverage with radio commentary by legendary broadcaster Mícheál Ó Muircheartaigh.

The legacy of previous teams and earlier depictions of Gaelic games is also a recurring feature of Comer's work; accompanied by newsreel and National Film Institute of Ireland archival footage, players refer repeatedly to the last team from Galway to lift the Sam Maguire in 1966 and the challenge of trying to emulate that success. This includes interviews with one of Galway's star players, Michael Donnellan, whose father (1966) and grandfather (1925) both played on All-Ireland-winning teams.

Previous cinematic depictions of Gaelic games are also recalled in the focus on the prematch ceremony, in particular the foregrounding of the tricolour and playing of the national anthem (taken from the RTÉ coverage of the match). As indicated previously, such scenes have featured throughout the history of Gaelic games on film, including in the very earliest surviving depictions (see Chapter One). However, Comer includes an innovative international aspect by cutting from television coverage of the prematch singing of 'Amhrán na bhFiann' in Croke Park to scenes of crowds in bars in New York, London and Tuam (County

Galway), all of whom mark the moment with considerable respect. The shot of the empty street outside the stadium intercut with these scenes also reaffirms another recurring trope in depictions of Gaelic games in indigenous productions: the ability of the games to provide a focus for national identification and cohesion.

GAELIC GAMES IN CONTEMPORARY FILM[5]

While today television is undoubtedly the primary medium through which moving images of Gaelic games are communicated, these sports continue to feature in contemporary film, including in some of the most commercially and critically acclaimed productions. Neil Jordan's Academy Award and the subsequent commercial success of *Interview with the Vampire* (1993) provided him with the box-office credibility to convince a major Hollywood studio to invest in an epic production on the life of one of the major figures in the Irish-independence movement, Michael Collins. Collins had strong connections with the GAA; his involvement with the organisation in London and with Irish republicanism developed simultaneously while he worked in the Post Office Savings Bank in West Kensington in the 1910s. He was sworn into the Irish Republican Brotherhood by prominent republican and chairman of London County Board Sam Maguire, a man whose name now adorns the major trophy in Gaelic football. During his time in London, Collins played hurling and football with the Geraldine GAA club, and as club treasurer acquired organisational and administrative skills that would serve him well during the War of Independence.[6]

Jordan's biopic, however, does not dwell on Collins' formative years and is concerned instead with the tumultuous events that followed the 1916 Rising. The film was controversial when released in Ireland in November 1996, not least because of the manner in which it portrayed the events surrounding 21 November 1920, better known today as Bloody Sunday, when British forces opened fire on a Gaelic-football match between Tipperary and Dublin in Croke Park. Interestingly, in light of the prominence of the sport in other international productions discussed earlier, in the original screenplay for *Michael Collins* it is hurling, not football, that Jordan describes as being played, with the unfortunate player killed on that day – Tipperary midfielder Michael Hogan – taunting the British armoured car with a hurley before being shot dead.[7]

Michael Collins was funded largely by the Hollywood studio Warner Bros., which invested $28 million in the production (including the elaborate reconstruction of the GPO in Dublin city, the republican headquarters during the Rising), and conscious of the need to provide epic cinema for an international audience, Jordan chose spectacle over substance in his reenactment of Bloody Sunday, shot at the Carlisle Grounds soccer stadium in Bray. As the film's producer, Stephen Woolley, has admitted, speaking of the attempt to raise funding from the studio, 'The reality is, to make this story … you have to make it an epic picture.'[8] Presumably Jordan at first considered that hurling would provide the greater spectacle (as we have already noted, hurling is by far the most depicted Gaelic game in international productions), but thought better of it in the final production. However, it is a fact that on Bloody Sunday British armoured cars did not invade Croke Park, though this is how Jordan depicts events on that day.[9]

Jordan has defended his use of armoured cars as he wanted this 'scene to last more than thirty seconds',[10] yet his choice of spectacle over fact is also apparent elsewhere in the film, including a scene which depicts the IRA's use of a car bomb, a weapon not used in the Irish conflict until the 1960s. The reality is that, for most audiences outside of Ireland, the particularities of the sport concerned or indeed the events of Bloody Sunday are less important than the entertainment value of the film they are watching; in Hollywood entertainment is everything.

It is instructive to compare the depiction of Gaelic games in *Michael Collins* to that in another account of the revolutionary period in Ireland, *The Wind that Shakes the Barley* (2006), in which veteran British independent film-maker Ken Loach eschews the epic pretensions of *Michael Collins* to focus on the impact of the revolutionary period on a small rural community in west Cork. *The Wind that Shakes the Barley* begins with a lengthy credit sequence of almost two minutes featuring hurling, in contrast to the less than twenty seconds of Gaelic football in *Michael Collins*. Loach offers an insight into his motivation for including this sequence in the film:

The game here is hurling, which is a Gaelic sport very much associated with the Irish sense of identity, and the playing of it was banned in this period, not banned because of the sport but banned because people were gathering in groups, and it was gathering into groups of people that was banned, so playing it was in a sense an act of defiance.[11]

The director's attention to detail is evident in this opening sequence, including the distinctive hurleys used and the dress of the players, with each player's team marked by the colour of his sash. Of course, the choice of a hurling sequence also allows Loach the opportunity to introduce the dramatic landscape of west Cork, though this is always a background (rather than being foregrounded as often occurs in international productions featuring Ireland) to the main interactions between the players on the field. Hurling enables Loach to introduce the community featured in the film and to emphasise the distinctiveness of their culture at a time when expressing your Irishness (whether through sport or language) could have serious consequences. This sequence is followed by a particularly violent encounter between the players and members of the Black and Tans, a special reserve force established during the War of Independence to support the local police force, the Royal Irish Constabulary. While brutally interrogating the players for breaking the law that prohibited groups of people from gathering, they eventually beat one of them to death for refusing to give his name in English.

VIOLENCE AND GAELIC GAMES

The depiction of Gaelic games in both *Michael Collins* and *The Wind that Shakes the Barley* also indicates a frequent association still found in contemporary cinematic representations: the juxtaposition of Gaelic games with moments of violence. These associations inevitably recall and are to some degree informed by established stereotypes discussed previously in this work; they also reflect the imperative within mainstream drama to provide dramatic moments of action. However, it is the degree to which context and motivation are provided for these associations (as with

The Wind that Shakes the Barley) that is a key determinant in evaluating the role of Gaelic games in specific films. Regrettably, this is too often not the case.

The hurling stick in particular has appeared in several contemporary films with the primary purpose of facilitating moments of violence, epitomised in the 2007 short simply called *The Hurling Stick* (2007). Here the game of hurling is given neither context nor development; the presence of the hurling stick in the film's title and narrative is entirely to facilitate violence. Two Irish-American hitmen – Mick (Josh Kelling) and Danny (Brian Thomas Evans) – meet up in a bar following Danny's return from a trip to Ireland. Danny gives the present of a hurling stick ('It's a traditional Irish game, I picked it up in Kilkenny for ya') to Mick, but he also tells him that he wants to leave his life of crime behind, in particular the most recent kill order he's just received. Mick insists they carry out their assignment, but when it turns out the assignment is for Danny to kill Mick, Mick defends himself with the hurling stick he just received. As he remarks after killing Danny with a strike of the hurley, 'Never give an Irishman a weapon and call it a game, Danny.'

While the hurling stick features threateningly in several prominent films (including *Ryan's Daughter* (1970) and *Disco Pigs* (2001)), the most dramatic example of its employment in this manner is the 2011 British crime thriller *Blitz*, adapted from the novel of the same name by Irish crime writer Ken Bruen. *Blitz* features a recurring character in Bruen's *oeuvre*, Sergeant Tom Brant (Jason Statham), a violent, hard-drinking and unconventional police officer whose 'weapon' of choice is a hurling stick. Indeed, the film opens with a very violent encounter between Brant and some car thieves in which he demonstrates the violent potential of a hurley. While beating each member of the gang, he informs them of the attributes of the game of hurling: 'This, lads, is a hurley, used in the Irish game of hurling; a cross between hockey and murder … A word of advice, girls: if you're picking the wrong fight, at least pick the right weapon.'

HORROR, HURLING AND BERTIE AHERN[12]

Given the recurring association of hurling with violence in contemporary film, it was inevitable that it would eventually feature within the genre most associated with violence: horror. However, in Irish director Conor McMahon's *Dead Meat* (2004), aspects of Gaelic games have not only been used to facilitate moments of violence, they have also contributed to the indigenisation of a global genre in a work critical of both established depictions of rural Ireland and the failures and complacencies of the Celtic Tiger period.

Since the mid-1990s, and particularly from the early 2000s, Irish film-makers have increasingly turned to horror to represent aspects of Irish society, culture and history. From Enda Hughes' *The Eliminator* (1996) to Stephen Bradley's *Boy Eats Girl* (2005), Patrick Kenny's *Winter's End* (2005), Billy O'Brien's *Isolation* (2006), Paddy Breathnach's *Shrooms* (2007) and *Red Mist* (2008), Aisling Walsh's *Daisy Chain* (2008), Justin O'Brien's *Ghostwood* (2008), Eric Courtney's *Seer* (2008), Conor McPherson's *The Eclipse* (2009), David Keating's *The Wake Wood* (2010), Jon Wright's *Grabbers* (2012) and Ivan Kavanagh's *The Canal* (2014), Irish directors have used this hugely popular and familiar genre to portray aspects of Irish life to audiences throughout the world.

As Barry Monahan has noted, 'as burgeoning national cinemas emerge into mainstream circuits of production and distribution, for reasons of economy, technology or aesthetic exploration, it is common to see degrees of address to established genres'.[13] Indeed, part of the appeal, and indeed comedy, of such films is how they play off familiar aspects of the genre itself. As Monahan again observes, 'The comedy works because in different ways the local semantics fail to sit comfortably with the generic syntax',[14] a description particularly relevant to a production described as 'the first Irish zombie/comedy film',[15] McMahon's *Dead Meat*, a work preceded by his similarly themed 2001 award-winning short *The Braineater*.

Dead Meat and *The Braineater* are heavily indebted to previous international horror films, including those by Sam Rami, Peter Jackson, George A. Romero and Lucio Fulci.[16] However, a striking feature in both is the use of elements and motifs associated with Gaelic games, in particular hurling, within their narratives. These films also, in common with other recent horror works, reject and critique previous touristic depictions of Ireland (an important determinant of representations of Ireland in international productions throughout the twentieth century, as noted in Chapter Three) while providing an 'allegorical moment' both for the exploration of trauma in Ireland's distant and more recent past and a critique of Celtic Tiger Ireland itself.

In Chapter Three we discussed the importance of nostalgic pastoralism in representations of Ireland, epitomised in John Ford's greatest commercial success, *The Quiet Man* (1952). The depiction of Ireland in *The Quiet Man* greatly influenced subsequent campaigns by the Irish tourist authority, Bord Fáilte (set up in the same year as *The Quiet Man's* release and now known as Fáilte Ireland), and continues to feature in contemporary tourist iconography (including postcards), some of which draw directly on the film itself.

The Ireland popularised by *The Quiet Man* is a pastoral idyll, often sparsely populated by amiable and loquacious characters with a penchant for music, alcohol and recreational fighting, and a reticence towards work, a country unprepared for, and challenged by, the arrival of modernity. Its legacy would influence subsequent filmic representations of Ireland, including works as diverse as *Darby O'Gill and the Little People* (Robert Stevenson, 1959), *Finian's Rainbow* (Francis Ford Coppola, 1968), *Far and Away* (Ron Howard, 1992), *Circle of Friends* (Pat O'Connor, 1995), *The Matchmaker* (Mark Joffe, 1997), *Waking Ned* (Kirk Jones, 1998), *The Boys from County Clare* (John Irvin, 2003), *PS I Love You* (Richard LaGravenese, 2007) and *Leap Year* (Anand Tucker, 2010). However, in recent Irish horror films this idyllic vision of Ireland is subverted within dark and disturbing works set in rural locales that feature little of the beauty of these earlier productions. Furthermore, in the figure of the zombie as featured in McMahon's *Dead Meat*, a critique of the failures and complacencies of Celtic Tiger Ireland is apparent.

As mentioned, McMahon's feature was preceded by the short *The Braineater*, a comic horror film in which the director's dystopian vision of rural Ireland was already apparent. The film depicts the tragic and surreal aftermath of a car accident that results in the death of a mother and father and the subsequent feralisation of their son, who survives by eating the brains of other humans and animals. When members of a local under-12 hurling team, on their way to a match with their eccentric coach Cathal Ceaunt (Eoin Whelan) – also featured in *Dead Meat* – encounter this unfortunate man many years later, several are killed before one, Cúchulainn-like,[17] fells his assailant with a powerful shot with his *sliotar*, ultimately decapitating him with his hurling stick.

Rural Ireland is often depicted in contemporary Irish horror film – including *The Braineater* – as a place far removed from the welcoming and reassuring locale represented in tourist iconography and contemporary Irish postcards. It is a space haunted by the hideous monsters of biological farming experiments (Billy O'Brien's *Isolation*) or a tortured girl's nightmares (Eric Courtney's *Seer*), populated by meat-eating zombies who appear without warning, attack and devour (*Dead Meat*), and tormented by the traumatised victims of clerical abuse who, it seems until the film's surprising climax, pick off their victims one by one (in Paddy Breathnach's *Shrooms*). Interestingly, in both *Dead Meat* and *Shrooms* it is tourists who are the central protagonists. In the latter, American students who have come to rural Ireland to experiment with drugs are all – bar one – horrifically killed, hardly a story Fáilte Ireland would wish to promote. In *Dead Meat*, Spanish tourist Helena (Marián Araújo), lost in the Leitrim countryside and assisted by the local gravedigger Desmond (David Muyllaert) and trainer of the local underage hurling team Cathal Ceaunt (Eoin Whelan), survives her ordeal of Leitrim's zombies (referred to by the hurling coach as 'ghowls') only to be locked up in a truck, like an animal, at the film's close.

It is the darker aspects of Ireland's past, despite the obvious lack of interest indicated by the tourist Helena in several scenes, that resonate within *Dead Meat*. In the locality, Desmond tells Helena at one point, Cromwell once ordered the hanging of fifty men and women, while as Ruth Barton has observed,

> … it is also a countryside dotted with ruined churches and round towers, symbols of an abandoned culture and religion. In such a landscape – and as reviewers remarked on the film's release, the landscape is one of the most distinctive aspects of this film[18] – the wandering bands of starving, homeless country people could easily be mistaken for famine victims come back to haunt the present. At the same time, McMahon's

perspective is resolutely metropolitan, viewing the countryside as the locus of an unspeakable horror.[19]

These landscape features – including 'ruined churches and round towers' – which often function within the touristic vision of Ireland as markers of a heroic and glorious past, in *Dead Meat* are haunted by a threatening contemporary evil. This horror echoes beyond the obvious living dead in *Dead Meat* and connects with a recurring theme across indigenous Irish cinema since the 1970s, including Fergus Tighe's *Clash of the Ash* discussed in the previous chapter. Irish film-makers have returned repeatedly to the rural, a place idealised by both tourist and sentimental nationalist in the past and present, to unearth stories of abuse and repression. For Barton, these works 'perform a public function of enabling their viewers to work through the legacy of Irish history in its most traumatic formulations'.[20]

Though there has been a tendency to marginalise horror film as a lower form of entertainment, too shocking to be considered academically or seriously, as Robin Wood has noted, precisely because of this perception of horror films as mere entertainment, 'full awareness stops at the level of plot, action and character, in which the most dangerous and subversive implications can disguise themselves and escape detection'.[21] For Adam Lowenstein, horror film has often provided the 'allegorical moment' or 'a shocking collision of film, spectator, and history',[22] while Bruce Kawin has contended that horror films

> function as nightmares for the individual viewer, as diagnostic eruptions for repressive societies, and as exorcistic or transcendent pagan rituals for supposedly post-pagan cultures. They can be analysed in all these ways because they represent a unique juncture of the personal, social, and mythic structures and because each of these structures has a conscious/official and unconscious/repressed dualism, whose dialectic finds expression in the act of masking.[23]

Though 'masked' through the comic postmodern play with form and content found in McMahon's film, both historical and more recent traumas nonetheless bubble beneath the playful surface narrative of *Dead Meat*. As already noted, at a number of points in the film there are references

Figures 8.2 & 8.3. Religious icons in *Dead Meat* (2004). Permission to reproduce images granted by director Conor McMahon

to past atrocities associated with Cromwell and the British presence in Ireland. However, Ireland's own more recent, though no less traumatic, experiences with established religion are evoked in recurring references to religious iconography in the film. In this context these features provide neither support nor comfort but appear almost entirely obsolete, apart from their use occasionally within the film as rudimentary weapons, as in one scene in which Helena defends herself from a zombie (who was once her boyfriend) with the assistance of a Sacred Heart picture. One of Helena's earliest encounters with the victims of the undead is her discovery in a dilapidated cottage of the bloodied dead body of an old woman clinging to her rosary beads. The house in which she finds this woman's body contains many religious icons (Figs 8.2 and 8.3), which appear repeatedly in shot, providing an ineffective backdrop to the

Figure 8.4. The hurling coach about to attack a zombie with his *camán* in *Dead Meat* (2004). Permission to reproduce image granted by director Conor McMahon

contemporary dystopian nightmare. As if to emphasise this point, in one sequence the zombie contemptuously flings some of these religious icons onto the floor of the cottage.

It is within this context that *Dead Meat* reimagines one of the most emotive of nationalist motifs – the hurling stick – as one of the weapons of choice for those few survivors in their attempts to escape their zombie pursuers. Indeed, the production was initially to include a hurling match with a zombie pitch invasion, but this proved to be logistically impossible within the microbudget parameters of the production.[24] Such was the impact of the hurling stick's use in an early screen test that McMahon recalls one spectator remarking, 'The hurley is the new chainsaw', quite possibly referring to a particular scene in which the hurling coach almost decapitates a zombie – who appears to have been a bride-to-be before her transformation – with a hurling stick, as he reaches from a jeep in which the tourist Helena and gravedigger Desmond are also fleeing the zombies (Fig. 8.4).

The use of the hurling stick here may superficially seem to perpetuate a stereotype familiar from international representations of the sport, as discussed earlier. However, in common with the Irish accents in the film, McMahon's choice of weapon – which typically in horror is the knife or chainsaw – further localises this prominent aspect of the genre. Furthermore, elsewhere in the film the presence of the hurling stick is nuanced by its evocation of the mythological figure of Cúchulainn, and its connection with local political developments, which may well be part of a larger critique of political failures in a time of apparent plenty. This is also evident in the neglect and decline of rural Ireland itself as depicted throughout the film, the promotion of unethical farming practices, and the evocative figure of the zombie.

Indeed, the figure of the zombie provides a highly suggestive motif for a film made at the height of the Celtic Tiger. From George Romero's reimagining of the zombie figure in *Night of the Living Dead* (1968), zombie films have been centrally concerned with social criticism. This criticism in *Dead Meat* is most explicitly made of intensive farming practices. Here the explanation offered for the infection of humans and their transformation into zombies is the spread of a particularly virulent strain of BSE, or mad cow disease, from animals to humans following the feeding of livestock with food acquired from the carcasses of dead animals. McMahon is here referring to the practice identified by scientists as responsible for the spread of BSE,[25] but there is a wider critique apparent of the modern capitalist means of food production in the West. As Felicity Lawrence notes in her study *Eat Your Heart Out: why the food business is bad for the planet and your health*:

Modern food production involves processes that, quite apart from having little care for real nutrition, drive people off the land, stimulate migration, increase inequalities and the depth of poverty, are corrosive of society, and depend on extravagant use of natural resources, from water to oil to land, that are running out. The politics of food is in other words not the art of shopping but the politics of modern globalised capitalism itself.[26]

While the horror genre in the 1950s has been associated with a fear of communist infiltration, evident in films such as *The Thing* (Christian Nyby, 1951) and *Them!* (Gordon Douglas, 1954),[27] the zombie has latterly been interpreted as a recurring symbol in film of the evils of capitalism. As Robin Wood notes, cannibalism 'represents the ultimate in possessiveness, hence the logical end of human relations under capitalism',[28] a point developed in his subsequent study *Hollywood from Vietnam to Reagan*, where he argues that zombies 'represent, on a metaphorical level, the whole dead weight of patriarchal consumer capitalism, from whose habits of behaviour and desire not even Hare Krishnas and nuns ... are

Figure 8.5. 2002 election-campaign poster for Fianna Fáil

exempt'.[29] Given the context within which *Dead Meat* was made, a Celtic Tiger Ireland marked by often ostentatious wealth and high consumerist spending encouraged by the neo-liberalist economic policies of successive Fianna Fáil-led governments and followed by a serious recession and one of the highest levels of both national and personal debt in Europe,[30] McMahon could hardly have chosen a more appropriate moment to employ such a resonant motif. At a time when the Celtic Tiger economy was dependent primarily on unbridled consumption that fed a property bubble, the collapse of which was at the centre of subsequent economic decline, McMahon depicts a world in which human life itself has become so devalued that human beings have become consumable. And if the criticism was not clear enough, the director offered a further significant piece of dialogue in an evocative scene in which we witness the hurling coach, Cathal Cheunt, defend the few uninfected survivors from an attacking mad cow, in the style of Cúchulainn, with his hurling stick and *sliotar*. While retrieving the *sliotar*, Cheunt utters 'A lot done, more to do' – a campaign slogan used by Fianna Fáil, and particularly associated with the party's then leader Bertie Ahern, prior to the 2002 election which returned the party to power (Fig. 8.5). The local significance of this statement's inclusion has been commented on by McMahon himself – 'That's a line only Irish people will probably get ... that was the taoiseach's slogan' – while the film's producer Ed King has described it as possibly a better tag line for the movie as a whole than that chosen on its release.[31]

In the contemporary era Gaelic games are primarily communicated via television, with the virtual world of YouTube and other online services increasingly important for audience engagement with these sports. Pat Comer's *A Year 'Til Sunday* may feature prominently televisual depictions of Gaelic games, yet it also reveals in its content and aesthetic the continuing indebtedness of contemporary depictions to developments in film production. Gaelic games also continue to feature in contemporary cinema, with major productions such as *Michael Collins* and *The Wind that Shakes the Barley* featuring these sports prominently as key markers of Irish culture and identity. Regrettably, the stereotypes associated with representations of Ireland and Irishness discussed earlier continue to appear in the contemporary period, where the hurling stick has featured in a range of films primarily to facilitate moments of violence. However, as evident in Conor McMahon's *Dead Meat*, hurling can also function within a larger critique of both established representations of rural Ireland and more recent developments. *Dead Meat* depicts a rural Ireland far removed from either nationalist mythology or the tourist gaze. Indeed, much as the tourist gaze has been associated with a particular vision of Ireland (discussed in Chapter Three), epitomised in the representation of the indigenous sport of hurling as rural, backward and potentially violent, *Dead Meat*, in common with other recent horror films, including Paddy Breathnach's *Shrooms*, may well constitute a counter-touristic vision, one in which hurling functions as a protective motif against the onslaught of voracious global capitalism. While international productions featuring Gaelic games have revealed the influence of the tourist gaze, it is the local gaze McMahon ultimately invites through his critical engagement with contemporary Irish politics and society and his playful and satiric evocation of mythological precedents and previous stereotypical representations. It is this exaggerated performative play with stereotypes which ultimately satirises previous depictions to produce a representation of both Ireland and Irish sport far removed from that of tourist-inflected productions.

9

Conclusion

Cinema and codified sports both emerged in the late nineteenth century. Sport featured prominently in the earliest attempts to capture movement photographically, with early cinema, from the 1890s onwards, frequently depicting sporting subjects. Sport as a cultural form already had a large following; in addition, action, drama and stars (all key aspects of popular cinema from the 1910s onwards) were also characteristics of sport. Hollywood had a major role in the popularisation of the sports-film genre, though sport has featured prominently in national cinemas across the globe. Much as sport can provide a focus for national identification (particularly through representative teams in popular pursuits such as Association football), representations of major sporting encounters and victories in film can also contribute to this process. If, as Susan Hayward suggests, film can function as a 'cultural articulation of a nation', textualising 'the nation and subsequently [constructing] a series of relations around the concepts, first, of state and citizen, then of state, citizen and other',[1] then depictions of sport on film may represent some of the most pertinent and popular examples of such an articulation, including depictions of Gaelic games considered in this book. However, Gaelic games (especially hurling) have also provided film-makers, particularly outside of Ireland, with a distinctive cultural signifier to seemingly affirm prevailing stereotypes concerning Ireland and Irish people, a feature that continues to be relevant in the contemporary era.

INCORPORATING THE CINEMATIC INTO
GAELIC GAMES: *LAOCHRA*

This book began with a reflection on the GAA's 1916 commemorative event *Laochra*, and it is to this event we now return to conclude. While Gaelic games today feature less prominently in film productions, the cinematic has been incorporated into major sporting events themselves, evident in the big stadium screens that are now a key feature of major games in Croke Park. A fascinating example of this integration (while simultaneously indicating the centrality of television today to people's engagement with Gaelic games) was the 2016 *Laochra* pageant, the GAA's 1916 commemorative event held in Croke Park on 24 April 2016. *Laochra* also offers an intriguing example of the integration of the national and international conceptions of Gaelic games in its ability to affirm both the Irish nation and a nationalist configuration of Irish identity while simultaneously drawing on established stereotypes concerning Ireland and Irish people. This is particularly evident in the foregrounding of violence and the affirmation of what might be described as a 'tourist gaze' on Ireland in the pageant's utopian rural focus.

As indicated at the outset, there were two principal modes of experiencing the *Laochra* event: one televisual (via TV broadcast by the Irish-language broadcaster TG4), the other theatrical, with significant cinematic elements for those present in Croke Park for the performance. The cinematic aspects were evident in the capturing of live performance (including re-enactments from episodes in Irish mythology featuring hurling, Irish dancing and song, and readings), rendered for television broadcast through pitchside camera and dynamic Steadicam sequences, and accompanied by pre-recorded and archival footage screened on three of the largest high-definition outdoor screens in Europe. The use of Steadicam to capture the event added a peculiarly cinematic element to *Laochra*; invented by the American cinematographer Garrett Brown, one of the first films in which Steadicam was used extensively was the seminal Oscar-winning sport drama *Rocky* (1976), a key text in redefining and further popularising the sport cinema genre.[2] With regard to the screens in the stadium, while two screens are normally featured in Croke Park (indicating the integration of the cinematic into this venue), a third

90-square-metre screen was added at the Hill 16 end, reducing the capacity (normally 82,300) to 81,000. Nonetheless, even at 81,000 this was the largest crowd ever to attend a National League final, which preceded *Laochra*. In addition to those in attendance in the stadium, the *Laochra* event and preceding Allianz Football League Division 1 and 2 finals attracted the largest ever audience for a TG4 broadcast, 'earning TG4 a share of 38% of all people viewing TV in Ireland … In total, almost three quarters of a million viewers (739,000)'.[3]

The cinematic/televisual aspects of the production reflect the background of the show's artistic director and producers. Artistic director Ruán Magan is an award-winning film-maker who has worked primarily in the documentary genre, including the three-part historical series *1916: the Irish rebellion* (2016). *Laochra* was produced by TV production company Tyrone Productions, one of the most successful producers of entertainment and documentary content on Irish television. The company was founded by John McColgan and Moya Doherty, the producers behind the international Irish-dance-themed theatrical phenomenon *Riverdance*, aspects of which were also evident in the *Laochra* event.

Laochra opens by immediately connecting elemental and stereotypical images of Irishness with Gaelic games. The pre-recorded footage which begins the TV version (and was shown on the screens in the stadium) opens with a shot of the gold-coloured GAA crest set against a background of water and fire (Fig. 9.1).

Figure 9.1. Opening shot of *Laochra* (2016). Image courtesy of Tyrone Productions Ltd

Figure 9.2. Ireland personified as woman in *Laochra* (2016). Image courtesy of Tyrone Productions Ltd

This dramatic initial image gives way to a shot of a red-haired woman (played by singer Sibéal Ní Chasaide) dressed in a green cape looking out upon an Irish landscape, which is dominated by water in the foreground and a dramatic mountain in the distance (Fig. 9.2).

As evident in Figure 9.2, this sequence evokes the familiar rural idyll evident in cinematic and touristic representations of Ireland, as discussed in Chapter Three. Its presence within *Laochra* also recalls the importance of pastoral iconography to nationalist configurations of Ireland and, indeed, rural Ireland as the central space associated with Gaelic games.

The initial opening shots are followed by a montage of images associated with Gaelic games, from crowd shots of supporters presumably on their way to a game, to shots of the prematch parades of legendary teams from counties Cork, Kerry and Kilkenny (including prominent former Cork and Kerry players Christy Ring and Páidí Ó Sé) and to scenes of Irish Volunteers drilling, a shot of the British army, and a return to the female figure seen at the beginning. There is in these scenes an inevitable marching towards what would appear to be a shared goal – despite the fact that some of the marchers actually have little in common, particularly the shots of the British army and the Irish Volunteers – a goal that seems bound up with the female personification of Ireland.

The pre-recorded opening sequence ends with a return to the female figure in the landscape before we enter the stadium to witness

Figure 9.3. Setanta playing hurling in *Laocha* (2016). Image courtesy of Tyrone Productions Ltd

Figure 9.4. Cúchulainn's death in *Laochra* (2016). Image courtesy of Tyrone Productions Ltd

the performed elements of the commemorative event, beginning with a re-enactment of aspects of the Setanta/Cúchulainn saga. Significantly, as found elsewhere in the production, physical combat and violence is celebrated in this scene in a lengthy fight sequence (integrated with hurling (Fig. 9.3)) as part of a recurring return to military elements throughout the pageant. Complemented by a stirring orchestral accompaniment, this initial re-enactment elevates violent and militaristic elements from Cúchulainn's life, culminating in the mythological figure's violent death (Fig. 9.4). The death of Cúchulainn is followed by readings of extracts

Figure 9.5. A map of Ireland is formed on the pitch during *Laochra* (2016). Image courtesy of Tyrone Productions Ltd

from speeches associated with leading political and cultural figures in Irish history, including the GAA's founder Michael Cusack. Cusack's words capture the juxtaposition of violence and sport evident throughout the commemorative event: 'A warlike race is ever fond of games requiring skill, strength and staying power.'

These readings are followed shortly thereafter by the recitation of the 1916 Proclamation of the Republic by thirty-two children, one from each county in Ireland and wearing the Gaelic-games jersey of their county. As discussed with regard to *Peil* and *Christy Ring* in Chapter Six, the foregrounding of children here provides an important point of identification for a large section of the intended audience of the film – children learning the skills of Gaelic games. However, these children are being inducted not just into Gaelic games, but also into defining features of Irish identity.

This includes a further key trope discussed already in this book with regard to earlier indigenous depictions of Gaelic games (Chapters Five and Six) and evident throughout the *Laochra* event – the depiction of the island of Ireland as a unified space. Indeed, this map of Ireland as depicted in Figure 9.5 is the centrepiece for much of the event.

The dynamic visual rendering of *Laochra* reveals the incorporation of the cinematic into contemporary sporting events, including through the employment of Steadicam and the importance of pre-recorded footage and big screens to the stadium performance. In common with previous indigenous cinematic depictions of Gaelic games, by both the National Film Institute of Ireland (Chapter Five) and Gael Linn (Chapter Six), the promotion and affirmation of the Irish nation and Irish identity are also key concerns. Indeed, the format of *Laochra* was structured to disguise and obscure the ruptures within Irish history and Irish politics. The show as a whole repeatedly worked to naturalise and normalise a narrative of Irish history and identity that placed the First World War and 1916 as parallel paths on this journey, largely ignoring the divided and contested nature of Irish history, identity and the island of Ireland itself.

Laochra also indicates the continuing relevance of a range of tropes associated with Gaelic games explored in this book, including the employment of these sports as a key marker of Irish identity; the fore-grounding of rural Ireland evident in cinematic and touristic represent-ations of the country; and the association of hurling with violence.

Gaelic games have now featured in film for well over one hundred years. These representations have evolved in that time in response to developments in the sports concerned, Irish society, and moving-image technology. Representations of both hurling and Gaelic football were popular attractions in early cinema. While few of these earliest depictions survive, those that do indicate an evolution in both the sports themselves and approaches to their representation, with patterns evident that continue to feature in contemporary depictions, including the focus on the ceremony preceding major encounters.

In the interwar years, the lack of an indigenous film industry meant that almost all depictions of Gaelic games emerged from international sources, including British newsreels and American productions. These films are important records of the evolving games, though they also reveal the persistence of particular stereotypes associated with Irish people, in particular their alleged proclivity for violence. This is evident in the predominant focus in American productions on hurling, and the foregrounding of violent incidents within the depictions.

The focus on hurling also reflects an increasingly important cultural and economic force as the twentieth century developed: tourism. As film became an ever more important mode of attracting tourists, and affirming their expectations, distinctive indigenous practices (such as hurling) featured as part of these representations. However, mainstream and particularly American cinema was also responding to developments within American society more generally, including the movement of ethnic communities such as Irish-Americans from the margins to the centre of American culture, a process to which prominent Irish-American film-makers, including John Ford, contributed. In this context, depictions of Gaelic games were part of a larger process concerned with assuaging concerns regarding the Irish, placing more threatening stereotypes in non-threatening and frequently comic contexts, resulting in sometimes farcical depictions of hurling in particular.

The popularity of American film internationally has ensured its influence on other film cultures, including in Ireland and Britain. As we saw with regard to the Rank Organisation's *Rooney*, stereotypical tropes similar to those found in American releases are evident here, including the association of Gaelic games with violence. The unconvincing depiction of hurling in *Rooney* (despite its inclusion of scenes from the 1957 All-Ireland final) also indicates both the challenge of integrating hurling successfully into a feature-length drama and the reality that the film's producers were less concerned with depicting the sport convincingly than with exploiting its inclusion to affirm prevailing Irish stereotypes.

While international film-makers continued to feature aspects of Gaelic games in their work as the twentieth century developed, an indigenous film culture finally began to coalesce in the years following the Second World War. The establishment of the National Film Institute of Ireland in 1945 was a key moment in this development, and the institute would be responsible from 1948 onwards for the first sustained period of indigenous filming of Gaelic games. The films produced provide us with crucial footage of the evolving games of hurling and Gaelic football and some of the greatest exponents of both codes, though they also reveal the employment of both film and Gaelic games in the larger project of affirming the Irish state and its social and religious leaders in a transitional period in Irish society.

By the late 1950s, the Irish-language organisation Gael Linn was also including Gaelic games in its monthly and later weekly newsreel series *Amharc Éireann*. In common with the films produced by the NFI, these works and the longer coaching films *Peil* and *Christy Ring* provide further fascinating records of both codes in the mid-twentieth century. The Gael Linn productions also reveal an organisation keen to employ Gaelic games in the promotion of Irish culture and identity and the affirmation of the religious, political and social leaders in Irish society in the period.

While both the NFI and Gael Linn may have employed Gaelic games primarily to affirm hegemonic configurations of the Irish nation, this process was never wholly achieved and was occasionally challenged within their depictions of Gaelic games in moments rarely directly acknowledged in commentary. As the 1960s developed, a critical turn became increasingly evident in the engagements of film-makers with Irish society and distinctive aspects of Irish culture, including Gaelic games. Peter Lennon's *Rocky Road to Dublin* and later Fergal Tighe's *Clash of the Ash* both reveal a postnationalist emphasis in their questioning of established constructions of Irish identity and their critically engaged depictions of Irish society in the 1960s and 1980s respectively.

Television is undoubtedly the principal medium through which audiences now encounter Gaelic games; however, references to, and depictions of, these sports still appear in contemporary cinema, including major international productions such as *Michael Collins* and *The Wind that Shakes the Barley*. As in previous decades these depictions provide directors with distinctive features of Irish culture. However, the stereotypical association of hurling in particular with violence still features, evident in contemporary films such as *Blitz*. Unsurprisingly perhaps given this historical association with violence, hurling has also featured within recent Irish horror productions, though (as evident in Conor McMahon's *Dead Meat*) these depictions may also function within a larger critique of both established representations of rural Ireland and more recent political developments.

Gaelic games may feature less today in cinema releases than in years gone by. However, the cinematic has now been integrated into major sporting events themselves, evident in the big screens that are now an important feature of major games at Croke Park. Furthermore, the rendering of games and other events in Croke Park draws heavily on technologies developed specifically for film production, including Steadicam, a prominent feature of the recording of the GAA's 1916 centenary pageant *Laochra*. While television is undoubtedly the key medium for contemporary renderings of Gaelic games, these representations are nonetheless indebted to the extraordinary legacy of the cinema and cinematic depictions of these sports.

Leabharlanna Poiblí Chathair Baile Átha Cliath
Dublin City Public Libraries

NOTES

INTRODUCTION

1. 'Dublin's League Final Win Brings Record-breaking Viewing Figures for TG4', http://www.tg4.ie/en/corporate/press/press-releases/2016-2/20-04-16-1/ (accessed 16 September 2017). It should be noted that the league finals featured counties Dublin, Kerry, Cavan and Tyrone – all with very large followings, which undoubtedly contributed to both the attendance and viewership.

2. Marta Braun, *Picturing Time: the work of Etienne-Jules Marey (1830–1904)* (Chicago: University of Chicago Press, 1992), pp. 66–7.

3. Brian Clegg, *The Man Who Stopped Time: the illuminating story of Eadweard Muybridge – pioneer photographer, father of the motion picture, murderer* (Washington, DC: Joseph Henry Press, 1997), p. 137.

4. This section draws on earlier research I conducted, and can be found in Chapter Two ('Early Cinema and the Emergence of the Sports Film') of my monograph *Sport and Film* (London: Routledge, 2013).

5. Luke McKernan, 'Sport and the First Films', in C. Williams (ed.), *Cinema: the beginnings and the future* (London: University of Westminster Press, 1996), p. 110.

6. For further on this, see Dan Streible, *Fight Pictures: a history of boxing and early cinema* (Berkeley, CA: University of California Press, 2008).

7. Sakbolé et al., 'Le Documentaire Africain/The African Documentary', *Ecrans d'Afrique*, vol. 16, 1996, pp. 45–55, http://www.africultures.com/revue_africultures/articles/ecrans_afrique/16/16_45.pdf (accessed 10 June 2017).

8. For more on the topic of sport, film and national culture, see Seán Crosson, 'The Sports Film and National Culture and Identity', in idem *Sport and Film* (London: Routledge, 2013).

9. Lincoln Allison, 'Sport and Nationalism', in Jay Coakley and Eric Dunning (eds), *Handbook of Sports Studies* (London: Sage Publications, 2002), p. 349.

10. Benedict Anderson, *Imagined Communities: reflections on the origin and spread of nationalism* (London: Verso, 1991 [1983]), p. 3.

11. Tom Nairn, *The Break-up of Britain: crisis and neo-nationalism* (London: New Left Books, 1977), p. 193.

12. For further on this, see Eric Hobsbawm and Terence Ranger (eds), *The Invention of Tradition* (Cambridge: Cambridge University Press, 1983), and Eric Hobsbawm, *Nations and Nationalism Since 1780: programme, myth, reality* (Cambridge: Cambridge University Press, 1992).

13. Eugene Weber, *Peasants into Frenchmen: the modernisation of rural France, 1870–1914* (London: Chatto & Windus, 1979).

14. Ernest Gellner, *Nations and Nationalism* (Oxford: Blackwell, 1983), pp. 37–8.

15. Anderson, *Imagined Communities*, p. 37.

16. Michael Billig, *Banal Nationalism* (London: Sage Publications, 1995), pp. 120–6.

17. See for example Andrew Higson, *Waving the Flag: constructing a national cinema in Britain* (Oxford: Clarendon, 1995), and Mette Hjort and Scott MacKenzie (eds), *Cinema & Nation* (London: Routledge, 2000).

18. Susan Hayward, *French National Cinema* (London: Routledge, 1993), p. x.

19. For further on this, see Seán Crosson, *Sport and Film* (London: Routledge, 2013), particularly Chapter Four.

20. James Chapman, *Past and Present: national identity and the British historical film* (London and New York: I.B. Tauris, 2005), p. 270.

21. Quoted in Jim Leach, *British Film* (Cambridge: Cambridge University Press, 2004), p. 23.

22. Nigel Andrews, David Churchill and Michael Blanden, 'The Hidden Spin-off of "Chariots"', *Financial Times*, Section I: Weekend Brief, 3 April 1982.

23. Alan Tomlinson, 'Images of Sport: situating *Chariots of Fire*', *British Society of Sports History Bulletin*, vol. 8, 1988, p. 32.

24. Mette Hjort and Scott MacKenzie (eds), *Cinema & Nation* (London: Routledge, 2000), p. 4.

25. For further on this and other relevant films, see Crosson, *Sport and Film*, particularly Chapter Six.

26. John Rickard, 'Lovable Larrikins and Awful Ockers', *Journal of Australian Studies*, no. 56, 1988, p. 82.

27. Murray G. Phillips and Gary Osmond, 'Filmic Sports History: Dawn Fraser, swimming and Australian national identity', *International Journal of the History of Sport*, vol. 26, no. 14, 2009, p. 2139.

28. Roland Barthes, 'The Tour de France as Epic', in idem, *The Eiffel Tower and Other Mythologies*, trans. Richard Howard (New York: Hill & Wang, 1979), p. 87.

29. This section draws on my previous research on this topic found in Chapter Eight ('The Sports Film and National Culture and Identity') of *Sport and Film* (London: Routledge, 2013).

30. This section draws on previous joint research undertaken with Philip Dine and published in Seán Crosson and Philip Dine, 'Sport and the Media in Ireland: an introduction', *Media History*, vol. 17, no. 2, 2011, pp. 109–16.

31. For more on this, see Seán Crosson, 'Gaelic Games and "the Movies"', in Mike Cronin, William Murphy and Paul Rouse (eds), *The Gaelic Athletic Association, 1884–2009* (Dublin: Irish Academic Press, 2009), pp. 111–36.

32. Mike Cronin, *Sport and Nationalism in Ireland: Gaelic games, soccer and Irish identity since 1884* (Dublin: Four Courts Press, 1999), p. 87.

33. As Sarah Benton has noted, 'the hurling stick was reborn as the symbol of man's throne, and of his gun in drills'. Sarah Benton, 'Women Disarmed: the militarization of politics in Ireland, 1913–23', *Feminist Review*, no. 50, summer 1995, p. 153.

34. T.W. Croke, 'To Mr Michael Cusack, Honorary Secretary of the Gaelic Athletic Association. The Palace, Thurles, 18 December 1884', http://jamesjoyce.omeka.net/exhibits/show/cyclops-parody-revival/item/80 (accessed 17 July 2015).

35. Paul Rouse, 'Journalists and the Founding of the GAA', *Media History*, vol. 17, no. 2, 2011, pp. 117–32.

36. Paul Rouse, 'Michael Cusack: sportsman and journalist', in Cronin et al. (eds), *The Gaelic Athletic Association*, p. 54.

37. Mark Duncan, 'The Camera and the Gael: the early photography of the GAA, 1884–1914', in Cronin et al. (eds), *The Gaelic Athletic Association*, pp. 106–7.

38. Luke Gibbons, 'From Megalith to Megastore: broadcasting and Irish culture', in *Transformations in Irish Culture* (Cork: Cork University Press in association with Field Day, 1996), p. 73. See also Marcus de Burca, *The GAA: a history* (Dublin: Cumann Lúthchleas Gael, 1980), p. 217.

39. Raymond Boyle, 'From Our Gaelic Fields: radio, sport and nation in post-partition Ireland', *Media, Culture and Society*, vol. 14, no. 4, 1992, p. 623.

40. S.J. Connolly (ed.), *The Oxford Companion to Irish History* (Oxford: Oxford University Press, 1999), p. 471.

41. Hugh Oram, *The Newspaper Book: a history of newspapers in Ireland, 1649–1983* (Dublin: Mo Books, 1983), p. 173.

42. Boyle, 'From Our Gaelic Fields', pp. 624, 631.

43. Mike Cronin, Mark Duncan and Paul Rouse, 'Media', in *The GAA: a people's history* (Cork: Collins Press, 2009), pp. 177–207.

44. This increased focus on sport cinema is evident in a range of academic works including Howard Good, *Diamonds in the Dark: America, baseball, and the movie* (Lanham, MD: Scarecrow Press, 1996); Aaron Baker and Todd Boyd (eds), *Out of Bounds: sports, media, and the politics of identity* (Bloomington, IN: Indiana University Press, 1997); Stephen C. Wood and J. David Pincus (eds), *Reel Baseball: essays and interviews on the national pastime, Hollywood and American culture* (Jefferson, NC: McFarland & Co., 2003); Michael Oriard, *King Football: sport and spectacle in the golden age of radio and newsreels, movies and magazines, the weekly and the daily press* (Chapel Hill, NC: University of North Carolina Press, 2004); Richard C. King and David J. Leonard (eds), *Visual Economies of/in Motion: sport and film (cultural critique)* (Bern: Peter Lang Publishing, 2006); Dan Streible, *Fight Pictures: a history of boxing and early cinema* (Berkeley, CA: University of California Press, 2008); Ron Briley, Michael K. Schoenecke and Deborah A. Carmichael (eds), *All-Stars & Movie Stars: sports in film & history* (Lexington, KY: University Press of Kentucky, 2008); Emma Poulton and Martin Roderick (eds), *Sport in Films* (New York: Routledge, 2009); Zachary Ingle and David M. Sutera (eds), *Gender and Genre in Sports Documentaries: critical essays* (Lanham, MD: Scarecrow Press, 2013); Zachary Ingle and David M. Sutera (eds), *Identity and Myth in Sports Documentaries: critical essays* (Lanham, MD: Scarecrow Press, 2013).

45. There are a significant number of non-academic studies of sports cinema, including Claudio Garioni, *Fuori Campo: il cinema racconta lo sport* (Rome: Delos Digital, 2017); Julien Camy and Gérard Camy, *Sport & Cinéma* (Paris: Éditions du Bailli de Suffren, 2016); William Russo, *Great Sports Stories: the legendary films* (Philadelphia, PA: Xlibris Corporation, 2005); Randy Williams, *Sports Cinema – 100 Movies: the best of Hollywood's athletic heroes, losers, myths, & misfits* (Pompton Plains, NJ: Limelight Editions, 2006).

46. See for example Taylor Downing, *Olympia* (London: BFI Publishing, 1992); Hannah B. Schaub, *Riefenstahls* Olympia: *körperideale – ethische verantwortung oder freiheit des künstlers?* (München: Wilhelm Fink Verlag, 2003); and María Graciela Rodríguez, 'Behind Leni's Outlook: a perspective on the film *Olympia* (1938)', *International Review for the Sociology of Sport*, vol. 38, no. 1, 2003, pp. 109–16.

47. See for example Steve Neale, '*Chariots of Fire*, Images of Men', *Screen*, vol. 23, nos 3–4, 1982, pp. 47–53; Martyn Bowden, 'Jerusalem, Dover Beach, and Kings Cross: imagined places as metaphors of the British class struggle in *Chariots of Fire* and *The Loneliness of the Long-distance Runner*', in Stuart C. Aitken and Leo E. Zonn (eds), *Place, Power, Situation and Spectacle: geography of film* (Lanham, MD and London: Rowman & Littlefield Publishers, 1994), pp. 69–100; and Ellis Cashmore, '*Chariots of Fire*: bigotry, manhood and moral certitude in an age of individualism', *Sport in Society*, vol. 11, nos 2–3, 2008, pp. 159–73.

48. See for instance Annie Jouan-Westlund, 'L'imaginaire Populaire Franco-Américain dans *Les Triplettes de Belleville*', *French Review*, vol. 79, no. 6, 2006, pp. 1195–1205; F. Place-Verghnes, 'Douce France? *Les Triplettes de Belleville*, de Sylvain Chomet', in Pierre Floquet (ed.), *CinémAction: «CinémAnimationS»* (Paris: Corlet Publications, 2007), pp. 97–103; and B. McCann, '"If It's Not Disney, What Is It?" Traditional animation techniques in *Les Triplettes de Belleville*', *French Studies Bulletin*, no. 108, 2008, pp. 59–62.

49. Glen Jones, '"Down on the Floor and Give Me Ten Sit-ups": British sports feature film', *Film & History*, vol. 35, no. 2, 2005, pp. 29–40.

50. J. Romaguera i Ramió, *Presencia del Deporteen el Cine Español: un primer inventario* (Sevilla: Fundación Andalucía Olímpica y Consejo Superior de Deportes, 2003).

51. John Cunningham, 'Foci, Fradi and the "Golden Team"', in *Hungarian Cinema from Coffee House to Multiplex* (London: Wallflower, 2004), pp. 183–8.

52. Alan McDougall, 'Eyes on the Ball: screening football in East German cinema', *Studies in Eastern European Cinema*, vol. 8, no. 1, 2017, pp. 4–18.

53. Graeme Turner, 'Cultural Studies and Film', in John Hill and Pamela Church Gibson (eds), *Film Studies: critical approaches* (Oxford: Oxford University Press, 2000), pp. 196–7.

54. In Gaelic games a 'minor' team refers to teams of under-18-year-olds from the county or club concerned.

55. Anthony Quinn, 'Rare Footage Captures Vibrant Lost Era', *Tyrone Times*, 15 October 2012.

56. Croke, 'To Mr Michael Cusack'.

CHAPTER 1

1. Tom Gunning, 'The Cinema of Attraction', *Wide Angle*, vol. 8, no. 3, 1986, pp. 63–70.

2. Clegg, *The Man Who Stopped Time*, p. 137.

3. Streible, *Fight Pictures*, p. 73.

4. For further on this, see Denis Condon, 'Irish Audiences Watch Their First US Feature: the Corbett–Fitzsimmons fight (1897)', in Ruth Barton (ed.), *Screening Irish-America* (Dublin: Irish Academic Press, 2009), pp. 135–47.

5. Kevin Rockett, *Irish Film Censorship: a cultural journey from silent cinema to Internet pornography* (Dublin: Four Courts Press, 2004), pp. 31–5.

6. Robert Monks, *Cinema Ireland: a database of Irish films and filmmakers, 1896–1986* [CD-ROM] (Dublin: National Library of Ireland, 1996).

7. See Denis Condon, *Early Irish Film, 1895–1921* (Dublin: Irish Academic Press, 2008), p. 165, for further on this.

8. Ibid. p. 166.

9. Denis Condon, 'Watching Gaelic Games on Screen in 1913', https://earlyirishcinema.com/2013/09/22/watching-Gaelic-games-on-screen-in-1913 (accessed 10 August 2017).

10. Condon, *Early Irish Film*, p. 167.

11. 'Assembly Rooms, Cork: Munster Hurling Final', *Evening Echo*, 31 October 1912, p. 2. Quoted in Condon, 'Watching Gaelic Games on Screen in 1913'.

12. Condon, 'Watching Gaelic Games on Screen in 1913'.

13. 'Opera House: Kerry v Louth', *Cork Examiner*, 3 July 1913.

14. *Evening Echo*, 12 July 1913. Quoted in Condon, *Early Irish Film*, p. 165.

15. For further on this, see Eoghan Corry, *The History of Gaelic Football* (Dublin: Gill & Macmillan, 2010), p. 1.

16. For more, see Corry, *The History of Gaelic Football*, p. 103.

17. An earlier intervention on this topic is available in Seán Crosson, '"For the honour of old Knock-na-gow I must win": representing sport in *Knocknagow* (1918)', *Screening the Past*, no. 33, 2012, http://www.screeningthepast.com/2012/02/%E2%80%9Cfor-the-honour-of-old-knock-na-gow-i-must-win%E2%80%9D-representing-sport-in-knocknagow-1918 (accessed 27 September 2018).

18. Kevin Rockett with Emer Rockett, *Film Exhibition and Distribution in Ireland, 1909–2010* (Dublin: Four Courts Press, 2011), p. 22. See also Kevin Rockett, Luke Gibbons and John Hill, *Cinema and Ireland* (London: Routledge, 1988), p. 6.

19. Charles Kickham, *Knocknagow* (Dublin: Gill & Macmillan, 1979). Further references to this text appear as page numbers in brackets.

20. Rockett et al., *Cinema and Ireland*, p. 21.

21. See Anonymous, 'Knocknagow: filming of Kickham's famous novel', *Irish Limelight*, May 1917, p. 6, for further on the debate on the date of the novel's setting prior to the shooting of the film.

22. Ibid.

23. The Briens have already been evicted in the novel and their grim existence in a 'miserable hovel' (Kickham, p. 255) is returned to repeatedly during the story.

24. Nicholas Allen, 'Cinema, Empire and Transition', *Modernist Cultures*, vol. 5, no. 1, 2010, p. 68.

25. *The Bioscope*, 16 October 1919, p. 58. Document located in the Tiernan McBride Library (document 1 in *Knocknagow* folder), Irish Film Institute.

26. Anonymous, 'Knocknagow on the Film, a Picture Play that Will Create a Furore in America', *Anglo-Celt*, 2 March 1918, p. 14.

27. Anonymous, 'Great Irish Film Week', *Watchword of Labour*, 27 December 1919 [n.p.].

28. Cronin et al., *The GAA*, p. 19.

29. There is also a mention of a tiger hunt in India at one point in the book (Kickham, p. 591).

30. Although bull-baiting was outlawed in 1835 with the passing of the Cruelty to Animals Act in the British parliament, it would appear to have continued to be a part of the rural culture Kickham describes in the 1850s.

31. Ikuo Abe, 'A Study of the Chronology of the Modern Usage of 'Sportsmanship' in English, American and Japanese Dictionaries', *International Journal of the History of Sport*, vol. 5, no. 1, 1988, pp. 3, 24.

32. Howard L. Nixon II, *Sport and the American Dream* (Champaign, IL: Leisure Press/Human Kinetics, 1984), p. 13.

33. Cronin et al., *The GAA*, pp. 18–19.

34. Seamus J. King, *A History of Hurling* (Dublin: Gill & Macmillan, 2005), p. 26.

35. Diarmuid O'Flynn, *Hurling: the warrior game* (Cork: Collins Press, 2008), p. 309.

36. King, *A History of Hurling*, p. 33.

37. Johnny Watterson and Lindie Naughton, *Irish Olympians, 1896–1992* (Dublin: Blackwater Press, 1992), p. 21.

38. Mark Quinn, *The King of Spring: the life and times of Peter O'Connor* (Dublin: Liffey Press, 2004), p. 167.

39. For further on the 'Irish Whales', see Larry McCarthy, 'Irish Americans in Sport: the twentieth century', in Joseph Lee and Marion R. Casey (eds), *Making the Irish American: history and heritage of the Irish in the United States* (New York: NYU Press, 2006), pp. 457–74; Ralph C. Wilcox, 'The Shamrock and the Eagle: Irish Americans and sport in the nineteenth century', in George Eisen and David Kenneth Wiggins (eds), *Ethnicity and Sport in North American History and Culture* (Westport, CT: Praeger Publishers, 1995), pp. 55–74; and Watterson and Naughton, *Irish Olympians*, pp. 5–6, 22–3.

40. Quinn, *The King of Spring*, p. 167. The Intercalated Olympic Games were to be a series of International Olympic Games held in Athens midway through the four-year cycle of the modern Olympic Games. However, they were only held in 1906.

41. *Irish Independent*, 11 July 1912.

42. *Nenagh Guardian*, 3 August 1912.

43. Watterson and Naughton, *Irish Olympians*, pp. 21–2.

44. Liam O'Callaghan has also identified the importance, particularly since the 1990s, of the assertion – and largely invention – of local allegiances and identities for provincial rugby-union teams in Ireland. See Liam O'Callaghan, '"The Red Thread of History": the media, Munster rugby and the creation of a sporting tradition', *Media History*, special issue: 'Sport and the Media in Ireland', vol. 17, no. 2, 2011, pp. 175–88.

45. Anonymous, 'The Other Rackard', *Irish Independent*, 28 March 2009.

46. For further on this, see Seán Crosson, 'Community Games', https://www.rte.ie/eile/brainstorm/2017/1107/918120-community-games (accessed 15 November 2017).

47. Fintan O'Toole, 'Can the Queen Win Over Croke Park?', *Observer*, 8 May 2011.

49. 'Club Planning and Development', http://www.gaa.ie/page/club_planning_and_development.html (accessed 27 October 2007).

49. 'Administration', http://www.gaa.ie/about-the-gaa/mission-and-vision (accessed 28 March 2011).

CHAPTER 2

1. This chapter owes a considerable debt to the joint research I undertook on this topic with Dónal McAnallen and the co-authored essay '"Croke Park Goes Plumb Crazy": Pathé newsreels and Gaelic games', published in the special issue of *Media History* on 'Sport and the Media in Ireland', vol. 17, no. 2, 2011, pp. 161–76. I am grateful to Dónal for his extensive input into that work, which informs this chapter, in particular the pioneering primary research he has undertaken of the GAA's records, minutes and overall historical development.

2. Barry Sheppard, '"As a Gael Should Meet Gaels": the Gaelic Athletic Association in the Irish Free State', *Irish Story*, 21 August 2012, http://www.theirishstory.com/2012/08/21/as-a-gael-should-meet-gaels-the-Gaelic-athletic-association-in-the-irish-free-state/#.

UnfMLFPgzY3 (accessed 24 May 2017); see also G. Ó Tuathaigh, 'The GAA as a Force in Irish Society', in Cronin et al. (eds), *The Gaelic Athletic Association*, p. 240.

3. For further on this, see Tim Carey, *Croke Park: a history* (Cork: Collins Press, 2013).

4. For further on this development, see de Búrca, *The GAA*, pp. 136–7, 150–1; and Jack Mahon, *A History of Gaelic Football* (Dublin: Gill & Macmillan, 2000), p. 65.

5. Ciara Chambers, *Ireland in the Newsreels* (Dublin: Irish Academic Press, 2012), p. 81.

6. Michael Chanan, *The Dream that Kicks: the prehistory and early years of cinema in Britain* (London: Routledge, 1996), p. 32.

7. Chambers, *Ireland in the Newsreels*, p. 13.

8. Ibid., p. 14.

9. Ibid.

10. Nicholas Pronay, 'British Newsreels in the 1930s: audience and producers', *History*, no. 56, 1971, p. 416.

11. Chambers, *Ireland in the Newsreels*, p. 110.

12. Fred Watts, 'Just "PIC and EVE"' (1928), quoted in Jenny Hammerton, *For Ladies Only? Eve's Film Review: Pathé Cinemagazine* (Hastings: The Projection Box, 2001), p. 117.

13. 'Objection to Films', *Irish Independent*, 6 August 1932; 'Action in Sligo', *Irish Independent*, 24 August 1932.

14. Uinseann Mac Eoin, *The IRA in the Twilight Years, 1923–1948* (Dublin: Argenta Publications, 1997), pp. 228–9.

15. 'Action in Sligo', *Irish Independent*, 24 August 1932.

16. Kevin Rockett, 'Film Censorship and the State', *Film Directions*, vol. 3, no. 9, 1980, p. 11.

17. Warning given by the Council of Irish Bishops at Maynooth in 1927, cited in J.H. Whyte, *Church and State in Modern Ireland* (Dublin: Gill & Macmillan, 1971), p. 27.

18. Rockett, *Irish Film Censorship*, p. 87.

19. Rockett et al., *Cinema and Ireland*, p. 6. Indeed, Rockett has identified a 'second Irish cinema building boom' as taking place between 1929 and 1939 (Rockett with Rockett, *Film Exhibition and Distribution in Ireland*, pp. 72–83).

20. T.J. Beere, 'Cinema Statistics in Saorstát Éireann', *Journal of the Statistical and Social Enquiry Society of Ireland*, no. 156, 1935/36, p. 85.

21. Ibid. p. 84.

22. Mark Tierney, *Modern Ireland* (Dublin: Gill & Macmillan, 1978), p. 201; Joseph Lee, *Ireland, 1912–1985: politics and society* (Cambridge: Cambridge University Press, 1989), pp. 184–201; Rockett with Rockett, *Film Exhibition and Distribution in Ireland*, p. 86.

23. Ciara Chambers in Episode One, *Éire na Nuachtscannán* (LM DÓC & TG4, 2017).

24. Mike Huggins, 'Projecting the Visual: British newsreels, soccer and popular culture, 1918–1939', *International Journal of the History of Sport*, vol. 24, no. 1, January 2007, p. 84.

25. See for example *Connacht Tribune*, 28 November 1931, where a notice is included for a screening of a Galway v London Gaelic football match at the Empire Theatre in Galway city.

26. This information is taken from a personal email communication with film historian Luke McKernan, 26 April 2007.

27. Linda Kaye's comments were made in Episode One, *Éire na Nuachtscannán* (LM DÓC & TG4, 2017).

28. For further on this issue, see ibid.

29. Chambers, *Ireland in the Newsreels*, pp. 138–9.

30. See Ulster GAA secretary's report for 1936, cited in minutes of GAA annual congress 1937, for criticism of the 'undue exploiting of occasional unseemly incidents at matches'.

31. *Daily Mail*, 3 October 1921.

32. See Seán McKeown, unpublished autobiography, Linen Hall Library, Belfast, pp. 112–13; and GAA annual congress minutes, 9 April 1939, for moves to control the reporting of Gaelic games in the British press.

33. 'Foreign Games in the Colleges', *Irish Times*, 26 April 1930.

34. Ibid. Dermot McMurrough was a twelfth-century king of Leinster who famously solicited help from the King of England, Henry II, and has long been accused of bringing the first English invaders into Ireland.

35. Seán McKeown, unpublished autobiography, pp. 112–13.

36. GAA annual congress minutes, 9 April 1939.

37. Ibid. In 1934, the recently established Belfast office of the BBC initially broadcast results of Gaelic games. However, these broadcasts were discontinued after protests from unionist listeners, including the then prime minister of Northern Ireland, James Craig. See Rex Cathcart, *The Most Contrary Region: the BBC in Northern Ireland, 1924–1984* (Belfast: Blackstaff Press, 1984), pp. 66–7.

38. Seán Ó Ceallacháin, *Seán Óg: his own story* (Dublin and London: Brophy Books, 1988), p. 213. The GAA and the radio authorities also disagreed repeatedly over the choice of commentators in the 1930s (Ó Ceallacháin, *Seán Óg*, pp. 221–2).

39. Central Council minutes, meeting of 25 June 1938; de Búrca, *The GAA*, pp. 172–3. See also the report of the Ulster GAA secretary for 1934 (contained in minutes of annual congress, 1935) in which criticism is evident of the prominence in newspapers of 'games alien to the soil … It seems a pity that our Dailies were not more concerned with the glory of Ireland within than seeking sensationalism from abroad.'

40. *Derry Journal*, 11 March 1921.

41. 'Reorganisation Meeting Under the Auspices of the Ulster Council, GAA, in Letterkenny', *Frontier Sentinel*, 19 December 1931.

42. 'Rank and File GAA Members', *Fermanagh Herald*, 22 April 1939.

43. Gael, 'Observer', *Fermanagh Herald*, 29 April 1939.

44. Miontuairiscí, An Chomhdháil Bhliantúil 1940; Central Council minutes, 27 April 1940.

45. *An Phoblacht*, 26 March 1932.

46. *Irish Independent*, 25 January 1937.

47. *Derry People*, 14 February 1936.

48. Ibid., 18 March 1933.

49. *Irish News*, 15 November 1927.

50. *Derry Journal*, 12 October 1934.

51. Letter from Aodh MacGabhann, Cavan GAA secretary, to county football team members, 2 October 1937, Cardinal Tomás Ó Fiaich Library & Archive.

52. GAA annual congress minutes, 20 April 1930.

53. Ibid.

54. *An Phoblacht*, 26 March 1932.

55. 'Gaelic Games Congress: good progress reported, some criticism of Ulster', *Irish Times*, 17 April 1933.

56. Ibid.

57. 'GAA Rulers Sit in Council', *Irish Press*, 17 April 1933.

58. GAA annual congress minutes, 21 April 1935.

59. Ibid.

60. Ibid.

61. Ibid.

62. The figure also includes some newsreel reports of non-competitive swims in Dublin, including swims on Christmas Day and New Year's Day.

63. Pathé also filmed Irish sports teams playing in other countries, particularly games featuring the Irish rugby team, but these are not featured in this survey.

64. Crosson and McAnallen, '"Croke Park Goes Plumb Crazy"', p. 163.

65. Personal email communication, 26 April 2007.

66. Ibid.

67. 'Ireland's National Game. And No Game for Weaklings! "Blackrock" Defeat "Redmonds" in Final of Hurling Championship, in which Both Sides Played "to the Last Ounce"', Pathé Gazette, 8 December 1927.

68. 'Hurling Final at Killarney', Pathé Gazette, 9 September 1937.

69. 'Gaelic Football at Dungannon', Gaumont Graphic, 15 May 1929.

70. For further on this issue, see Dónal McAnallen's contribution to Episode Five of the documentary series *Éire na Nuachtscannán* (LM DÓC & TG4, 2017).

71. 'Training for the Tailteann Games', Pathé Gazette, 24 April 1922.

72. See Huggins, 'Projecting the Visual', pp. 96–7, for a consideration of the support of newsreels of Association football in Britain for the prevailing status quo in British life.

73. 'Commandant McKeon Starts Game Between Dublin and Leix at Croke Park, Ireland', Pathé Gazette, 1 October 1921.

74. 'Ireland Has Racing Despite Its Little "War"! Government Yields to Public Pressure and "Daily Express" Campaign and Grants – One Day!', Pathé Gazette, 21 November 1921.

75. The fact that a ceasefire had been agreed the previous July may have also contributed to this description.

76. 'Rebel Spoil Sports Defied. Mr Tim Healy (Governor General) and Mr Cosgrave (President) Attend Punchestown Races', Pathé Gazette, 19 April 1923.

77. Huggins, 'Projecting the Visual', p. 93.

78. See, for example, 'To Fight Again – All-Ireland Hurling Final Ends in Draw at Croke Park, Dublin', Pathé Gazette, 5 September 1934, for Archbishop Harty of Cashel throwing in the ball; cf. letter from Harty to Pádraig Ó Caoimh, Ard-Rúnaí Cumann Lúthchleas Gael (GAA), 24 August 1934, in GAA Central Council minutes, meeting of 1 September 1934. See also 'Football Final in Dublin – Galway Defeat Dublin in Hard Fought Battle at Croke Park', Pathé Gazette, 27 September 1934.

79. 'Hurling Final at Killarney', Pathé Gazette, 9 September 1937.

80. Huggins, 'Projecting the Visual', p. 82.

81. 'Gaelic Football – Kerry Defeat Kildare by 9 Points to 2 at Croke Park', Pathé Gazette, 20 October 1930. A further relevant example of a political protest captured by a newsreel at a major Gaelic game was revealed to me in a personal interview with Mattie Gilsenan (19 July 2008), the captain of the first Meath Gaelic-football team to reach an All-Ireland final in 1939. Following a viewing of the British Movietone footage of this All-Ireland ('Irish Football Final: Kerry v Meath – No Sound', British Movietone News, 26 September 1939), Gilsenan revealed that the banner being carried during the parade of teams preceding the game was an IRA protest.

82. 'Kilkenny Wins All-Ireland Hurling Final at Croke Park Before a Record Crowd', Pathé Gazette, 20 September 1923.

83. 'Enormous Crowds Watch Dublin Defeat Kerry in All-Ireland Football Final', Pathé Gazette, 9 October 1924.

84. 'Ireland's National Game – Record Crowd See Cork Defeat Kilkenny in All-Ireland Hurling Final', Pathé Gazette, 1 November 1926; 'Ireland's National Game – Enormous Crowd See Dublin Beat Cork by 20 Points to 6 in "Fast and Furious" All-Ireland Hurling Final', Pathé Gazette, 11 September 1927; 'Ireland's National Game – And No Game for Weaklings!'. Pathé Gazette, 8 December 1927.

85. Further information on John Gordon Lewis and his work is available on the British Universities Film & Video Council website: http://bufvc.ac.uk/newsonscreen/search/index.php/person/544 (accessed 3 September 2018).

86. 'Dublin – Irish Hurling Year', Pathé Gazette, 1930–39; the All-Ireland hurling final featured between Limerick and Kilkenny took place on 6 September 1936.

87. 'Cavan Defeat Kildare – Exclusive Pictures of All-Ireland Football Final at Croke Park', Pathé Gazette, 26 September 1935.

88. 'Gaelic Football in New York', Pathé Gazette, 28 May 1939.

89. 'All Ireland Football Final', Pathé Gazette, 21 October 1937.

90. 'All-Ireland Football Final at Croke Park, Dublin', Pathé Gazette, 1 October 1936.

91. This information was given in a personal interview on 19 July 2008 with Mattie Gilsenan, captain of Meath's All-Ireland football final team of 1939, who remembers watching the newsreel footage of the game afterwards, with a local individual providing live commentary on the images.

92. 'Cavan Defeat Kildare', Pathé Gazette, 26 September 1935.

93. 'Dublin – Irish Hurling Year', Pathé Gazette, 1930–39.

94. '60,000 at Croke Park', Irish Press, 27 September 1937.

95. J.J. Barrett, In the Name of the Game (Dublin: Dub Press, 1997), p. 658; cf. 'Enormous Crowds Watch Dublin Defeat Kerry', Pathé Gazette, 9 October 1924.

96. Michael O'Hehir, *My Life and Times* (Dublin: Blackwater Press, 1996), pp. 7–8; cf. 'All Ireland Football Final Replay', Pathé Gazette, 27 October 1938.

97. Pathé Gazette, 8 December 1927.

98. 'To Fight Again', Pathé Gazette, 5 September 1934.

99. 'All-Ireland Hurling Final', Pathé Gazette, 8 September 1938.

100. See for example cataloguer's notes for 'All Ireland Hurling Final', Pathé Gazette, 8 September 1938, and 'To Fight Again', Pathé Gazette, 5 September 1934.

101. Peter Martin, *Censorship in the Two Irelands, 1922–1939* (Dublin: Irish Academic Press, 2006), pp. 165–6.

102. 'Kerry and Cavan Play Gaelic Football and Live to Fight Again', British Movietone News, 30 September 1937.

103. 'De Valera Attends Irish Games', British Movietone News, 9 July 1936.

104. 'Sport – Irish Hurling', British Movietone News, 12 November 1951.

105. 'Gaelic Football in America', Gaumont British News, 6 June 1938. Quoted in Chambers, *Ireland in the Newsreels*, p. 138.

106. Huggins, 'Projecting the Visual', p. 90.

107. 'All Ireland Football Final', Pathé Gazette, 30 September 1937.

108. 'Cavan Defeat Kildare', Pathé Gazette, 26 September 1935.

109. Nicholas Pronay, 'The Newsreels: the illusion of actuality', in Paul Smith (ed.), *The Historian and Film* (Cambridge: Cambridge University Press, 1976), p. 98.

110. 'Gaelic Football – Galway v Cork at Terenure', Pathé Gazette, 17 January 1924.

111. Oriard, *King Football*.

112. Huggins, 'Projecting the Visual', pp. 80–102.

113. Oriard, *King Football*, p. xi.

114. Andy Watters and Neil Loughran, *The Little Book of Gaelic Football* (Stroud, UK: History Press, 2014), p. 15.

115. 'Gaelic Football – Colour', British Movietone News, 31 October 1976, https://www.youtube.com/watch?v=qeJg_e6cjkI (accessed 15 November 2017).

CHAPTER 3

1. Ronald L. Davis, *John Ford: Hollywood's old master* (Norman, OK: University of Oklahoma Press, 1995), p. 25.

2. Ibid.

3. Ibid.

4. Ibid., p. 26.

5. Joseph McBride, *Searching for John Ford* (New York: St Martin's Press, 2001), p. 61.

6. Davis, *John Ford*, p. 26.

7. Martin McLoone, *Irish Film: the emergence of a contemporary cinema* (London: British Film Institute, 2000), p. 48.

8. John Urry, *The Tourist Gaze* (London: Sage, 2001), pp. 1–2.

9. V.Y. Mudimbe, *The Idea of Africa* (Bloomington and Indianapolis, IN: Indiana University Press, 1994), p. 6.

10. Urry, *The Tourist Gaze*, p. 3.

11. Jonathan Culler, 'Semiotics of Tourism', *American Journal of Semiotics*, vol. 1, no. 1, 1981, p.127.

12. John Arundel and Maurice Roche, 'Media Sport and Local Identity: British rugby league and Sky TV', in Maurice Roche (ed.), *Sport, Popular Culture and Identity* (Oxford: Meyer & Meyer, 2000), p. 84.

13. Gerry Smyth, *Space and the Irish Cultural Imagination* (Basingstoke and New York: Palgrave, 2001), p. 35. See also Dean MacCannell, *The Tourist: a new theory of the leisure class* (London: Macmillan, 1976), for a discussion on the importance of 'the search for the authentic' among tourists.

14. Rockett et al., *Cinema and Ireland*, p. xii.

15. For further on this, see Luke Gibbons, 'Romanticism, Realism and Irish Cinema', in Rockett et al., *Cinema and Ireland*, pp. 194–257.

16. An earlier intervention on this topic is available in Seán Crosson, '"Shillalah Swing Time … You'll Thrill Each Time a Wild Irishman's Skull Shatters": representing hurling in American cinema, 1930–1960', in Ruth Barton (ed.), *Screening Irish-America: representing Irish-America in film and television* (Dublin: Irish Academic Press, 2009), pp. 148–64.

17. Fox Movietone and Pathé both covered the 1936 challenge game between All-Ireland hurling champions Limerick and New York as well as several other visits by Irish teams to the US. See for example 'Hurling Match – Limerick Wins in New York', Pathé Gazette, 4 June 1936, and 'Gaelic Football in New York', British Movietone News, 6 June 1938.

18. John Lewis, 'Who Was Ted Husing?', http://www.tedhusing.net/Ted_Husing/Who_Was_Ted_Husing/Who_Was_Ted_Husing.html (accessed 10 May 2016).

19. This was not Husing's last association with hurling; in 1940 he provided the narration for the Paramount short *Grantland Rice Sportlight: the sporting Irish* directed by Jack Eaton, a film that features a range of Irish sports, including street bowling and fox hunting before climaxing with footage from the 1938 All-Ireland hurling final at Croke Park between Dublin and Waterford.

20. 'Warner Bros. Short Subjects', *AAP Catalog* (New York: Associated Artists Productions Corp., 1957), pp. 51–2.

21. For further information on Martin Kennedy, see http://web.archive.org/web/20080808182045/http://www.premierview.ie/martin_kennedy.html (accessed 3 September 2018).

22. See for example the *Meath Chronicle*, 21 February 1931; 14 March 1931, p. 4.

23. Richard Ward, 'Extra Added Attractions: the short subjects of MGM, Warner Brothers and Universal', *Media History*, vol. 9, no. 3, 2003, p. 226.

24. Gael, 'A Gross Libel', *Fermanagh Herald*, 18 February 1939.

25. The exact date is unclear as records of shorts exhibited are few and little coverage was given to them in the media. However, according to the Irish censor's (James Montgomery) notes in the *Record of Films Censored* (no. 12367), held in the National Archives of Ireland, *Hurling* was censored on 12 November 1937 and an *Irish Press* report from February 1938

indicated that the film had 'recently been shown' (Anonymous, 'Unfairly Treated, GAA Discussion on Land Commission and Playing Fields', *Irish Press*, 14 February 1938).

26. Minutes of the meeting of the Central Council of the GAA, held at Croke House on 12 February 1938, at 8.30 p.m. at which Mr R. O'Keeffe presided. Minutes held in the Gaelic Museum, Dublin. I want to acknowledge the assistance of Dónal McAnallen in finding information, including these minutes, relating to the reaction of the GAA to this film. A report of the Central Council meeting is also given in Anonymous, 'Unfairly Treated', p. 10.

27. Notes provided in film-censor's records, no. 12367. The film was censored on 12 November 1937 and the notes indicated that GAA representatives met with a representative of MGM on 11 March 1938 concerning the film.

28. *Connaught Tribune* special correspondent, 'Our American Letter, Ireland's Ancient Game, Hurling Film to be Made', *Connaught Tribune*, 1 August, 1936.

29. Ward, 'Extra Added Attractions', p. 225. Even the pioneering British documentarist John Grierson commented on 'the very frequent beauty and very great skill of exposition … in the sports shorts from Metro-Goldwyn-Mayer' which have brought 'the popular lecture to a pitch undreamed of, and even impossible in the days of the magic lantern' (John Grierson, 'First Principles of Documentary' (1932), in Catherine Fowler (ed.), *The European Cinema Reader* (London and New York: Routledge, 2002), p. 40).

30. Publicity sheet with the author. I want to acknowledge the kind assistance of collector Paul Balbirnie in supplying me with a copy of it.

31. I realise that this sport is more commonly referred to as lacrosse today, but this is the spelling given on the publicity sheet.

32. Publicity sheet kindly provided to the author by collector Paul Balbirnie.

33. Anonymous, 'Unfairly Treated'.

34. Ibid.; minutes of the meeting of the Central Council of the GAA, held at Croke House on 12 February 1938.

35. Stephanie Rains, *The Irish-American in Popular Culture (1945–2000)* (Dublin: Irish Academic Press, 2007), p. 150.

36. McLoone, *Irish Film*, pp. 44–59.

37. Appadurai is describing here the process through which the old stabilities of place and people are more and more 'shot through with … the woof of human motion, as more persons and groups deal with the realities of having to move, or fantasies of wanting to move'. Arjun Appadurai, *Modernity at Large* (Minneapolis: University of Minnesota Press, 1996), p. 33.

38. Ibid., p. 49.

39. Beth Zdriluk, '"My Favorite Mask Is Myself": presentation, illusion and the performativity of identity in Wellesian performance', *Film Journal*, vol. 1, no. 9, 2004, http://web.archive.org/web/20040821014301/http://www.thefilmjournal.com/issue9/wellesperformance.html (accessed 15 April 2017).

40. See McBride, *Searching for John Ford*, pp. 577–8.

41. Luke Gibbons, *The Quiet Man* (Cork: Cork University Press, 2002), p. 91.

42. *Irish Times* reporter, 'Tourist Industry Has Prospects of Record Year', *Irish Times*, 14 July 1956.

43. Anonymous, 'Justin B. Herman Dead at 76; writer and producer of films', *New York Times*, 10 December 1983, http://query.nytimes.com/gst/fullpage.html?res=9C04E3DE1638F933A25751C1A965948260&sec=&pagewanted=print (accessed 10 June 2014).

44. Even though the film was described in the press on its release as a 'documentary', the subject matter itself is clearly fictionalised, as the above narrative summary indicates.

45. Barry trained fourteen Cork teams (thirteen in hurling and one in football (1946)) and one Limerick hurling team (1934) to All-Ireland victory between 1926 and 1966. See Jim Cronin, 'Jim Barry', in *Making Connections: a Cork GAA miscellany* (Cork: Cork County Board, 2005), pp. 55–63.

46. This information was kindly supplied to the author in an interview with Jimmy Brohan, one of the Cork players depicted in the film.

47. Anonymous, 'First Showing of Two Films About Ireland', *Irish Times*, 19 July 1956.

48. Anonymous, 'Film and the Irish Tourist Industry', *Irish Independent*, 19 July 1956.

49. Benedict Kiely, 'The Tourists and the Screen', *Irish Press*, 23 July 1956.

50. The elite level of Gaelic games is represented by senior county players in both hurling and Gaelic football.

51. The Cinema Correspondent, 'The Business Jungle', *Irish Times*, 23 July 1956.

52. Smyth, *Space and the Irish Cultural Imagination*, pp. 36–7. Smyth is quoting from Joep Leerssen, *Remembrance and Imagination: patterns in the historical and literary representation of Ireland in the nineteenth century* (Cork: Cork University Press, 1996), p. 226.

53. McBride, *Searching for John Ford*, pp. 577–8.

54. *Irish Independent*, 1 May 1956. See also *Irish Press*, 1 May 1956.

55. Anonymous, *Irish Independent*, 2 May 1956. See also *Irish Press*, 2 May 1956.

56. *Irish Times*, 4 May 1956.

57. Ibid.

58. Myles na Gopaleen, 'GAATHLETES', *Irish Times*, 18 May 1956.

59. Myles na Gopaleen, 'Ford-Proconsul', *Irish Times*, 14 May 1956.

60. I want to thank Charles Barr for bringing this collection to my attention and providing me with copies of materials from it, including this cartoon.

61. Anita Sharp-Bolster, 'Shamrocks and Moons', *Irish Independent*, 30 April 1957.

62. Anonymous, 'Mystery Abbey Extra Was – John Ford!', *Evening Press*, 8 May 1956. Included in the Lord Killanin Collection in the Irish Film Institute.

63. The name Flann O'Brien was itself a pseudonym for the author, born Brian Ó Núalláin in 1911 in County Tyrone.

64. Tag Gallagher, *John Ford: the man and his films* (Berkeley, CA: University of California Press, 1986), p. 543.

65. Lewis Coser, *The Functions of Social Conflict* (Glencoe, IL: Free Press, 1956).

66. John Hill, 'The Quiet Man: Ford mythology and Ireland', in Seán Crosson and Rod Stoneman (eds), *The Quiet Man ... and Beyond: reflections on a classic film, John Ford, and Ireland* (Dublin: Liffey Press, 2009), pp. 191–2.

67. Dean MacCannell, 'Staged Authenticity: arrangements of social space in tourist settings', *American Journal of Sociology*, vol. 79, no. 3, 1973, p. 595.

68. Anonymous, 'Dublin Letter: too much "blarney"', *Cork Examiner*, 19 July 1956.

69. McLoone, *Irish Film*, pp. 44–59.

70. Quotation taken from narration of *Foreign Sports in the US*, New York: Motion Picture Section, New York Field Office, 1959.

CHAPTER 4

1. Rockett with Rockett, *Film Exhibition and Distribution in Ireland*, pp. 147–8.

2. See for example the *Cork Examiner*, 19 April 1958.

3. Sandra Brennan, 'George Pollock', *New York Times*, All Movie Guide, http://movies2.nytimes.com/gst/movies/filmography.html?p_id=106786 (accessed 26 August 2015).

4. Brown, incidentally, has a rather intriguing connection with Irish cinema, including *The Quiet Man*. He was the first husband of Maureen O'Hara, who, though not at all interested in Brown, married him, her autobiography suggests, to stop him hassling her to do so, a rather novel approach to rejecting a potential suitor. The marriage was never consummated and was quickly annulled when O'Hara's mother found out. See Maureen O'Hara with John Nicoletti, *'Tis Herself: a memoir* (London: Simon & Schuster/Townhouse, 2004), pp. 27–9, 33–4.

5. Kevin Rockett, 'A State Called Irish National Cinema', Projecting the Nation: National Cinema in an International Frame Conference, Irish Film Centre, Dublin, 16 November 1996.

6. Kevin Rockett, 'An Irish Film Studio', in *Cinema and Ireland* (London: Routledge, 1988), p. 107. He is summarising the remarks of L. MacG, 'No Disgrace to Our Touchy Temperaments', *Sunday Review*, 15 March 1959.

7. 'Ireland's First Film Studio', *Irish Press*, 13 March 1958.

8. 'Room for Irish Film Industry', *Irish Times*, 14 March 1958.

9. Eamonn Sweeney, *Breaking Ball* (Motive Television for RTÉ, 2000–06), script kindly provided to the author by Cormac Hargaden, producer of the RTÉ series.

10. Seán Moran, 'Waterford Associated with Celebrities', *Irish Times*, 19 August 2008.

11. 'Three Days of Heaven', *Cork Examiner*, 20 November 1957.

12. 'Film Stars at Mansion House', *Irish Press*, 10 October 1957.

13. An Fear Rua, 'Rooney: "The Darlin' of the Lay-ay-dees"', 1 January 2000, http://www.anfearrua.com/viewdoc.aspx?id=156 (accessed 10 March 2015).

14. Ibid.

15. David Rowe, 'If You Film It, Will They Come? Sports on film', *Journal of Sport & Social Issues*, vol. 22, no. 4, 1998, p. 355.

16. For further on the Alf Tupper character, see Jeffrey Hill, '"I Like to Have a Go at the Swanks": Alf Tupper and English society, 1945–1990', in Philip Dine and Seán Crosson (eds), *Sport, Representation, and Evolving Identities in Europe* (Bern: Peter Lang Publishing, 2010), pp. 79–100.

17. 'Marathon Hurling', *Strabane Chronicle*, 21 September 1957.

18. 'Six Hour Hurling "Final" at Croke Park', *Irish Independent*, 9 September 1957.

19. 'Kilkenny Arts Festival', *Waterford Today*, 8 August 2007, http://www.waterford-today.ie/index.php?option=com_content&task=view&id=962&Itemid=10172&ed=75 (accessed 26 August 2016).

20. 'President Attends Film Showing', *Irish Times*, 14 March 1958.

21. 'This Week's Films', *Cork Examiner*, 7 April 1958.

22. John D. Hickey, 'Kilkenny's 14th Win Was Unforgettable', *Irish Independent*, 2 September 1957.

23. Bosley Crowther, 'Screen: Irish comedy; John Gregson starred in Sutton's "Rooney"', *New York Times*, 6 June 1958, http://www.nytimes.com/movie/review?res=9903E1D71F3AEF34BC4E53DFB0668383649EDE (accessed 15 January 2015).

24. Our Film Critic, 'This Dublin Scene Is No Travesty', *Irish Independent*, 17 March 1958.

25. Benedict Kiely, 'Cameras on Croke Park', *Irish Press*, 17 March 1958.

CHAPTER 5

1. I want to acknowledge the generous support of the staff of the Irish Film Archive, including Kasandra O'Connell, Sunniva O'Flynn and Rebecca Grant, in the completion of this chapter, including the archive's permission to use screencaps from their films and records featured here. I also want to thank Bill Morrison, former senior publicity officer with Bord Fáilte, and Professor Mike Cronin, academic director, Boston College Ireland, for information provided regarding Bord Fáilte and Aer Lingus. Aspects of this chapter appeared previously in Seán Crosson, '"Ar Son an Náisiúin": the National Film Institute of Ireland's All-Ireland films', *Éire-Ireland*, special issue on Irish sport, vol. 48, nos 1 & 2, 2013, pp. 193–212.

2. Pope Pius XI, 'Vigilanti Cura: encyclical letter of Pope Pius Xi on the motion picture', The Holy See, http://www.vatican.va/holy_father/pius_xi/encyclicals/documents/hf_p-xi_enc_29061936_vigilanti-cura_en.html (accessed 10 May 2015).

3. Ruth Barton, *Irish National Cinema* (London: Routledge, 2004), p. 67.

4. John Grierson, 'A Film Policy for Ireland', *Studies: an Irish quarterly review*, vol. 37, no. 147, September 1948, p. 283.

5. Ibid., p. 288.

6. Ibid., p. 285.

7. Ibid., p. 289.

8. Ibid., p. 283.

9. 'All Ireland Final Film', *Tuam Herald*, 3 November 1956.

10. In 1999, a panel of GAA past presidents and journalists selected what they regarded as the greatest hurling and football players since the foundation of the association in the GAA hurling and football teams of the millennium.

11. See for example 'Competitions for Sixty Juvenile Hurling Teams', *Kerryman*, 27 March 1965, for a report on the use of the NFI All-Ireland-final films for instructional purposes in county Kerry.

12. 'Official Bulletin Reports Progress of Hurling Drive', *Irish Independent*, 2 March 1965.

13. 'Competitions for Sixty Juvenile Hurling Teams', *Kerryman*, 27 March 1965.

14. G.J. McCanny, letter to Mr Prenderville, Gaelic Athletic Association, 5 October 1977. Irish Film Institute (IFI), item number 16245, box 317.

15. G.J. McCanny, draft letter to Mr M. de Prionnbhiol, Gaelic Athletic Association, 25 July 1975. IFI, item number 16256, box 317.

16. These details were given by Seán O'Sullivan in the documentary series *Memories in Focus* (Peter Canning, *Memories in Focus* (Dublin: RTÉ, 1995)).

17. Robert Monks, personal interview, 17 April 2008.

18. 'Gaelic Fields and Forum', *Meath Chronicle*, 9 October 1954.

19. 'All Ireland Final Film', *Tuam Herald*, 3 November 1956.

20. 'Final Crowd May Be a Record', *Irish Independent*, 23 September 1960.

21. 'London Calling', *Irish Independent*, 27 October 1961; G.J. McCanny, draft letter to Mr Ó Síocháin, Gaelic Athletic Association, 8 August 1969. IFI, item number 16267, box 317; Tom Hyde (National Film Institute), letter to unknown recipient, 24 October 1967. IFI, item number 16292, box 317.

22. 'Rome Showing for Irish Films', *Irish Press*, 21 July 1960.

23. Mick Dunne, 'US Viewers to See Hurling', *Irish Press*, 14 July 1964.

24. 'Croke Park Can Hold 76,000 for Final', *Irish Independent*, 20 September 1957; Kenneth Wolstenholme, 'Why Keep This Great Game Such a Big Secret?', *Sunday Press*, 13 September 1959.

25. 'Italian Award for Film of GAA Matches', *Irish Independent*, 7 March 1956; 'People and Places', *Irish Press*, 9 January 1961.

26. Minutes of Finance and General Purposes Committee Meeting, National Film Institute of Ireland, 3 January 1958. Irish Film Institute.

27. Louis Marcus, letter to Luke Dodd, head of Irish Film Archive, 14 October 1998. IFI, ARC 52; Monks, personal interview, 17 April 2008.

28. Peter Canning, *Memories in Focus* (Dublin: RTÉ, 1995); Patrick J. Cummins, *"Emergency" Air Accidents – South-East Ireland, 1940–1945* (Waterford: Aviation History Ireland, 2003), p. 45.

29. Harvey O'Brien, *The Real Ireland: the evolution of Ireland in documentary film* (Manchester: Manchester University Press, 2004), p. 79.

30. Canning, *Memories in Focus*.

31. O'Brien, *The Real Ireland*, p. 79.

32. Brian McIlroy, 'Interview with George Fleischmann', in *Irish Cinema: an illustrated history* (Dublin: Anna Livia Press, 1988), pp. 109–10.

33. Larry Hartenian, 'The Role of Media in Democratizing Germany: United States occupation policy, 1945–1949', *Central European History*, vol. 20, no. 2, June 1987, p. 184.

34. Boyle, 'From Our Gaelic Fields, pp. 623–36.

35. Richard D. Mandell, *The Nazi Olympics* (Urbana, IL: University of Illinois Press, 1987).

36. Taylor Downing, *Olympia* (London: BFI, 1992), p. 30.

37. Kissing the bishop's ring was a traditional ceremonial practice within the Catholic Church to indicate reverence to the bishop concerned.

38. Huggins, 'Projecting the Visual', pp. 96–7.

39. Crosson and McAnallen, '"Croke Park Goes Plumb Crazy"'.

40. Eoghan Corry, *The GAA Book of Lists* (Dublin: Hodder Headline Ireland, 2005), pp. 371–412.

41. King, *A History of Hurling*, p. 125.

42. Breandán Ó hEithir, *Over the Bar* (Dublin: Poolbeg, 1991), p. 140.

43. King, *A History of Hurling*, p. 125.

44. 'Galway Board's Statement', *Irish Independent*, 16 September 1953.

45. As George Petrie noted, 'the aisling poems used the "guise of a love-song put on to conceal treason"' (George Petrie, *The Ancient Music of Ireland* (Dublin: M.H. Gill, 1855), p. 37).

46. Hill 16 was not constructed from the ruins of the 1916 Rising; it was known originally as Hill 60 in remembrance of a First World War encounter at Gallipoli but was renamed after the 1916 Rising.

47. Seán Ó Síocháin, Letter to Desmond Hand, National Film Institute, 12 August 1965. IFI, item number 16280, box number 317.

48. J.J. O'Brien, Letter to Tom Hyde, National Film Institute, 30 August 1968. IFI, item number 16283, box number 317.

49. McCanny, draft letter to Mr Ó Síocháin, 8 August 1969.

50. Tom Hyde, Letter to J.J. O'Brien, General Film Distributors Ltd, 5 September 1968. IFI, item number 16283, box number 317.

51. Bill Morrison, 'Re. Bord Fáilte's Use of the National Film Institute's All-Ireland Films', email to Seán Crosson, 12 April 2012; Mike Cronin, 'Re. Aer Lingus Screening of National Film Institute's All-Ireland Films', email to Seán Crosson, 11 April 2012.

52. Terence Brown, *Ireland: a social and cultural history, 1922–2002* (London: Harper Perennial, 2004), pp. 199–226.

53. Dick Hogan, 'Emigration Study Reverses the Perspective', *Irish Times*, 1 February 2000.

54. Corry, *The GAA Book of Lists*, pp. 371–412.

CHAPTER 6

1. For further on this, see B. Mairéad Pratschke, 'A Look at Irish-Ireland: Gael Linn's 'Amharc Éireann' films, 1956–64', *New Hibernia Review*, vol. 9, no. 3, 2005, pp. 17–38.

2. '1950–1959', http://www.gael-linn.ie/default.aspx?treeid=256 (accessed 15 March 2016).

3. For a notice for a game between Leitrim and Roscommon in the Gael Linn senior football tournament, see the *Leitrim Observer*, 18 September 1965.

4. O'Brien, *The Real Ireland*, p. 105.

5. Anonymous, 'Thoughts and Tidings: Gael Linn film', *Derry People*, 8 September 1956.

6. This was confirmed to me by Máire Harris of Gael Linn, phone conversation on 21 April 2015.

7. Huggins, 'Projecting the Visual', pp. 96–7.

8. For further on these protests against the turnover tax by women, see Donal Fallon, 'Dublin Women Take to the Streets, 1963', *Come Here To Me! Dublin life & culture*, 10 June 2012, https://comeheretome.com/2012/06/10/dublin-women-take-to-the-streets-1963 (accessed 10 February 2016).

9. This section draws on research previously published in Seán Crosson 'Configuring Irishness through Coaching Films: *Peil* (1962) and *Christy Ring* (1964)', *Sports Coaching Review*, vol. 5, no. 1, 2016, pp. 14–28

10. Laura Hills and Eileen Kennedy, 'Ready, Set, Action: representations of coaching through film', in Paul Potrac, Wade Gilbert and Jim Denison (eds), *Routledge Handbook of Sports Coaching* (London: Routledge, 2013) p. 41.

11. Hayward, *French National Cinema*, p. x.

12. Pratschke, 'A Look at Irish-Ireland', p. 36.

13. Corry, *The GAA Book of Lists*, pp. 371–412.

14. Simon J. Bronner, *Creativity and Tradition in Folklore: new directions* (Logan, UT: Utah State University Press, 1992), p. 1.

15. Corry, *The History of Gaelic Football*, p. 3.

16. Louis Marcus, 'The Making of *Christy Ring* and *Peil*', DVD notes to *Christy Ring/Peil* (Dublin: Gael Linn, 2008).

17. John D. Hickey, 'Football Film Is Great Success', *Irish Independent*, 27 November 1962.

18. Marcus, 'The Making of *Christy Ring* and *Peil*'.

19. Hickey, 'Football Film Is Great Success', p. 17.

20. Marcus, 'The Making of *Christy Ring* and *Peil*'.

21. Anonymous, 'Premiere of "Christy Ring" film in Cork', *Cork Examiner*, 17 October 1964.

22. Ibid.

23. Pádraig Puirséal, 'Hurling Sorcery on the Screen', *Irish Press*, 23 October 1964.

24. Ibid.

CHAPTER 7

1. Extracts from this chapter appeared previously in Seán Crosson, 'Anticipating a Postnationalist Ireland: representing Gaelic games in *Rocky Road to Dublin* (1968) and *Clash of the Ash* (1987)', in Irene Gilsenan Nordin and Carmen Zamorano Llena (eds), *Redefinitions of Irish Identity: a postnationalist approach* (Oxford: Peter Lang, 2010), pp. 85–102.

2. Brown, *Ireland: a social and cultural history*, p. 255.

3. Richard Kearney, *Postnationalist Ireland* (London: Routledge, 1996), p. 61.

4. Ibid.

5. Ibid.

6. Quoted in ibid., p. 64.

7. Kearney is quoting (p. 64) from Kenneth Frampton, 'Towards a Critical Regionalism: six points for an architecture of resistance', in Hal Foster (ed.), *The Anti-aesthetic: essays on postmodern culture* (Seattle, WA: Bay Press, 1983), p. 21.

8. McLoone, *Irish Film*, p. 161. See also Martin McLoone, 'Ireland and Cinema', in John Hill and Pamela Church Gibson (eds), *The Oxford Guide to Film Studies* (Oxford: Oxford University Press, 1998), p. 512.

9. Paul Duane, *The Making of Rocky Road to Dublin* (Dublin: Loopline Films, 2004).

10. Incidentally, the visit of Taoiseach Jack Lynch to the same set shortly after would lead to the appointment of Huston to chair a Film Industry Committee, the report of which would recommend, and eventually contribute to, the establishment of the Irish Film Board in 1981,

a central institution in encouraging and funding film-making in Ireland, including Fergus Tighe's *Clash of the Ash*.

11. Fredric Jameson, 'Postmodernism and Consumer Society', in *The Cultural Turn: selected writings on the postmodern, 1983–1998* (London: Verso, 1998), p. 18.

12. Luke Gibbons, 'The Rocky Road to Modernity', *History Ireland*, vol. 14, no. 1, January/February 2006, p. 48.

13. Lennon makes reference to this comment in Paul Duane's *The Making of Rocky Road to Dublin* (Dublin: Loopline Films, 2004).

14. Ibid.

15. Quoted on the website of First Run Icarus Films, http://www.frif.com/new2005/dub.html (accessed 16 October 2016).

16. Lennon made this comment in Paul Duane's *The Making of Rocky Road to Dublin* (Dublin: Loopline Films, 2004).

17. According to Lennon, 'No cinema manager in Ireland wanted to offend the parish priest.' Peter Lennon, 'Portrait of a Brainwashed Society', *Guardian*, 11 April 2004.

18. Philip Molloy, 'The Lost Snapshot of an Ireland They Didn't Want You to See', *Irish Independent*, 1 October 2005.

19. Lennon, 'Portrait of a Brainwashed Society', p. 15.

20. Vincent Browne, 'The Rocky Road to Dublin', *Film West*, no. 24, Summer 1996, p. 34.

21. Lennon, 'Portrait of a Brainwashed Society'.

22. Carol Murphy, 'Peter Lennon's Rocky Road', *Film Ireland*, http://www.filmireland.net/exclusives/rockyroadtodublin.htm (accessed 15 September 2015).

23. I want to acknowledge the assistance of Dónal McAnallen in identifying Mac Lua, who is uncredited in Lennon's film.

24. Brendan Mac Lua, *The Steadfast Rule: a history of the GAA ban* (Dublin: Cúchulainn Press, 1967), p. 106.

25. Ibid., p. 107.

26. Cheryl Herr, *The Field* (Cork: Cork University Press, 2000), p. 53.

27. Desmond Fennell, 'Choosing Our Self Image (The Problem of Irish Identity)', *Crane Bag*, vol. 7, no. 2, 1983, p. 193.

28. Seanad Éireann, 'Adjournment Matter – Irish Film Board', vol. 116, 14 July 1987, http://historical-debates.oireachtas.ie/S/0116/S.0116.198707140008.html (accessed 15 September 2016).

29. Molly McAnailly Burke, 'The Mischief of Moxley', *Sunday Independent*, 5 September 1991.

30. Rockett et al., *Cinema and Ireland*, p. 274.

31. Anthony O'Neill, 'A Certain Tendency of the Irish Cinema', *Film West*, no. 36, 1999, p. 16.

32. Cathal Black, 'Cathal Black Interview with Vincent Browne', *Film West*, no. 24, spring 1996, p. 22.

33. Anonymous, 'Video Releases', *Irish Times*, 29 July 2000, Weekend Section.

34. Ibid.

35. Paddy Woodworth, 'Sporting Rebels', *Sunday Press*, 8 February 1987.

36. Stephanie MacBride, 'Clash of the Ash Wins at L'Orient', *Film Base News*, no. 3, September/October 1987), p. 9.

37. Rockett et al., *Cinema and Ireland*, p. 268.

38. Kearney, *Postnationalist Ireland*, p. 64.

39. At its 2003 annual congress, for example, the then president of the GAA, Seán Kelly, remarked on 'the importance of the local GAA club to the Association. The GAA club is the cornerstone of the Association and the needs of the GAA Club must be addressed.' See 'Club Planning and Development', http://www.gaa.ie/page/club_planning_and_development.html (accessed 27 October 2015).

40. Sweeney, *Breaking Ball*.

41. Woodworth, 'Sporting Rebels'.

42. These details and those that follow are from a personal interview by the author with Tighe on 20 August 2007.

43. This information is available on the website of St Colman's College, Fermoy, http://www.stcolmanscollege.com/history.htm (accessed 20 November 2015).

44. Fergus Tighe, *Clash of the Ash* (script, 1986). Held in the Tiernan McBride Library in the Irish Film Institute, p. 3.

45. Ibid., p. 31.

CHAPTER 8

1. For instance, in 2017 the most watched event on RTÉ up to 18 September was the All-Ireland Gaelic football final. For more on this, see 'All-Ireland Senior Football Final Most Watched Show on Irish TV', http://www.rte.ie/about/en/press-office/press-releases/2017/0918/905698-all-ireland-senior-football-final-most-watched-show-on-irish-tv (accessed 10 November 2017).

2. For further on Dogme, see Jack Stevenson, *Dogme Uncut* (Santa Monica, CA: Santa Monica Press, 2003), or Mette Hjort and Scott MacKenzie (eds), *Purity and Provocation: Dogme '95* (London: British Film Institute, 2008).

3. Comer referred to his admiration for Wiseman in a guest lecture to students of the Huston School of Film & Digital Media, NUI Galway on 5 October 2017.

4. Tom Humphries, 'Comer's Epic of Cinéma Vérité', *Irish Times*, 30 November 1998.

5. Extracts from the following section have appeared previously in Seán Crosson, 'Gaelic Games and "the Movies"', in Mike Cronin, William Murphy and Paul Rouse (eds), *The Gaelic Athletic Association, 1884–2009* (Dublin: Irish Academic Press, 2009), pp. 111–36.

6. Edward O'Mahony, *Michael Collins: his life and times*, http://www.generalmichaelcollins.com/pages/Michael_Collins.html (accessed 20 August 2016).

7. Neil Jordan, *Michael Collins: screenplay and film diary* (London: Vintage, 1996), p. 126.

8. *The South Bank Show* – 'Michael Collins episode'.

9. Paul Bew, 'The Role of the Historical Adviser and the Bloody Sunday Tribunal', *Historical Research*, vol. 78, no. 199, 2005, p. 125.

10. *The South Bank Show* – 'Michael Collins episode'.

11. Ken Loach commentary on DVD release of *The Wind that Shakes the Barley* (2006).

12. Extracts from the following section have previously appeared in Seán Crosson, 'Horror, Hurling, and Bertie: aspects of contemporary Irish horror cinema', *Kinema*, no. 37, 2012, pp. 65–83.

13. Barry Monahan, 'Attack of the Killer Cows! Reading genre and context in *Isolation* (2005)', *Estudios Irlandeses*, no. 2, 2007, p. 264.

14. Ibid.

15. Dana Och, 'Straying from the Path: horror and Neil Jordan's *The Company of Wolves*', in Brian McIlroy (ed.), *Genre and Irish Cinema: Ireland and transnationalism* (London: Routledge, 2007), p. 193.

16. For a discussion of these influences, see 'Butcher', 'A Wonderful Sam Saimi Irish Inspired Zombie Fest', http://www.killerreviews.com/staff_review.php?movieid=2528 (accessed 22 July 2016). See also Wayne Simmons, 'Interview with Conor McMahon', http://zagginterviews. blogspot.com/2006/02/conor-mcmahon.html (accessed 27 March 2016) for McMahon's own comments on the film's homage to previous horror films.

17. One of the most famous episodes associated with the mythological figure Cúchulainn involves him defending himself from an attacking hound with his hurling stick and *sliotar*, the ball used in the game.

18. For relevant reviews, see 'Butcher', 'A Wonderful Sam Saimi Irish Inspired Zombie Fest'. Also Simmons, 'Interview with Conor McMahon'.

19. Ruth Barton, 'Boy Eats Girl (2006)', *Estudios Irlandeses*, no. 1, 2007, p. 162.

20. Ruth Barton, *Irish National Cinema* (London: Routledge, 2004), p. 131.

21. Robin Wood, 'An Introduction to the American Horror Film', in Bill Nichols (ed.), *Movies and Methods, Volume II* (Berkeley, CA: University of California Press, 1985), p. 203.

22. Adam Lowenstein, *Shocking Representation: historical trauma, national cinema and the modern horror film* (New York: Columbia University Press, 2005), p. 3.

23. Bruce Kawin, 'The Mummy's Pool', in Leo Braudy and Marshall Cohen (eds), *Film Theory and Criticism: introductory readings* (Oxford: Oxford University Press, 1999), p. 680.

24. The film was the first to be produced under the Irish Film Board's microbudget initiative. In the 'making of' documentary, *Mad Cows and Zombies* (2004), included on the DVD release of *Dead Meat*, Brendan McCarthy, who was then head of production and development at the Irish Film Board and expressed his concern that horror was a neglected genre in Irish film, describes *Dead Meat* as the first microbudget film funded by the board as well as the first horror film the board was involved with.

25. 'What Was the Epidemic Caused By?', http://www.bsereview.org.uk/bse/epidemic-caused. html (accessed 15 December 2017).

26. Quoted in Alexander Cockburn, 'A Bitter Harvest', *Sunday Times*, Culture, 13 July 2008.

27. Wood, 'An Introduction to the American Horror Film', p. 210.

28. Ibid., p. 213.

29. Robin Wood, *Hollywood from Vietnam to Reagan* (New York: Columbia University Press, 1986), p. 118.

30. As Fintan O'Toole noted in 2007, 'National debt as a percentage of GDP fell from 87.7 per cent in 1990 to 20.4 per cent in 2006. But lending by credit institutions to private households has more than trebled from €39 billion in 2000 to €134 billion in 2006. Outstanding indebtedness on credit cards stood at €1.5 billion at the end of 2002. At the end of 2006, it was €2.7 billion. Ireland has acquired the highest ratio of personal debt to GNP in the euro zone' (Fintan O'Toole, 'Fruit of the Boom Years Squandered', *Irish Times*, 20 November 2007). See also Paul Cullen, 'Household Debt Up Due to Mortgage Borrowing', *Irish Times*, 30 April 2009.

31. Both of these comments are taken from the director's commentary to the DVD release of *Dead Meat*.

CHAPTER 9

1. Hayward, *French National Cinema*, p. x.

2. Crosson, *Sport and Film*, pp. 93–8.

3. 'Dublin's League Final Win Brings Record-Breaking Viewing Figures for TG4', http://www.tg4.ie/en/corporate/press/press-releases/2016-2/20-04-16-1 (accessed 16 September 2017). It should be noted that the league finals featured Dublin, Kerry, Cavan and Tyrone – all counties with very large followings, which undoubtedly contributed to both the attendance and viewership.

BIBLIOGRAPHY

Abe, Ikuo, 'A Study of the Chronology of the Modern Usage of "Sportsmanship" in English, American and Japanese Dictionaries', *International Journal of the History of Sport*, vol. 5, no. 1, 1988, pp. 3–28

Allen, Nicholas, 'Cinema, Empire and Transition', *Modernist Cultures*, vol. 5, no. 1, 2010, pp. 65–78

Allison, Lincoln, 'Sport and Nationalism', in Jay Coakley and Eric Dunning (eds), *Handbook of Sports Studies* (London: Sage Publications, 2002), pp. 344–55

Althusser, Louis, *Lenin and Philosophy, and Other Essays*, trans. Ben Brewster (New York: Monthly Review Press, 1972)

Anderson, Benedict, *Imagined Communities: reflections on the origin and spread of nationalism* (London: Verso, 1991 [1983])

Andrews, Nigel, David Churchill and Michael Blanden, 'The Hidden Spin-off of "Chariots"', *Financial Times*, Section I: Weekend Brief, 3 April 1982

An Fear Rua, 'Rooney: "The Darlin' of the Lay-ay-dees"', 1 January 2000, http://www.anfearrua.com/viewdoc.aspx?id=156 (accessed 10 March 2015)

Anon., '1950–1959', Gael-linn.ie, http://www.gael-linn.ie/default.aspx?treeid=256 (accessed 15 March 2016)

——, '60,000 at Croke Park', *Irish Press*, 27 September 1937

——, 'Action in Sligo', *Irish Independent*, 24 August 1932

——, 'Administration', GAA.ie, http://www.gaa.ie/about-the-gaa/mission-and-vision (accessed 28 March 2011)

——, 'All-Ireland Final Film', *Tuam Herald*, 3 November 1956

——, 'All-Ireland Senior Football Final Most Watched Show on Irish TV', http://www.rte.ie/about/en/press-office/press-releases/2017/0918/905698-all-ireland-senior-football-final-most-watched-show-on-irish-tv (accessed 10 November 2017)

——, 'Assembly Rooms, Cork: Munster hurling final', *Evening Echo*, 31 October 1912

——, 'Club Planning and Development', http://www.gaa.ie/page/club_planning_and_development.html (accessed 27 October 2007)

——, 'Competitions for Sixty Juvenile Hurling Teams', *Kerryman*, 27 March 1965

——, 'Croke Park Can Hold 76,000 for Final', *Irish Independent*, 20 September 1957

——, 'Dublin Letter: too much "blarney"', *Cork Examiner*, 19 July 1956

——, 'Dublin's League Final Win Brings Record-breaking Viewing Figures for TG4', http://www.tg4ie/en/corporate/press/press-releases/2016-2/20-04-16-1 (accessed 15 November 2017)

——, 'Film and the Irish Tourist Industry', *Irish Independent*, 19 July 1956

——, 'Film Stars at Mansion House', *Irish Press*, 10 October 1957

——, 'Final Crowd May be a Record', *Irish Independent*, 23 September 1960

——, 'First Showing of Two Films About Ireland', *Irish Times*, 19 July 1956

——, 'Football Film', *Irish Press*, 24 November 1962

——, 'Foreign Games in the Colleges', *Irish Times*, 26 April 1930

——, 'GAA Rulers Sit in Council', *Irish Press*, 17 April 1933

——, 'Gaelic Fields and Forum', *Meath Chronicle*, 9 October 1954

——, 'Gaelic Games Congress: good progress reported, some criticism of Ulster', *Irish Times*, 17 April 1933

——, 'Interview with Conor McMahon', http://www.killerreviews.com/interview_dead_meat.asp (accessed 27 September 2008)

——, 'Ireland's First Film Studio', *Irish Press*, 13 March 1958

——, 'Irish Films for Olympic Games', *Irish Independent*, 21 July 1961

——, 'Italian Award for Film of GAA Matches', *Irish Independent*, 7 March 1956

——, 'Justin B. Herman Dead at 76; writer and producer of films', *New York Times*, 10 December 1983, http://query.nytimes.com/gst/fullpage.html?res=9C04E3DE1638F933A25751C1A965948260&sec=&pagewanted=print (accessed 10 June 2014)

——, 'Kilkenny Arts Festival', *Waterford Today*, 8 August 2007, http://www.waterford-today.ie/index.php?option=com_content&task=view&id=962&Itemid=10172&ed=75 (accessed 26 August 2016)

——, 'Knocknagow: filming of Kickham's famous novel', *Irish Limelight*, May 1917

——, '"Knocknagow" on the Film: a picture play that will create a furore in America', *Anglo-Celt*, 2 March 1918

——, 'London Calling', *Irish Independent*, 27 October 1961

——, 'Marathon Hurling', *Strabane Chronicle*, 21 September 1957

——, 'Mystery Abbey Extra Was – John Ford!', *Evening Press*, 8 May 1956

——, 'Objection to Films', *Irish Independent*, 6 August 1932

——, 'Official Bulletin Reports Progress of Hurling Drive', *Irish Independent*, 2 March 1965

——, 'Opera House: Kerry v Louth', *Cork Examiner*, 3 July 1913

——, 'People and Places', *Irish Press*, 9 January 1961

——, 'Premiere of "Christy Ring" Film in Cork', *Cork Examiner*, 17 October 1964

——, 'President Attends Film Showing', *Irish Times*, 14 March 1958

——, 'Rank and File GAA Members', *Fermanagh Herald*, 22 April 1939

——, 'Reorganisation Meeting under the Auspices of the Ulster Council, GAA, in Letterkenny', *Frontier Sentinel*, 19 December 1931

——, 'Rome Showing for Irish Films', *Irish Press*, 21 July 1960

——, 'Room for Irish Film Industry', *Irish Times*, 14 March 1958

——, 'Six Hour Hurling "Final" at Croke Park', *Irish Independent*, 9 September 1957

——, 'The Other Rackard', *Irish Independent*, 28 March 2009

——, 'The Team at Theatre Royal, Tralee', *Kerryman*, 5 July 1913

——, 'This Week's Films', *Cork Examiner*, 7 April 1958

——, 'Three Days of Heaven', *Cork Examiner*, 20 November 1957

——, 'Thoughts and Tidings: Gael Linn film', *Derry People*, 8 September 1956

——, 'Tourist Industry Has Prospects of Record Year', *Irish Times*, 14 July 1956

——, 'Unfairly Treated: GAA discussion on Land Commission and playing fields', *Irish Press*, 14 February 1938

——, 'Video Releases', *Irish Times*, 29 July 2000, Weekend Section

——, 'What Was the Epidemic Caused By?', http://www.bsereview.org.uk/bse/epidemic-caused.html (accessed 15 December 2017)

Appadurai, Arjun, *Modernity at Large* (Minneapolis: University of Minnesota Press, 1996)

Arundel, John, and Maurice Roche, 'Media, Sport and Local Identity: British rugby league and Sky TV', in Maurice Roche (ed.), *Sport, Popular Culture and Identity* (Oxford: Meyer & Meyer, 2000), pp. 57–91

Babington, Bruce, *The Sports Film: games people play* (London and New York: Wallflower Press, 2014)

Baker, Aaron, *Contesting Identities: sports in American film* (Champaign, IL: University of Illinois Press, 2003)

Baker, Aaron, and Todd Boyd (eds), *Out of Bounds: sports, media, and the politics of identity* (Bloomington, IN: Indiana University Press, 1997)

Barrett, J.J., *In the Name of the Game* (Dublin: Dub Press, 1997)

Barthes, Roland, 'The Tour de France as Epic', in idem, *The Eiffel Tower and Other Mythologies*, trans. Richard Howard (New York: Hill & Wang, 1979), pp. 87–8

Barton, Ruth, *Irish National Cinema* (London: Routledge, 2004)

——, 'Boy Eats Girl (2006)', *Estudios Irlandeses*, no. 1, 2007, pp. 162–3

Beere, T.J., 'Cinema Statistics in Saorstát Éireann', *Journal of the Statistical and Social Enquiry Society of Ireland*, no. 156, 1935/36, pp. 83–106

Benton, Sarah, 'Women Disarmed: the militarization of politics in Ireland, 1913–23', *Feminist Review*, no. 50, summer 1995, pp. 148–72

Bew, Paul, 'The Role of the Historical Adviser and the Bloody Sunday Tribunal', *Historical Research*, vol. 78, no. 199, 2005, p. 125

Billig, Michael, *Banal Nationalism* (London: Sage Publications, 1995)

Black, Cathal, 'Cathal Black Interview with Vincent Browne', *Film West*, no. 24, 1996, pp. 22–4

Bowden, Martyn, 'Jerusalem, Dover Beach, and Kings Cross: imagined places as metaphors of the British class struggle in *Chariots of Fire* and *The Loneliness of the Long-distance Runner*', in Stuart C. Aitken and Leo E. Zonn (eds), *Place, Power, Situation and Spectacle: geography of film* (Lanham, MD, and London: Rowman & Littlefield Publishers, 1994), pp. 69–100

Boyle, Raymond, 'From Our Gaelic Fields: radio, sport and nation in post-partition Ireland', *Media, Culture and Society*, vol. 14, no. 4, 1992, pp. 623–36

Braun, Marta, *Picturing Time: the work of Etienne-Jules Marey (1830–1904)* (Chicago: University of Chicago Press, 1992)

Brennan, Sandra, 'George Pollock', *New York Times*, All Movie Guide, http://movies2nytimes.com/gst/movies/filmography.html?p_id=106786 (accessed 26 August 2015)

Briley, Ron, Michael K. Schoenecke and Deborah A. Carmichael (eds), *All-Stars & Movie Stars: sports in film & history* (Lexington, KY: University Press of Kentucky, 2008)

Bronner, Simon J., *Creativity and Tradition in Folklore: new directions* (Logan, UT: Utah State University Press, 1992)

Brown, Terence, *Ireland: a social and cultural history, 1922–2002* (London: Harper Perennial, 2004)

Browne, Vincent, 'The Rocky Road to Dublin', *Film West*, no. 24, summer 1996, pp. 34–6

'Butcher', 'A Wonderful Sam Saimi Irish Inspired Zombie Fest', http://www.killerreviews.com/staff_review.php?movieid=2528 (accessed 22 July 2016)

Camy, Julien, and Gérard Camy, *Sport & Cinéma* (Paris: Éditions du Bailli de Suffren, 2016)

Carey, Tim, *Croke Park: a history* (Cork: Collins Press, 2013)

Cashmore, Ellis, 'Chariots of Fire: bigotry, manhood and moral certitude in an age of individualism', *Sport in Society*, vol. 11, nos 2–3, 2008, pp. 159–73

Cathcart, Rex, *The Most Contrary Region: the BBC in Northern Ireland, 1924–1984* (Belfast: Blackstaff, 1984)

Chambers, Ciara, *Ireland in the Newsreels* (Dublin: Irish Academic Press, 2012)

Chapman, James, *Past and Present: national identity and the British historical film* (London and New York: I.B. Tauris, 2005)

Cinema Correspondent, 'The Business Jungle', *Irish Times*, 23 July 1956

Clegg, Brian, *The Man Who Stopped Time: the illuminating story of Eadweard Muybridge – pioneer photographer, father of the motion picture, murderer* (Washington, DC: Joseph Henry Press, 2007)

Cockburn, Alexander, 'A Bitter Harvest', *Sunday Times*, Culture, 13 July 2008

Condon, Denis, 'Irish Audiences Watch Their First US Feature: the Corbett-Fitzsimmons fight (1897)', in Ruth Barton (ed.), *Screening Irish-America* (Dublin: Irish Academic Press, 2009), pp. 135–47

——, 'Watching Gaelic Games on Screen in 1913', https://earlyirishcinema.com/2013/09/22/watching-Gaelic-games-on-screen-in-1913 (accessed 10 August 2017)

——, *Early Irish Film, 1895–1921* (Dublin: Irish Academic Press, 2008)

Connolly, John, and Paddy Dolan, 'Sport, media and the Gaelic Athletic Association: the quest for the "youth" of Ireland', *Media, Culture & Society*, vol. 34, no. 4, 2012, pp. 407–23.

Connolly, S.J. (ed.), *The Oxford Companion to Irish History* (Oxford: Oxford University Press, 1999)

Corry, Eoghan, *The GAA Book of Lists* (Dublin: Hodder Headline, 2005)

——, *The History of Gaelic Football* (Dublin: Gill & Macmillan, 2010)

Coser, Lewis, *The Functions of Social Conflict* (Glencoe, IL: Free Press, 1956)

Croke, T.W., 'To Mr Michael Cusack, Honorary Secretary of the Gaelic Athletic Association. The Palace, Thurles, 18 December 1884', http://multitext.ucc.ie/d/Archbishop_Croke__the_GAA_November_1884 (accessed 15 September 2016)

Cronin, Jim ('Jim Barry'), *Making Connections: a Cork GAA miscellany* (Cork: Cork County Board, 2005), pp. 55–63

Cronin, Mike, '"Is it for the Glamour?" Masculinity, nationhood and amateurism in contemporary projections of the Gaelic Athletic Association', in W. Balzano, A. Mulhall and M. Sullivan (eds), *Irish Postmodernisms and Popular Culture* (London: Palgrave Macmillan, 2007)

——, 'Projecting the Nation through Sport and Culture: Ireland, Aonach Tailteann and the Irish Free State, 1924–32', *Journal of Contemporary History*, vol. 38, no. 3, 2003, pp. 395–411

——, *Sport and Nationalism in Ireland: Gaelic games, soccer and Irish identity since 1884* (Dublin: Four Courts Press, 1999)

——, Mark Duncan and Paul Rouse, 'Media', in *The GAA: a people's history* (Cork: Collins Press, 2009)

Crosson, Seán, 'Anticipating a Postnationalist Ireland: representing Gaelic games in *Rocky Road to Dublin* (1968) and *Clash of the Ash* (1987)', in Irene Gilsenan Nordin and Carmen Zamorano Llena (eds), *Redefinitions of Irish Identity: a postnationalist approach* (Oxford: Peter Lang, 2010), pp. 85–102

——, '"Ar Son an Náisiúin": the National Film Institute of Ireland's All-Ireland films', *Éire-Ireland*, special issue on Irish sport, vol. 48, nos 1 & 2, 2013, pp. 193–212

——, 'Configuring Irishness through Coaching Films: *Peil* (1962) and *Christy Ring* (1964)', *Sports Coaching Review*, vol. 5, no. 1, 2016, pp. 14–28

——, 'Community Games', https://www.rte.ie/eile/brainstorm/2017/1107/918120-community-games (accessed 15 November 2017)

——, and Dónal McAnallen, '"Croke Park Goes Plumb Crazy": Pathé newsreels and Gaelic games', *Media History*, vol. 17, no. 2, 2011, pp. 161–76

——, '"For the honour of old Knock-na-gow I must win": representing sport in *Knocknagow* (1918)', *Screening the Past*, no. 33, 2012, http://www.screeningthepast.com/2012/02/%E2%80%9Cfor-the-honour-of-old-knock-na-gow-i-must-win%E2%80%9D-representing-sport-in-knocknagow-1918 (accessed 27 September 2018)

——, 'Gaelic Games and "the Movies"', in Mike Cronin, William Murphy and Paul Rouse (eds), *The Gaelic Athletic Association, 1884–2009* (Dublin: Irish Academic Press, 2009), pp. 111–36

——, 'Horror, Hurling, and Bertie: aspects of contemporary Irish horror cinema', *Kinema*, no. 37, 2012, pp. 65–83

——, '"Shillalah Swing Time … You'll Thrill Each Time a Wild Irishman's Skull Shatters": representing hurling in American cinema, 1930–1960', in Ruth Barton (ed.), *Screening Irish-America: representing Irish-America in film and television* (Dublin: Irish Academic Press, 2009), pp. 148–64

——, and Philip Dine, 'Sport and the Media in Ireland: an introduction', *Media History*, vol. 17, no. 2, 2011, pp. 109–16

——, *Sport and Film* (London: Routledge, 2013)

Crowther, Bosley, 'Screen: Irish comedy; John Gregson starred in Sutton's "Rooney"', *New York Times*, 6 June 1958, http://www.nytimes.com/movie/review?res=9903E1D71 F3AEF34 BC4E53DFB0668383649EDE (accessed 15 January 2015)

Cullen, Paul, 'Household Debt Up Due to Mortgage Borrowing', *Irish Times*, 30 April 2009

Culler, Jonathan, 'Semiotics of Tourism', *American Journal of Semiotics*, vol. 1, no. 1, 1981, pp. 127–40

Cummins, Patrick J., 'Emergency' Air Accidents – South-East Ireland, 1940–1945 (Waterford: Aviation History Ireland, 2003), p. 45

Cunningham, John, 'Foci, Fradi and the "Golden Team"', in idem, Hungarian Cinema From Coffee House to Multiplex (London: Wallflower, 2004), pp. 183–8

Davis, Ronald L., John Ford: Hollywood's old master (Norman, OK: University of Oklahoma Press, 1995)

De Búrca, Marcus, The GAA: a history (Dublin: Cumann Lúthchleas Gael, 1980)

Dine, Philip, and Seán Crosson (eds), Sport, Representation, and Evolving Identities in Europe (Bern: Peter Lang Publishing, 2010)

Downing, Taylor, Olympia (London: BFI Publishing, 1992)

Duncan, Mark, 'The Early Photography of the GAA, 1884–1914', in Mike Cronin, William Murphy and Paul Rouse (eds), The Gaelic Athletic Association, 1884–2009 (Dublin: Irish Academic Press, 2009), pp. 93–110

Dunne, Mick, 'US Viewers to See Hurling', Irish Press, 14 July 1964

Fallon, Donal, 'Dublin Women Take to the Streets, 1963', Come Here To Me! Dublin life & culture, 10 June 2012, https://comeheretome.com/2012/06/10/dublin-women-take-to-the-streets-1963 (accessed 10 February 2016)

Farrell, Rebecca E., Across the Water: teaching Irish music and dance at home and abroad (Lanham, MD: R&L Education, 2010)

Felle, Tom, 'Gay Pound Cashes in on GAA's Manhood', Sunday Independent, 7 October 2001

Fennell, Desmond, 'Choosing Our Self Image (The Problem of Irish Identity)', Crane Bag, vol. 7, no. 2, 1983, pp. 191–6

Free, Marcus, 'Diaspora and Rootedness: amateurism and professionalism in media discourses of Irish soccer and rugby in the 1990s and 2000s', Éire-Ireland, vol. 48, nos 1 & 2, 2013, pp. 211–29

Frampton, Kenneth, 'Towards a Critical Regionalism: six points for an architecture of resistance', in Hal Foster (ed.), The Anti-aesthetic: essays on postmodern culture (Seattle, WA: Bay Press, 1983), pp. 16–31

Gael, 'Observer', Fermanagh Herald, 29 April 1939, p. 10

Gael, 'A Gross Libel', Fermanagh Herald, 18 February 1939

Gallagher, Tag, John Ford: the man and his films (Berkeley, CA: University of California Press, 1986)

'Galway Board's Statement', Irish Independent, 16 September 1953

Garioni, Claudio, Fuori Campo: il cinema racconta lo sport (Rome: Delos Digital, 2017)

Gellner, Ernest, Nations and Nationalism (Oxford: Blackwell, 1983)

Gibbons, Luke, 'From Megalith to Megastore: broadcasting and Irish culture', Transformations in Irish Culture (Cork: Cork University Press in association with Field Day, 1996), pp. 70–81

——, The Quiet Man (Cork: Cork University Press, 2002)

——, 'The Rocky Road to Modernity', History Ireland, vol. 14, no. 1, January/February 2006, pp. 48–50

Good, Howard, Diamonds in the Dark: America, baseball, and the movie (Lanham, MD: Scarecrow Press, 1996)

Grierson, John, 'A Film Policy for Ireland', *Studies: an Irish quarterly review*, vol. 37, no. 147, September 1948, pp. 283–91

Grierson, John, 'First Principles of Documentary' (1932), in Catherine Fowler (ed.), *The European Cinema Reader* (London and New York: Routledge, 2002), pp. 39–44

Gunning, Tom, 'The Cinema of Attraction', *Wide Angle*, vol. 8, no. 3, 1986, pp. 63–70

Hammerton, Jenny, *For Ladies Only? Eve's film review: Pathé Cinemagazine* (Hastings: The Projection Box, 2001)

Hartenian, Larry, 'The Role of Media in Democratizing Germany: United States occupation policy, 1945–1949', *Central European History*, vol. 20, no. 2, June 1987, p. 184

Hayward, Susan, *French National Cinema* (London: Routledge, 2005)

Herr, Cheryl, *The Field* (Cork: Cork University Press, 2000)

Hickey, John D., 'Football Film Is Great Success', *Irish Independent*, 27 November 1962

——, 'Kilkenny's 14th Win Was Unforgettable', *Irish Independent*, 2 September 1957

Higson, Andrew, *Waving the Flag: constructing a national cinema in Britain* (Oxford: Clarendon Press, 1995)

Hill, John, 'The Quiet Man: Ford mythology and Ireland', in Seán Crosson and Rod Stoneman (eds), *The Quiet Man ... and Beyond: reflections on a classic film, John Ford, and Ireland* (Dublin: Liffey Press, 2009), pp. 178–99

Hills, Laura, and Eileen Kennedy, 'Ready, Set, Action: representations of coaching through film', in Paul Potrac, Wade Gilbert and Jim Denison (eds), *Routledge Handbook of Sports Coaching* (London: Routledge, 2013), pp. 40–51

Hjort, Mette, and Scott MacKenzie, *Cinema and Nation* (London: Routledge, 2000)

——, and Scott MacKenzie (eds), *Purity and Provocation: Dogme '95* (London: British Film Institute, 2008)

Hobsbawm, Eric, *Nations and Nationalism Since 1780: programme, myth, reality* (Cambridge: Cambridge University Press, 1992)

——, and Terence Ranger (eds), *The Invention of Tradition* (Cambridge: Cambridge University Press, 1983)

Hogan, Dick, 'Emigration Study Reverses the Perspective', *Irish Times*, 1 February 2000

Huggins, Mike, 'Projecting the Visual: British newsreels, soccer and popular culture, 1918–1939', *International Journal of the History of Sport*, vol. 24, no. 1, 2007, pp. 80–102

Humphries, Tom, 'Comer's Epic of Cinéma Vérité', *Irish Times*, 30 November 1998

Hutchinson, John, *Modern Nationalism* (London: Fontana Press, 1987)

Ingle, Zachary, and David M. Sutera (eds), *Gender and Genre in Sports Documentaries: critical essays* (Lanham, MD: Scarecrow Press, 2013)

——, and David M. Sutera (eds), *Identity and Myth in Sports Documentaries: critical essays* (Lanham, MD: Scarecrow Press, 2013)

Jameson, Fredric, 'Postmodernism and Consumer Society', in idem, *The Cultural Turn: selected writings on the postmodern, 1983–1998* (London: Verso, 1998), pp. 1–20

Johnston, Dillon, *Irish Poetry After Joyce* (Syracuse: Syracuse University Press, 1997)

Jones, Glen, '"Down on the Floor and Give Me Ten Sit-ups": British sports feature film', *Film & History*, vol. 35, no. 2, 2005, pp. 29–40

Jouan-Westlund, Anni, 'L'imaginaire Populaire Franco-Américain dans *Les Triplettes de Belleville*', *French Review*, vol. 79, no. 6, 2006, pp. 1195–1205

Kawin, Bruce, 'The Mummy's Pool', in Leo Braudy and Marshall Cohen (eds), *Film Theory and Criticism: introductory readings* (Oxford: Oxford University Press, 1999), pp. 679–91

Kearney, Richard, *Postnationalist Ireland* (Routledge: London, 1996)

Keenan, Marie, *Child Sexual Abuse and the Catholic Church: gender, power and organisational culture* (Oxford: Oxford University Press, 2012)

Kickham, Charles, *Knocknagow* (Dublin: Gill & Macmillan, 1979 [1873])

Kiely, Benedict, 'Cameras on Croke Park', *Irish Press*, 17 March 1958

———, 'The Tourists and the Screen', *Irish Press*, 23 July 1956

King, Seamus J., *A History of Hurling* (Dublin: Gill & Macmillan, 2005)

King, Richard C., and David J. Leonard (eds), *Visual Economies of/in Motion: sport and film (cultural critique)* (Bern: Peter Lang Publishing, 2006)

Leach, Jim, *British Film* (Cambridge: Cambridge University Press, 2004)

Lee, Joseph, *Ireland, 1912–1985: politics and society* (Cambridge: Cambridge University Press, 1989)

Leerson, Joep, *Remembrance and Imagination: patterns in the historical and literary representation of Ireland in the nineteenth century* (Cork: Cork University Press, 1996)

Lennon, Peter, 'Portrait of a Brainwashed Society', *Guardian*, 11 April 2004

Lewis, John, 'Who Was Ted Husing?', http://www.tedhusing.net/Ted_Husing/Who_Was_Ted_Husing/Who_Was_Ted_Husing.html (accessed 10 May 2016)

Lowenstein, Adam, *Shocking Representation: historical trauma, national cinema and the modern horror film* (New York: Columbia University Press, 2005)

MacBride, Stephanie, '"Clash of the Ash" Wins at L'Orient', *Film Base News*, no. 3, September–October 1987, p. 9

Mac Eoin, Uinseann, *The IRA in the Twilight Years, 1923–1948* (Dublin: Argenta Publications, 1997)

Mac Lua, Brendan, *The Steadfast Rule: a history of the GAA ban* (Dublin: Cúchulainn Press, 1967)

Mahon, Jack, *A History of Gaelic Football* (Dublin: Gill & Macmillan, 2000)

Mandell, Richard D., *The Nazi Olympics* (Urbana, IL: University of Illinois Press, 1987)

Marcus, Louis, 'The Making of *Christy Ring* and *Peil*', DVD notes to *Christy Ring/Peil* (Dublin: Gael Linn, 2008)

Martin, Peter, *Censorship in the Two Irelands, 1922–1939* (Dublin: Irish Academic Press, 2006)

McAnailly Burke, Molly, 'The Mischief of Moxley', *Sunday Independent*, 5 September 1991

McBride, Joseph, *Searching for John Ford: a life* (New York: St Martin's Press, 2001)

McCann, B., '"If It's Not Disney, What Is It?" Traditional animation techniques in *Les Triplettes de Belleville*', *French Studies Bulletin*, no. 108, 2008, pp. 59–62

MacCannell, Dean, 'Staged Authenticity: arrangements of social space in tourist settings', *American Journal of Sociology*, vol. 79, no. 3, 1973, pp. 589–603

———, *The Tourist: a new theory of the leisure class* (London: Macmillan, 1976)

MacG., L., 'No Disgrace to Our Touchy Temperaments', *Sunday Review*, 15 March 1959

McCarthy, Larry, 'Irish Americans in Sport: the twentieth century', in Joseph Lee and Marion R. Casey (eds), *Making the Irish American: history and heritage of the Irish in the United States* (New York: NYU Press, 2006), pp. 457–74

McCarthy, Colm et al., *Report of the Special Group on Public Service Numbers and Expenditure Programmes, Volume II: Detailed Papers* (Dublin: Government Publications Sales Office, 2009)

McDevitt, Patrick F., 'Muscular Catholicism: nationalism, masculinity and Gaelic team sports, 1884–1916', *Gender & History*, vol. 9, no. 2, August 1997, pp. 262–84

McDougall, Alan, 'Eyes on the Ball: screening football in East German cinema', *Studies in Eastern European Cinema*, vol. 8, no. 1, 2017, pp. 4–18

McIlroy, Brian, 'Interview with George Fleischmann', in *Irish Cinema: an illustrated history* (Dublin: Anna Livia Press, 1988), pp. 109–13

McKernan, Luke, 'Sport and the First Films', in C. Williams (ed.), *Cinema: the beginnings and the future* (London: University of Westminster Press, 1996), pp. 107–16

McLoone, Martin, 'Ireland and Cinema', in John Hill and Pamela Church Gibson (eds), *The Oxford Guide to Film Studies* (Oxford: Oxford University Press, 1998), pp. 510–15

——, *Irish Film: the emergence of a contemporary cinema* (London: British Film Institute, 2000)

Molloy, Philip, 'The Lost Snapshot of an Ireland They Didn't Want You To See', *Irish Independent*, 1 October 2005

Monahan, Barry, 'Attack of the Killer Cows! Reading genre and context in *Isolation* (2005)', *Estudios Irlandeses*, no. 2, 2007, pp. 264–6

Monks, Robert, *Cinema Ireland: a database of Irish films and filmmakers, 1896–1986* [CD-ROM] (Dublin: National Library of Ireland, 1996)

Moran, Seán, 'Waterford Associated with Celebrities', *Irish Times*, 19 August 2008

Murphy, Carol, 'Peter Lennon's Rocky Road', *Film Ireland*, http://www.filmireland.net/exclusives/rockyroadtodublin.htm (accessed 15 September 2015)

na Gopaleen, Myles, 'GAATHLETES', *Irish Times*, 18 May 1956

——, 'Ford-Proconsul', *Irish Times*, 14 May 1956

Nairn, Tom, *The Break-up of Britain: crisis and neo-nationalism* (London: New Left Books, 1977)

Neale, Steve, '"Chariots of Fire", Images of Men', *Screen*, vol. 23, nos 3–4, 1982, pp. 47–53

Newell, Beth, '"Ebony Saint" or "Demon Black"? Racial stereotypes in Jim Sheridan's *In America*', in Kevin Rockett and John Hill (eds), *Film History and National Cinema* (Dublin: Four Courts Press, 2005), pp. 143–53

Nixon II, Howard L., *Sport and the American Dream* (Champaign, IL: Leisure Press/Human Kinetics, 1984)

O'Brien, Harvey, *The Real Ireland: the evolution of Ireland in documentary film* (Manchester: Manchester University Press, 2004)

O'Callaghan, Liam, '"The Red Thread of History": the media, Munster rugby and the creation of a sporting tradition', *Media History*, special issue: 'Sport and the Media in Ireland', vol. 17, no. 2, 2011, pp. 175–88

Ó Ceallacháin, Seán, *Seán Óg: his own story* (Dublin and London: Brophy Books, 1988)

Och, Dana, 'Straying from the Path: horror and Neil Jordan's *The Company of Wolves*', in Brian McIlroy (ed.), *Genre and Irish Cinema: Ireland and transnationalism* (London: Routledge, 2007), pp. 191–202

O'Flynn, Diarmuid, *Hurling: the warrior game* (Cork: Collins Press, 2008)

O'Hara, Maureen, with John Nicoletti, *'Tis Herself: a memoir* (London: Simon & Schuster/ Townhouse, 2004)

Ó hEithir, Breandán, *Over the Bar* (Dublin: Poolbeg, 1991)

O'Hehir, Michael, *My Life and Times* (Dublin: Blackwater Press, 1996)

O'Mahony, Edward, *Michael Collins: his life and times*, http://www.generalmichaelcollins.com/pages/Michael_Collins.html (accessed 20 August 2016)

O'Neill, Anthony, 'A Certain Tendency of the Irish Cinema', *Film West*, no. 36, 1999, pp. 16–17

Oram, Hugh, *The Newspaper Book: a history of newspapers in Ireland, 1649–1983* (Dublin: Mo Books, 1983)

Oriard, Michael, *King Football: sport and spectacle in the golden age of radio and newsreels, movies and magazines, the weekly and the daily press* (Chapel Hill, NC: University of North Carolina Press, 2004)

O'Toole, Fintan, 'Can the Queen Win Over Croke Park?', *Observer*, 8 May 2011

——, 'Fruit of the Boom Years Squandered', *Irish Times*, 20 November 2007

Ó Tuathaigh, Gearóid, 'The GAA as a Force in Irish Society', in Mike Cronin, William Murphy and Paul Rouse (eds), *The Gaelic Athletic Association, 1884–2009* (Dublin: Irish Academic Press, 2009), pp. 237–56

Our Film Critic, 'This Dublin Scene is No Travesty', *Irish Independent*, 17 March 1958

Petrie, George, *The Ancient Music of Ireland* (Dublin: M.H. Gill, 1855)

Phillips, Murray G., and Gary Osmond, 'Filmic Sports History: Dawn Fraser, swimming and Australian national identity', *International Journal of the History of Sport*, vol. 26, no. 14, 2009, pp. 2126–42

Pius XI, Pope, 'Vigilanti Cura: encyclical letter of Pope Pius Xi on the motion picture', http://www.vatican.va/holy_father/pius_xi/encyclicals/documents/hf_p-xi_enc_29061936_vigilanti-cura_en.html (accessed 10 May 2015)

Place-Verghnes, F., 'Douce France? *Les Triplettes de Belleville*, de Sylvain Chomet', in Pierre Floquet (ed.), *CinémAction: «CinémAnimationS»* (Paris: Corlet Publications, 2007), pp. 97–103

Poulton, Emma, and Martin Roderick (eds), *Sport in Films* (New York: Routledge, 2009)

Pratschke, B.M., 'A Look at Irish-Ireland: Gael Linn's "Amharc Éireann" films, 1956–64', *New Hibernia Review*, vol. 9, no. 3, 2005, pp. 17–38

Pronay, Nicholas, 'British Newsreels in the 1930s: audience and producers', *History*, no. 56, 1971, pp. 411–18

——, 'The Newsreels: the illusion of actuality', in Paul Smith (ed.), *The Historian and Film* (Cambridge: Cambridge University Press, 1976), pp. 95–119

Puirséal, Pádraig, 'Hurling Sorcery on the Screen', *Irish Press*, 23 October 1964

Quinn, Anthony, 'Rare Footage Captures Vibrant Lost Era', *Tyrone Times*, 15 October 2012, http://www.tyronetimes.co.uk/news/rare-footage-captures-vibrant-lost-era-1-4367722 (accessed 16 July 2017)

Quinn, Mark, *The King of Spring: the life and times of Peter O'Connor* (Dublin: Liffey Press, 2004)

Raftery, Mary, and Eoin O'Sullivan, *Suffer the Little Children: the inside story of Ireland's industrial schools* (London and New York: Continuum International Publishing Group, 2002)

Rains, Stephanie, *The Irish-American in Popular Culture (1945–2000)* (Dublin: Irish Academic Press, 2007)

Rickard, John, 'Lovable Larrikins and Awful Ockers', *Journal of Australian Studies*, no. 56, 1988, pp. 78–85

Rockett, Kevin, 'An Irish Film Studio', *Cinema and Ireland* (London: Routledge, 1988), pp. 95–126

———, 'Film Censorship and the State', *Film Directions*, vol. 3, no. 9, 1980, pp. 11–15

———, *Irish Film Censorship: a cultural journey from silent cinema to Internet pornography* (Dublin: Four Courts Press, 2004)

———, Luke Gibbons and John Hill, *Cinema and Ireland* (London and New York: Routledge, 1988)

———, with Emer Rockett, *Film Exhibition and Distribution in Ireland, 1909–2010* (Dublin: Four Courts Press, 2011)

Rodríguez, María Graciela, 'Behind Leni's Outlook: a perspective on the film *Olympia* (1938)', *International Review for the Sociology of Sport*, vol. 38, no. 1, 2003, pp. 109–16

Romaguera i Ramió, J., *Presencia del Deporteen el Cine Español: un primer inventario* (Sevilla: Fundación Andalucía Olímpica y Consejo Superior de Deportes, 2003)

Rouse, Paul, 'Journalists and the Founding of the GAA', *Media History*, vol. 17, no. 2, 2011, pp. 117–32

———, 'Michael Cusack: sportsman and journalist', in Mike Cronin, William Murphy and Paul Rouse (eds), *The Gaelic Athletic Association, 1884–2009* (Dublin: Irish Academic Press, 2009), pp. 47–59

———, *Sport and Ireland: a history* (Oxford: Oxford University Press, 2015)

Smith, Anthony D., *The Ethnic Origins of Nations* (Oxford: Blackwell, 1986)

Rowe, David, 'If You Film It, Will They Come? Sports on film', *Journal of Sport & Social Issues*, vol. 22, no. 4, 1998, pp. 350–9

Russo, William, *Great Sports Stories: the legendary films* (Philadelphia, PA: Xlibris Corporation, 2005)

Sakbolé et al., 'Le Documentaire Africain/The African Documentary', *Ecrans d'Afrique*, vol. 16, 1996, pp. 45–55

Schaub, Hannah B., *Riefenstahl's Olympia: körperideale – ethische verantwortung oder freiheit des künstlers?* (München: Wilhelm Fink Verlag, 2003)

Sheppard, Barry, '"As a Gael Should Meet Gaels": the Gaelic Athletic Association in the Irish Free State', *Irish Story*, 21 August 2012, http://www.theirishstory.com/2012/08/21/as-a-gael-should-meet-gaels-the-Gaelic-athletic-association-in-the-irish-free-state/#.UnfMLFPgzY3 (accessed 24 May 2017)

Seanad Éireann, 'Adjournment Matter: Irish Film Board', vol. 116, 14 July 1987, http://historical-debates.oireachtas.ie/S/0116/S.0116198707140008html (accessed 15 September 2016)

Simmons, Wayne, 'Interview with Conor McMahon', http://zagginterviews.blogspot.com/2006/02/conor-mcmahon.html (accessed 27 July 2016)

Smyth, Gerry, *Space and the Irish Cultural Imagination* (Basingstoke and New York: Palgrave, 2001)

Special Correspondent, 'Our American Letter, Ireland's Ancient Game: hurling film to be made', *Connaught Tribune*, 1 August 1936

St Colman's College, Fermoy, http://www.stcolmanscollege.com/history.htm (accessed 20 November 2015)

Stevenson, Jack, *Dogme Uncut* (Santa Monica, CA: Santa Monica Press, 2003)

Streible, Dan, *Fight Pictures: a history of boxing and early cinema* (Berkeley, CA: University of California Press, 2008)

Tierney, Mark, *Croke of Cashel: the life of Archbishop Thomas William Croke, 1823–1902* (Dublin: Gill & Macmillan, 1976)

Tierney, Mark, *Modern Ireland* (Dublin: Gill & Macmillan, 1978)

Tighe, Fergus, *Clash of the Ash* (script, 1986). Held in the Tiernan McBride Library in the Irish Film Institute

Tomlinson, Alan, 'Images of Sport: situating *Chariots of Fire*', *British Society of Sports History Bulletin*, vol. 8, 1988, pp. 27–41

Tudor, Deborah V., *Hollywood's Vision of Team Sports: heroes, race, and gender* (New York and London: Garland Publishing, 1997)

Turner, Graeme, 'Cultural Studies and Film', in John Hill and Pamela Church Gibson (eds), *Film Studies: critical approaches* (Oxford: Oxford University Press, 2000), pp. 196–7

Urry, John, *The Tourist Gaze* (London: Sage, 2001)

Ward, Richard, 'Extra Added Attractions: the short subjects of MGM, Warner Brothers and Universal', *Media History*, vol. 9, no. 3, 2003, pp. 221–44

Watterson, Johnny, and Lindie Naughton, *Irish Olympians, 1896–1992* (Dublin: Blackwater Press, 1992)

Watters, Andy, and Neil Loughran, *The Little Book of Gaelic Football* (Stroud, UK: History Press, 2014)

Weber, Eugene, *Peasants into Frenchmen: the modernisation of rural France, 1870–1914* (London: Chatto & Windus, 1979)

Whyte, J.H., *Church and State in Modern Ireland* (Dublin: Gill & Macmillan, 1971)

Wilcox, Ralph C., 'The Shamrock and the Eagle: Irish Americans and sport in the nineteenth century', in George Eisen and David Kenneth Wiggins (eds), *Ethnicity and Sport in North American History and Culture* (Westport, CT: Praeger Publishers, 1995), pp. 55–74

Williams, Randy, *Sports Cinema – 100 Movies: the best of Hollywood's athletic heroes, losers, myths and misfits* (Pompton Plains, NJ: Limelight Editions, 2006)

Wolstenholme, Kenneth, 'Why Keep this Great Game Such a Big Secret?', *Sunday Press*, 13 September 1959

Wood, Robin, 'An Introduction to the American Horror Film', in Bill Nichols (ed.), *Movies and Methods, Volume II* (Berkeley, CA: University of California Press, 1985), pp. 195–219

——, *Hollywood from Vietnam to Reagan* (New York: Columbia University Press, 1986)

Wood, Stephen C., and J. David Pincus (eds), *Reel Baseball: essays and interviews on the national pastime, Hollywood and American culture* (Jefferson, NC: McFarland & Co., 2003)

Woodworth, Paddy, 'Sporting Rebels', *Sunday Press*, 8 February 1987

Zdriluk, Beth, '"My Favorite Mask Is Myself": presentation, illusion and the performativity of identity in Wellesian performance', *Film Journal*, vol. 1, no. 9, 2004, http://web.archive.org/web/20040821014301/http://www.thefilmjournal.com/issue9/wellesperformance.html (accessed 15 April 2017)

Zhang, Yingjin, *Chinese National Cinema* (New York: Routledge, 2004)

Zhang, Zhen, *An Amorous History of the Silver Screen: Shanghai cinema, 1896–1937* (Chicago: University of Chicago Press, 2005)

Zhou, Xuelin, *Young Rebels in Contemporary Chinese Cinema* (Hong Kong: Hong Kong University Press, 2007)

FILMOGRAPHY

A Nation Once Again Dir. Brendan Stafford. Dublin: National Film Institute of Ireland, 1946

Any Given Sunday Dir. Oliver Stone. Burbank, California: Warner Bros., 1999

Atlantean Dir. Bob Quinn. Conamara: Cinegael, 1983

Blitz Dir. Elliott Lester. Santa Monica, California: Lionsgate, 2011

Boy Eats Girl Dir. Stephen Bradley. Dublin: Element Films, 2005

Boys from County Clare, The Dir. John Irvin. Culver City, California: Samuel Goldwyn Films, 2003

Braineater, The Dir. Conor McMahon. Dublin, DLIADT, 2001

Canal, The Dir. Ivan Kavanagh. Dublin: Treasure Entertainment, 2014

Chariots of Fire Dir. Hugh Hudson. Los Angeles, California: 20th Century Fox, 1981

Christy Ring Dir. Louis Marcus. Dublin: Gael Linn, 1964

Circle of Friends Dir. Pat O'Connor. US: Savoy Pictures, 1995

Clash of the Ash, The Dir. Fergus Tighe. Dublin: Circus Films, 1987

Crying Game, The Dir. Neil Jordan. London: Palace Pictures, 1992

Daisy Chain Dir. Aisling Walsh. Dublin: Subotica Entertainment, 2008

Darby O'Gill and the Little People Dir. Robert Stevenson. Burbank, California: Walt Disney Pictures, 1959

Das Wunder von Bern (*The Miracle of Bern*) Dir. Sönke Wortmann. Geiselgasteig: Bavaria Film International, 2003

Dawn! Dir. Ken Hannam. Sydney: Aquataurus Film Corp., 1979

Dead Meat Dir. Conor McMahon. Dublin: Three Way Productions, 2004

Disco Pigs Dir. Kirsten Sheridan. London: Renaissance Films, 2001

Eclipse, The Dir. Conor McPherson. Dublin: Treasure Entertainment, 2009

Eliminator, The Dir. Enda Hughes. Belfast: Cousins Pictures, 1996

Far and Away Dir. Ron Howard. Los Angeles, California: Universal Pictures, 1992

Finian's Rainbow Dir. Francis Ford Coppola. Burbank, California: Warner Bros., 1968

Flåklypa Grand Prix (*Pinchcliffe Grand Prix*) Dir. Ivo Caprino. Stockholm: Sandrew Metronome, 1975

Foreign Sports in the US. New York: Motion Picture Section, New York Field Office, 1959

GAA Football Gold: All-Ireland final highlights, 1947–1959. Dublin: Irish Film Institute, 2011

GAA Gold: All-Ireland Hurling Championship Finals, 1948–1959. Dublin: Irish Film Institute, 2010

Ghostwood Dir. Justin O'Brien. Dublin: Maxim Pictures Ltd, 2008

Good Bye Lenin! Dir. Wolfgang Becker. Berlin: X Verleih AG, 2003

Grabbers Dir. Jon Wright. Dublin: Samson Films, 2012

Grantland Rice Sportlight: the sporting Irish Dir. Jack Eaton. Hollywood, California: Paramount Pictures, 1940

Hoosiers Dir. David Anspaugh. Los Angeles, California: Orion Pictures, 1986

Hurling Dir. David Miller. Beverly Hills, California: Metro-Goldwyn-Mayer, 1936

Hurling Stick, The Dir. Vincent Grashaw. Long Beach, California: Dragovista, 2007

Invictus Dir. Clint Eastwood. Burbank, California: Warner Bros., 2009

Ireland, Isle of Sport Dir. Kenneth Fairbairn. London: Rayant Pictures, 1961

Isolation Dir. Billy O'Brien. Dublin: Element Films, 2006

Knocknagow Dir. Fred O'Donovan. Dublin: Film Company of Ireland, 1918

Lamb Dir. Paulin Soumanou Vieyra. Bénin, Sénégal: Cinémathèque Afrique, 1963

Laochra Dir. Ruán Magan. Dublin: Tyrone Productions, 2016

Leap Year Dir. Anand Tucker. Universal City, California: Universal Pictures, 2010

Les Triplettes de Belleville (*Belleville Rendez-vous*) Dir. Sylvain Chomet. Paris: Diaphana Films, 2003

Loneliness of the Long-distance Runner, The Dir. Tony Richardson. London: Woodfall Film Productions, 1962

Mad Cows and Zombies Dir. Katie Lincoln. Dublin: Three Way Productions Ltd, 2004

Making of Rocky Road to Dublin, The Dir. Paul Duane. Dublin: Loopline Films, 2004

Matchmaker, The Dir. Mark Joffe. London: Working Title Films, 1997

Memories in Focus Dir. Peter Canning. Dublin: RTÉ, 1995

Men Boxing Dirs William K.L. Dickson and William Heisey. West Orange, New Jersey: Edison Studios, 1891

Michael Collins Dir. Neil Jordan. Burbank, California: Warner Bros., 1996

N Lán 5 Háo (*Woman Basketball Player No. 5*) Dir. Xie Jin. Shanghai: Tian Ma Film Studio, 1957

Offside Dir. Jafar Panahi. Tehran: Jafar Panahi Film Productions, 2006

Olympia Dir. Leni Riefenstahl [Triad Productions Corporation DVD, 2008]. Berlin: Olympia-Film, 1938

Peil Dir. Louis Marcus. Dublin: Gael Linn, 1962

Program, The Dir. David S. Ward. Burbank, California: Touchstone Pictures, 1993

PS I Love You Dir. Richard LaGravenese. Los Angeles, California: Alcon Entertainment, 2007

Quiet Man, The Dir. John Ford. Studio City, California: Republic Pictures, 1952

Red Mist Dir. Paddy Breathnach. London: Generator Entertainment, 2008

Rising of the Moon, The Dir. John Ford. Dublin: Four Provinces Productions, 1957

Rocky Dir. John G. Avildsen. Los Angeles, California: United Artists, 1976

Rocky Road to Dublin Dir. Peter Lennon. Paris: Victor Herbert, 1968

Rooney Dir. George Pollock. London: Rank Organisation, 1958

Ryan's Daughter Dir. David Lean. Los Angeles, California: Metro-Goldwyn-Mayer, 1970

Seer Dir. Eric Courtney. Dublin: Jim Cahill, 2008

Shrooms Dir. Paddy Breathnach. Dublin: Treasure Entertainment, 2007

Slap Shot Dir. George Roy Hill. Los Angeles, California: Universal Pictures, 1977

South Bank Show, The – '*Michael Collins* episode'. Dir. Tony Knox. London: LWT Programme for ITV, 1996

Sports Slants, episode no. 4, Narrator: Ted Husing. Burbank, California: Vitaphone Varieties for Warner Bros., 1931

Sports Thrills, episode no. 5, Narrator: Ted Husing. Burbank, California: Vitaphone Varieties for Warner Bros., 1932

This Sporting Life Dir. Lindsay Anderson. London: Rank Organisation, 1963

Three Kisses Dir. Justin Herman. Los Angeles, California: Paramount Pictures, 1955

Ti Yu Huang Hou (*Queen of Sports*) Dir. Yu Sun. Hong Kong: Lian Hua Film Company, 1934

Trobriand Cricket Dirs Gary Kildea and Jerry Leach. Government of Papua New Guinea/ University of Cambridge Museum of Archaeology & Ethnography, 1975

The Wake Wood Dir. David Keating. London: Hammer Films, 2010

Waking Ned Dir. Kirk Jones. Los Angeles, California: Fox Searchlight Pictures, 1998

Wind that Shakes the Barley, The Dir. Ken Loach. Paris: Pathé Distribution, 2006

Winter's End Dir. Patrick Kenny. Dublin: Winter's End Ltd, 2005

Young Cassidy Dirs Jack Cardiff and John Ford. Los Angeles, California: Metro-Goldwyn-Mayer, 1965

NEWSREEL EPISODES

'All-Ireland Football Final', Pathé Gazette, 30 September 1937

'All-Ireland Football Final', Pathé Gazette, 21 October 1937

'All-Ireland Football Final at Croke Park, Dublin', Pathé Gazette, 1 October 1936

'All-Ireland Hurling Final', Pathé Gazette, 8 September 1938

'Cavan Defeat Kildare – Exclusive Pictures of All-Ireland Football Final at Croke Park', Pathé Gazette, 26 September 1935

'Commandant McKeon Starts Game Between Dublin and Leix at Croke Park, Ireland', Pathé Gazette, 1 October 1921

'Enormous Crowds Watch Dublin Defeat Kerry in All-Ireland Football Final', Pathé Gazette, 9 October 1924

'De Valera Attends Irish Games', British Movietone News, 9 July 1936

'Dublin – Irish Hurling Year', Pathé Gazette, 1930–39

'Football Final in Dublin – Galway Defeat Dublin in Hard Fought Battle at Croke Park', Pathé Gazette, 27 September 1934

'Gaelic Football at Dungannon', Gaumont Graphic, 15 May 1929

'Gaelic Football – Colour', British Movietone News, 31 October 1976

'Gaelic Football – Galway v Cork at Terenure', Pathé Gazette, 17 January 1924

'Gaelic Football in New York', Pathé Gazette, 28 May 1939

'Gaelic Football in New York', British Movietone News, 6 June 1938

'Gaelic Football – Kerry Defeat Kildare by 9 Points to 2 at Croke Park', Pathé Gazette, 20 October 1930

'Hurling Final at Killarney', Pathé Gazette, 9 September 1937

'Hurling Match – Limerick Wins in New York', Pathé Gazette, 4 June 1936

'Ireland Has Racing Despite Its Little "War"! Government Yields to Public Pressure and "Daily Express" Campaign and Grants – One Day!', Pathé Gazette, 21 November 1921

'Ireland's National Game. And No Game for Weaklings! "Blackrock" Defeat "Redmonds" in Final of Hurling Championship, in Which Both Sides Played "to the Last Ounce"', Pathé Gazette, 8 December 1927

'Ireland's National Game. Enormous Crowd See Dublin Beat Cork by 20 Points to 6 in "Fast and Furious" All-Ireland Hurling Final', Pathé Gazette, 11 September 1927

'Ireland's National Game. Record Crowd See Cork Defeat Kilkenny in All-Ireland Hurling Final', Pathé Gazette, 1 November 1926

'Irish Football Final: Kerry v Meath – No Sound', British Movietone News, 26 September 1939

'Kerry and Cavan Play Gaelic Football and Live to Fight Again', British Movietone News, 30 September 1937

'Rebel Spoil Sports Defied. Mr Tim Healy (Governor General) and Mr Cosgrave (President) Attend Punchestown Races', Pathé Gazette, 19 April 1923

'Sport – Irish Hurling', British Movietone News, 12 November 1951

'"To Fight Again" – All-Ireland Hurling Final Ends in Draw at Croke Park, Dublin', Pathé Gazette, 5 September 1934

'Training for the Tailteann Games', Pathé Gazette, 24 April 1922

INDEX

Illustrations are indicated by page numbers in bold.